CREATOR
SUSTAINER
PROTECTOR
GOD
ﷲ

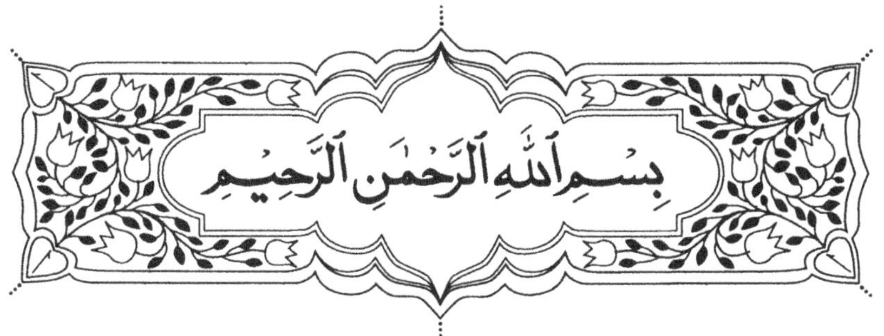

A Song of Muhammad ﷺ

by

M. R. Bawa Muhaiyaddeen ﱞ

THE FELLOWSHIP PRESS

Philadelphia, Pennsylvania

Library of Congress Cataloging-in-Publication Data

Muhaiyaddeen, M. R. Bawa.
    A song of Muhammad �®ﷺ / by M. R. Bawa Muhaiyaddeen.
      p. cm.
    ISBN 0-914390-49-X   ISBN 0-914390-50-3 (pbk)
    1. Muhammad, Prophet, d. 632--Poetry. 2. Sufi poetry. I. Title.

894' .81117--dc20   96-13365
                                                                  CIP

Printed in the United States of America
by THE FELLOWSHIP PRESS
Bawa Muhaiyaddeen Fellowship
First Printing

Muhammad Raheem Bawa Muhaiyaddeen ﴾ﻗﺪﺲ﴿

Introduction

There is an imperishable place in the human heart where three worlds meet, a convergence, the world of souls, this world and the hereafter. To understand *A Song of Muhammad* ﷺ, to know who the Prophet Muhammad ﷺ truly is, Muhammad Raheem Bawa Muhaiyaddeen ﵁ invites us directly into that place, showing us on our passage in how to lose the individuated self, to be rid of those attributes which separate us from the absolute, the One. This is an ecstatic song of mysteries to contemplate and a song of secrets revealed.

There was indeed a beloved Prophet ﷺ, born in Mecca and buried in Medina. This song celebrates him, his birth, this *maulid* tells us something of the extraordinary events in the first twenty years he spent as a man on this earth, what he said, what he did, what he taught. But this song also celebrates that Muhammad ﷺ who first manifested at the beginning of creation as Nūr Muhammad, the luminosity from whom God created everything. It is for that reason *A Song of Muhammad* ﷺ opens with an exalted explanation of the universal beginning.

And who is this remarkable being who brings us direct experience of Allah and His creation, of the Prophet ﷺ and his life? To enter the world of Bawa Muhaiyaddeen is to leave history and enter mystery, the imperishable heart. Usually, when asked to speak about himself on a personal level Bawa Muhaiyaddeen who came as the *Qutb*, the light of God's explanation for this age, he would brush such questions aside, directing attention instead to the ocean of *'ilm*, the divine wisdom which is without history. What we can say about him however, is that he was first identified in the early decades of this century as a mystic, a sage living in a remote jungle of Sri Lanka, that he lived in Colombo and Jaffna for many years before, as God willed, first coming to America. From 1971 until 1986 when he left his body behind, he divided his time between Sri Lanka and America.

This song was a spontaneous recital sung in Tamil over a fairly short period of time near the beginning of the sixties, part song, part spoken elaboration in eastern style. More than thirty years later it was translated into English by Dr. Ajwad Macan-Markar and Mrs. Rajes Ganesan. May these words which are not ordinary words be inscribed on our hearts with letters of light.

Sharon Marcus, 1996

Contents

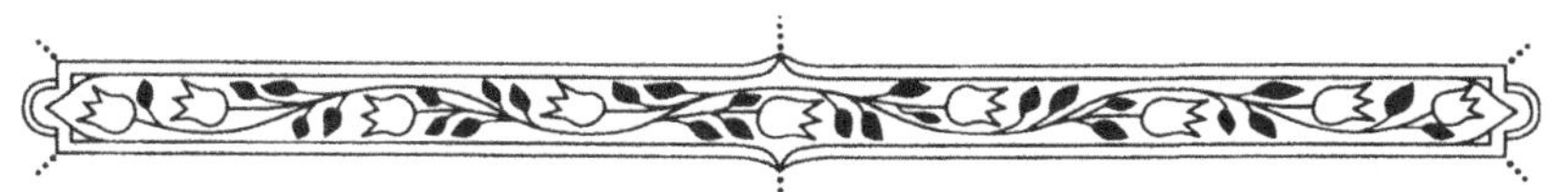

CHAPTER I

The Birth of Muhammad ﷺ

The Birth of Muhammad ⊕

Light of the jeweled crown, light which fills the heart,
Gracious and blissful Lord who fills us,
The ecstasy within love, most precious gem of this world,
A fruit filled with goodness, that Āthi, that Jōthi
Who plays a victorious drum of grace and bliss —
When will the day come, when will I reach You
Without play and destiny, but still
Overcoming play and destiny, when will I serve,
When will I reach the feet of the Lord
Who is the gem of my eye?
There is a reason many enlightened beings appeared
In different forms, from time to time on this earth
They came one after the other to give us good counsel,
To make us understand the most direct way
To cut the evils that had to be cut;
They comforted us, made us delight in that state of bliss,
They rid us of our sorrows, our poverty and illness,
Letting us experience the sweet taste of honey,
Planting the flag of victory forever;
They made each of our hearts resplend

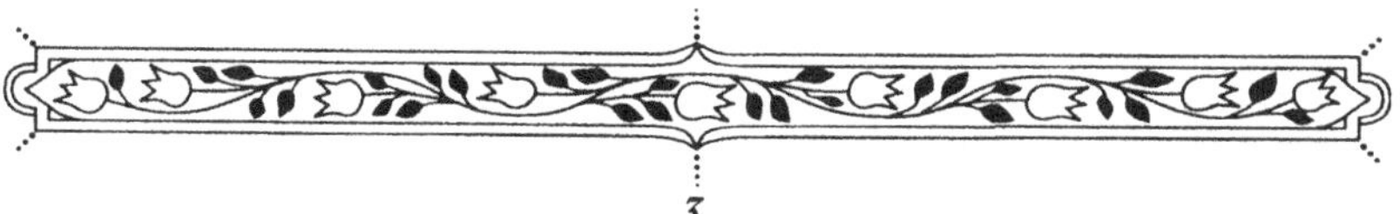

And the beauty of our state victorious, blissful forever.

How can I ever describe
Those divine words of that One, the Rahmān?
Before He created the world
It was His intention to create wise prophets,
The Āthi intended to create the world
According to His plan,
The Āthi, the primal One, the Jōthi
Was moved to display His state of justice and law,
It was His intention to create all lives in this state,
The Āthi intended to create prophets
Who would be destroyed again and again
Then be recreated again and again in the five yugas.
This was the way He intended to create
All the radiant celestial beings, all the wise men,
The earth, the next world, the heavens,
The divine kingdom, the kingdom of hell
And everything else.

He took the two pearls pervading His gracious spirit
And inserted them on the forehead as protection,
As helpers for this world and the kingdom of God,
He made them radiant pearls who became helpers,
Revealing them in the days of antiquity
When there were no separate books of religion.
He intended to create all lives
In a marvelous way to satisfy the yearning lives.

The causal One remained
The formless One in a formless state,
He remained alone, Himself,
The unique Āthi, the primal One.
With His melting intention He made
Three overpowering eyes appear as flames,
He made two of these eyes celestial beings,
Dēvas, with His grace, one the light of the moon
And the other the light of the sun.
To create this world and *ākhirah*, the next world,
He made resplendent Nūr Muhammad
Radiate in a masculine form
And all other beings in a feminine form,
Declaring, "I will make you, O Muhammad,
The praise of all divine scriptures,
To all created lives in these worlds you will be male."
And He declared further, "All those beings
Which are to be created from you
Will be female in relation to you."
The gracious, blissful Lord of all three worlds
Uttered these sweet honeyed words,
The divine words of the guru,
And when He had pronounced these sweet words
He gazed with His most gracious eyes,
The unquestionable Lord
In the form of His gracious sternness
Opened that gnostic eye with determination,
The eye on the forehead

Which could look to the right and to the left,
He looked straight at radiant, subtle Nūr Muhammad
Who melted like water spreading over the worlds,
And the primal One, the Āthi saw
This melted water running over the worlds.
On that day the primal One said,
"O Muhammad this water is for all the worlds,
This is grace which quenches the thirst of fervor,
All the treasures are found in your state,
All the glorious lives are within you, look!"
The Nūr Muhammad of the Āthi, the primal One,
Heard these gracious, holy words of the Ruler,
The gracious Lord of all three worlds,
And what had been water became a pearl.
The Āthi observed the water had now become a pearl,
The primal One saw this,
Threw the pearl into seven good seas
And enclosed it within the vessel of *hikmat* or wisdom
From which came forth copper, gold, iron, silver, lead
And the fire-like light of the metals.
When the Āthi saw this He created the eight heavens,
The eight spheres of the sky, seven oceans
And the earth which is the world.
When He looked blissfully with His eye of grace
Through the causal light,
The tree of *yaqīn* or certitude appeared as His grace,
And He placed mighty Muhammad ﷺ
In the form of a peacock on that tree,

Then He created all lives as a trial,
Putting the indescribable Muhammad ☾
Inside each of them.
"O Muhammad," the primal One said,
"You will be My pearl everywhere,
You will be My right eye, see O pearl,
O male pearl, the pearl which appears
With beauty from my left will be the female pearl,
The pearl which will rise on the right is the male pearl,
For all lives the creative seed or sperm
Will come from you."
The Jōthi, the Āthi said more, "I will be the One
To radiate as brilliance, while for Me
You will have a beautiful feminine form,
For all lives in the world you will be masculine,
But I will be that God
Who is the Father and the Creator."

This was the way He created the peacock,
He gave the tree of *yaqīn* four branches,
Centered lofty Muhammad ☾
In the form of the peacock
Among those four branches, then
Looked intently at him with His eye of grace
And the peacock trembled, he shuddered;
When he shuddered and trembled
His entire body began to sweat
And drops of sweat fell everywhere;

The one hundred and twenty-four thousand
Precious drops of sweat that fell from him
Became the one hundred and twenty-four thousand
Prophets of the Āthi for the triple worlds,
For the world of grace
And the heavenly kingdom of the Āthi.
And more, through these precious drops of sweat,
With exaltedness He created the heavenly world;
From the drops of sweat that fell from his forehead
He created each and every thing,
The oceans, the earth, the world and the netherworlds,
He created all this from the drops of sweat
That fell when Āthi Muhammad melted.
Three hundred and thirteen
Other drops separated from them
And became the *mursalūn nabīs,*
Prophets He sent to the world.
He created jinns and fairies from the fire on this earth.
All this was created from the drops
Of sweat that fell from Muhammad ☉.

As the Āthi gazed more intently the kingdom of God,
The hells, the heavens and the fourteen worlds
Came into existence,
Each one created from the drops
Of Muhammad's sweat ☉.
On the day Muhammad ☉
Was placed within to give clarity

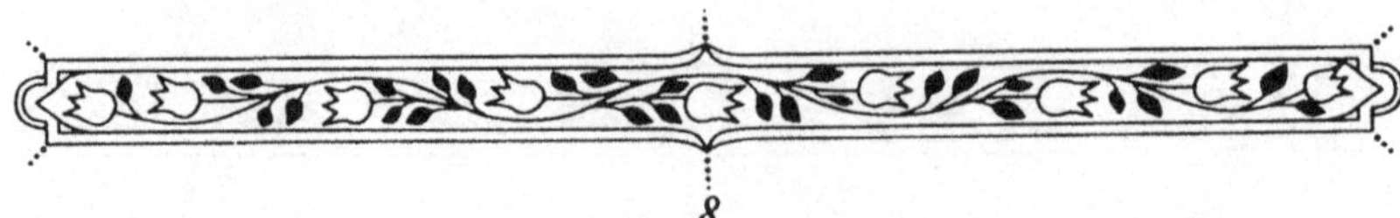

God said, "Yā Muhammad who came

As the Yā Rasūl, the four branches

Which appeared on the tree of *yaqīn*

Are the four religions,

And I will send resplendent prophets

From you O Muhammad to this world,

I will send four perfected *nabīs* to the four religions.

If people have the intention,

If they pray to Me meltingly,

I will connect them to Me again,

But if they become self-important

I will reduce them to charcoal in the fires of hell.

Through you I will control them all,

Realize this O Muhammad, the four branches

Will become the four holy, primal religions."

Then He created the four mirrors of modesty

With His gracious hands, with exaltedness;

Through His grace the Āthi

Placed these four mirrors of modesty

Around the peacock on all four sides;

When the peacock saw himself in the four mirrors

Placed in the four directions

He began to tremble and shudder with emotion,

Praising his own beauty, but when

He saw drops of sweat pouring down

He became sorrowful.

Trembling in that state the peacock saw his own legs

And felt ashamed because they looked like sticks,

He felt embarrassed looking down.
Nūr Muhammad as the peacock bent his head
In embarrassment and cried out,
"O Āthi You made me so beautiful,
But why did you make my legs so ugly,
O Rahmān who is the eye of plenitude,
Most praiseworthy One,
Why did you make my legs so dark, so ugly?"
Then God gave these gracious words of explanation,
"O my eminent Nūr Muhammad,
Through your sweat I will make all creations,
I will create the world and all the celestial beings;
All those created from you
Whose hearts and qualities are not purified
Will be created in the dark ugly color of your legs,
This is a sign of hell for those creations, understand this."

When mighty Nūr Muhammad,
The messenger of the one Rahmān
In the form of a peacock heard the words of his Lord,
His heart was disturbed, he cried out and wailed.
In that state he fainted and woke up,
Then two drops of his sweat fell
From which the Āthi created the moon and the sun.
He created every word from this truth,
He created all lives, the earth, lands, the netherworlds,
The 'arsh, the throne, the *kursī*, the eye of wisdom,
The *qalam*, the pen, the heavens,

The hells and the fourteen worlds,

Celestial beings, wise beings,

Three hundred and thirty million heavenly beings,

Forty-eight thousand *rishis* or wise beings,

Three hundred and thirteen *mursalūn nabīs*,

One hundred and twenty-four thousand prophets,

Enlightened beings, believers,

Virtuous women and the seventy-three groups,

He created them all from the sweat

Of Muhammad which fell everywhere.

When He had created the shining hells,

The heavens, everything,

He looked again with authority

At this beautiful peacock

And made him a precious pearl.

With His divine words the primal One said,

"O resplendent Muhammad I created you as the male

In this world, the wealth of everything,

The treasure in all souls,

I will have you live in all the flowering shrubs,

I will make you the fruit that is sweeter than honey,

I will make you indescribable, clear nectar,

I will make you the exalted remedy,

I will make you flavorful honey,

I will have you fill the body completely,

I will make you a lamp inside and out,

I will make you the key to every explanation,

I will make you the life of every visible thing,

I will make you permanent and beautiful,
On the day of direct questioning
I will make you the only help."
Muhammad ☾ understood the state
Which was indicated,
Which had the clarity of this quality,
Which was imprinted with the six tastes
On the eye of the forehead.

Once this was finished the skies could be seen shining.
Can one tongue even reciting continually
Tell all there is to be told?
Can my tongue enumerate all these events one by one?
Aiyō, so many many illuminating things,
Aiyō, how can I describe them?
If I were to go on describing this
Till the end of my life, would I ever come to the end?
O that treasured honey, the all-curing remedy,
I speak and speak of it,
How can I describe this honey,
Sweet everywhere in the world,
How can I ever adequately describe
Your divine gracious Muhammad,
This primal Muhammad ☾?

The primal One, the Āthi said,
"I will create Adam and then Eve
In the meaningful religion of Zabūr,

I will be the original pearl and
I will make you the child within that pearl,
The one who resplends,
The radiance which shines, the excellent gem.
I will plant you firmly in the religion of Zabūr
As the being who is eternal,
The radiance, as the flame, the gem,
As the unequaled treasure,
The sweetest honey, as nectar,
As plenitude, the beauty of the body, the form of *insān*,
I will create you as radiant *insān* or man
In a form which takes shape again and again
To control the uncontrollable males, the souls,
The clever, mighty ones,
The demons of arrogance which jump and roll around
And ghosts who are enemies —
Understand this King Muhammad,
Through you I will control them all."
And the primal One said more,
"Take this spear of maya, illusion,
I will create a state of mind with you,
Of the sweat that fell from the five-colored peacock
Existing in your beauty
I will create all the different living creatures on earth,
With exaltedness, with five letters,
With five letters which represent the five colors.
O Āthi Muhammad I gave you five colors,
And of the sweat that fell from you

I intend to create everything, *insān* or man as well,
That man who will be made of the five elements;
Understand this," said the all-pervading One.
"Of the sweat that fell
From your five beautiful colors I will create man,
I will create five attributes of that man
And make them the five elements,
And I will make you his soul O Nūr Muhammad,
I will make you the beauty of his face,
I will make him beautiful; understand this well.
It becomes your obligation
To show him the right and the left,
To show him My grace and draw him to Me,"
So said the Āthi.

While Āthi Muhammad was a peacock of five colors,
From the sweat that fell off him
The Āthi created *'ālam* and *arwāh,*
The visible and invisible,
The grass, the shrubs, weeds, trees, everything else,
He created the three worlds,
The eight directions and six angles,
Placing the five colors
Which were the five elements in them.
O mind, understand He created
That primal Āthi Muhammad
In the most exquisite form,
And the drops of sweat which fell

From this beautiful male became the sperm,

And the form of the Āthi Muhammad

Would be the soul in each life.

Understand this, listen, it is told this way,

Understand clearly that these five colors would become

The five elements and the five faces;

The heart would be a mirror.

Look at the middle eye shining above the breast

Of the peacock and between its two wings,

You will see it is a mirror

Made from a mixture of green, blue and rose,

This is the intention of man.

At the center is the heart which appears as five colors,

What appears as five colors is the house of six angles,

Understand this is the six-pointed house of man.

If you examine it you will see many different forms,

If you analyze it with your divine analytic wisdom

You will see six faces radiating within,

One of them is Annal Nūr Muhammad.

What fell as the seed of sweat

Is that one face, the face of grace,

The five colors pasted on it are the five elements.

This is why the peacock is called

Aru muham, the one with six faces,

O my people understand the meaning of six faces,

This is true praise,

The concept of *aru muham* which fills the heart —

In fact this is the real form of man,

Understand this with the clarity of pure honey.

Before man was created with this exaltedness,
The Āthi, the primal One created
The light of the eye on his forehead,
When He gazed at it with His lofty gnostic eye
Of true wisdom it became a peacock.
He placed the four mirrors of modesty in the peacock,
Representing in man the qualities of modesty,
Fear of wrongdoing, sincerity and reserve,
These four qualities are a treasure in man,
Understand O mind
This state which is so good,
This restraint is the mark of man.
O those who were born with me,
This is a clear explanation.

"From today that peacock will be described
As created from you O Muhammad,
O Muhammad I created you
As the exemplar for the world and also as food,
Now I will create your father Adam,
And from him I will create your mother Āminah,
From them I will create all mankind
Who must try to understand this with clarity.
The one who is to be iblīs or satan, your enemy
Will spread his umbrella of evil everywhere;
Cast him out, he will come as your enemy,

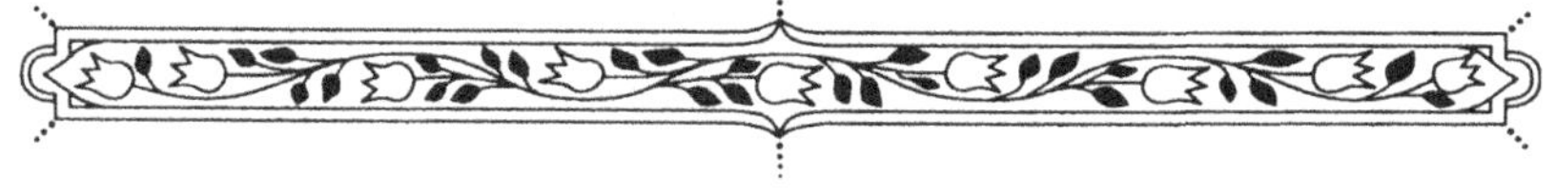

He will call you,
He will make you notice him,
He will entice you this way.
Because he will do that, to make your words
The most exalted in the world, to make
The whole body as sweet as honey,
To give clarity, I gave a sign:
Peacocks do not mate, the young are produced
From the sweat of the male,
Realize this, understand it is a sign,
An example I have given you,
The peacock and peahen never mate,
But the peahen lays its eggs and hatches its young
Who appear with five radiant colors, a radiant sign;
Till this world and *ākhirah* which is the hereafter end,
This sign will never be obscured,"
So said the Āthi, the primal One.

In this way, with this sign, Muhammad ☪ was created at the very beginning in the form of a peacock. All the universes, water, fire, air, earth, gold were created from him, the Āthi created each and every thing from Muhammad ☪. The five colors of the peacock represent the five elements, the ugly legs of the peacock represent the evil thoughts of man; whoever develops this darkness will enter hell. From the five colors the five elements rose, and the sweat that fell from Nūr Muhammad in the form of a peacock became the *āthmām*, the souls, life. This *āthmām* becomes the sperm in each man. Muhammad ☪ fills all beings, the sperm

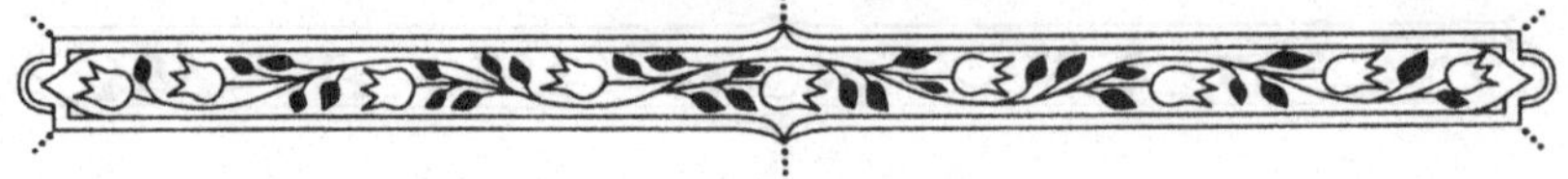

comes from him; that sperm responsible for procreation came from Nūr Muhammad as the peacock when it fell in drops of sweat. Even today this is what melts and falls from man, from grass, weeds, everything. Arrogance explodes and discharges sperm which is the mark of creation; if it does not explode that way there is no procreation. This is the great secret of Muhammad's blissful appearance ☙ which cannot easily be explained.

Muhammad ☙ who came at the time of the beginning is called Nūr Muhammad. He appeared first as enlightened beings in the religion of Zabūr, Hinduism, and later in the religions of Jabrāt, fire worship, Injīl, Christianity and finally in the religion of Furqān, Islam. In each reappearance he had a different name, two hundred and one such appearances in all. It is impossible to describe the age and form of Muhammad ☙, impossible to describe his powers as the enlightened being.

The four branches of the tree of *yaqīn*, certitude, became the four religions and the four scriptures. The tree which grew from Muhammad ☙ ends in Muhammad ☙, the tree was created from Muhammad ☙ and ends in Muhammad ☙, keep that in mind. With clarity of mind, in an exalted way, understand this precious all-encompassing treasure. For the perfection of your heart understand the state of virtuous Muhammad ☙. He is that brilliant lamp which dispels all darkness. To reach, to grasp that lamp we need a *meignāna guru nāthan*, a true lord of the gurus.

Appa, my brothers and sisters, it is not possible to describe the magnificence of Muhammad ☙, nevertheless I will tell you his story now, and perhaps something about his birth and history.

When the words of the guru penetrate you in a way
Which transforms your qualities,

It is like the inner sweetness of honey,
Your mind overflows with beauty and receives peace,
It understands this greatness, it understands
There is only one religion and one family of God;
When your mind cuts away
The differences of *you* and *I*,
When it proclaims there is only One,
You truly belong to God's family;
When you think meltingly of the Āthi,
Intending Him alone with a tender heart,
When you understand this state,
Realizing it with clarity,
You become light;
When your mind forgets itself,
Drinking only that sweet honey,
Singing the praise that the unique One is the only One,
Destroying the four thousand,
Four hundred and forty-eight poisonous nerves,
You become a God-realized being —
In the words of the Āthi,
You become a knower of that state beyond religions;
When your intention melts, when your heart melts,
When you realize the state of the Āthi
And love all lives in the same way,
You become a *nabī*, a prophet of the primal Āthi.
Those who say with determination
That One is the only One,
Who find mental clarity and do service

Will have the form of a blissful god in this world;
Those who recognize and understand
Who Muhammad ☪ is,
Who follow the practices of his teachings
Become the light of the Āthi, the primal One.
When you understand your state and correct it,
When you start upon that straight, true path, when you
See the grace and delve into it praising the Āthi,
You become as sweet as nectar,
You acquire the form of radiance
Endowed with the grace of the Āthi,
When you treat all lives as your own,
Understanding the true taste of that bliss
You become a virtuous man, a ruler of all lives;
When your mind begins to melt and flow,
When it has the clarity and sweetness of honey,
Recognizing and understanding the truth,
Proclaiming the truth as truth,
Exclaiming that the Āthi is One, only One,
When you melt in that state
You become *manu-Īsan*, man-God.
Whoever reaches, whoever establishes
The state of man-God,
Doing good both day and night with a melting heart
Will be the sweet friend of the Āthi;
When you arrive at the clear path,
When you are filled with your inheritance,
When your heart loves the Āthi

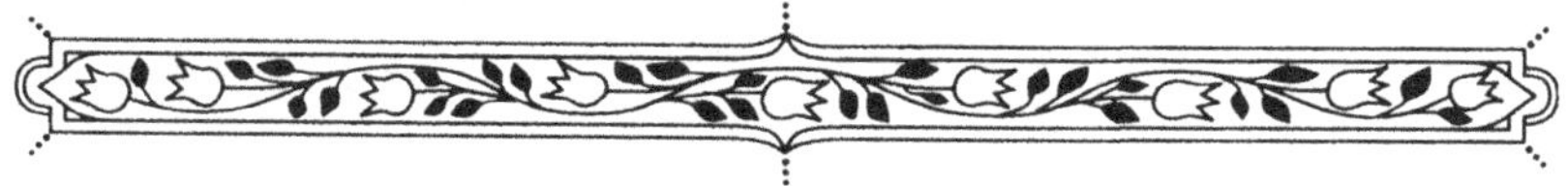

Who is the gem of your eye,

And when your perception has clarity,

You will be a divine being in the world.

Try to understand everything I sang of earlier. As He decreed, this was the way Allah created Muhammad ﷺ. To create the world, to create Adam ﷺ He transformed Muhammad ﷺ into a peacock, creating everything from him. God created goats, cattle, all other living things, and with great care He created everything else, oceans, lands, earth, the netherworld, the *'arsh*, the throne, the *kursī*, the eye of wisdom, the *qalam*, the pen, heavens, hells and fourteen worlds.

From the peacock He created the tree of *yaqīn*, certitude, and the four branches of this tree which represent the four religions. He also created the mirrors of modesty from this tree, God created these mirrors within man so that he would have four virtuous qualities in his life, fear of wrongdoing, reserve, modesty and sincerity, qualities which would be complete within man. He created that wonderful Muhammad ﷺ in this way and from him He created clarity. He created Muhammad ﷺ even before He created the four religions.

After creating Muhammad ﷺ He decided to create the *sifāt* or the manifestation. Once He had created Muhammad ﷺ He created everything else from him, deciding then to create Adam ﷺ. He created heavens, hells, Adam ﷺ, and then it was His intention to create Muhammad ﷺ within Adam. As a result of this intention, from His creation of Adam, Muhammad became his progeny through Āminah ﷺ, who is called Īswari in Tamil. He had Muhammad ﷺ conceived in the womb of Āminah ﷺ, and in the history of the world Muhammad ﷺ appeared, reappeared,

appeared and reappeared many times, each of his appearances occurring in a different time period. Every prophet descended to the world at a time when the people followed iblīs or satan, when they altered justice and flew the flag of injustice. Iblīs created many images to distract the people in every part of the world.

While all this happened God formed the intention to send down Muhammad ☾ as the final prophet. He descended as the final prophet, Muhammad ☾ in his two hundred and first appearance, born in Mecca. He was conceived in Āminah's womb ☾ and grew there. When she was four months pregnant his father 'Abdullāh ☾ died on a trade mission. In the fourth month of Āminah's pregnancy ☾ Muhammad's father ☾ died.

Muhammad ☾ was born as a light without any afterbirth, was born into this world without blemish. He came to the world of man as the last prophet, to correct the people, to discard every evil, make them walk the good, true path. It has been said there will be no more prophets.

When Āminah ☾ was four months pregnant, 'Abdullāh ☾ who is called Īswaran in Tamil died. That Muhammad ☾, formerly in the six-pointed house was born this way, born into the world at the tenth month of her pregnancy. Just before his birth Āminah ☾ felt labor pains. Since there was no one to take care of her, no one to ask how she felt, celestial maidens descended from the heavens to help her with the delivery and white pigeons descended from the heavens too, stroking her abdomen to ease the severe labor pains. As this was going on black clouds surrounded her and then a white cloud descended; when that happened Muhammadur-Rasūl ☾ was born into the world. He was born in a silken, white robe, he was born on a Monday night wearing a white robe. There was no afterbirth but Āminah ☾ was momentarily unconscious, and while she was so, celestial angels came down at God's command to carry noble Muhammad ☾ up to the heavens.

The eight heavens were decorated and the seven hells were closed as he was carried around the heavens by celestial angels then bathed in the water of paradise; they dressed him in a white robe, cradled him and rained flowers upon him. God commanded the angels to take him back down to the world before Āminah regained consciousness. All the angels and celestial beings in the heavens blessed him, decorated him, named him Muhammad and bestowed three signs upon him, a key in his hand, a light on the nape of his neck and a mark, also on the nape of his neck.

Now God addressed him, "O precious Prophet exalted in three worlds, with this light on the nape of your neck, *Nabī* with long arms, O mighty one, O *Qutb* may your praises fill the universes." So said Allah, the mighty One. As He said this Allah, the mighty One kissed him with the kiss of grace while heavenly angels blessed him to protect him from the evil eye. Then they brought Muhammad back down to Āminah before she regained consciousness.

"A radiant Rasūl, a Messenger, Nabī Muhammad

Has come, a gem for the world,

A gem for this world has come,

He has come as a gem for this world,

Born as man-God resplending in the world

He has come as a pearl for all those who were born

As children of Adam,

As a light for everyone,

As a lamp within the radiant *qalb*, the heart, the breast,

As a lamp and overflowing grace,

As a guru for the true and just path,

As a most beautiful light

For the One of eternal bliss, he has come,
The beautiful grace exalted in the world,
A gem loved by the heavens,
A gem which fills everything,
A gem precious to everything."
They said this cradling the baby
And singing a lullaby,
There was happiness in the heavenly world
As noble Muhammad ﷺ slept.
They sang the words, "*Lā ilāha ill-Allāhu*,
Nothing exists but God, You are God;
O noble Muhammad," they said,
Decorating the heavens with flowers,
Singing *Lā ilāha ill-Allāhu* to this *Nabī* ﷺ.
They resonated with praises
Of resplendent Muhammad ﷺ,
And with an exquisite prayer
Recited *dhikr* and *salawāt,*
The remembrance of God and His praise.
With beauty and bliss they recited
The name, the *dhikr* as sweet as honey,
And everyone in the heavenly world
Gathered around to kiss him,
The moon and the sun stopped at their zenith
And everyone said, "O Mahmūd!"
They said he was a *Nabī,*
A Prophet of good, true wisdom,
They called him the pearl of clarity, saying

He was the light of the three worlds,

The light of grace.

He was cradled in gold,

O the *Nabī* who rules the universes,

They blessed him with a pearl

And gave our *Nabī* the name Rasūl Muhammad .

Reciting sweet words of honey

They fed him the milk of grace

Saying, "O *rathina* Muhammad,

O gem-like Muhammad."

All the heavenly beings blessed him,

The heavenly angels, the houris,

Celestial beings, everyone in heaven

Cradled Muhammad singing,

"*Ar-ararro, ar-arro,*

O Muhammadūay, gem of all the souls in *ākhirah*, sleep,

O Muhammad mingled in everything in this world,

The light of *gnānam*, of wisdom

Who rules that place at the center,

O true and just Muhammadūay who never sleeps,

Teaching the radiant words

Of the Āthi, leading people on the right path,

O that messenger *Nabī* of Annal Rahmān,

The great and merciful One,

As the light in the eye on the forehead,

As the one who knows the recipient and recites,

O that *Nabī* who is mingled within the primal One,

As the one who is trustworthy,

Who has conquered three evils,
The guru who teaches the five true and just *kalimahs*,
Words of prayer as precious as the eyes,
O Guru Muhammadūay conceived in Āminah's womb,
Born without afterbirth or blemish,
You were born through the *dhikr*,
O Muhammadūay for all lives, at all times,
Within that transcendent love of all lives
You are the complete treasure of all lives,
O Muhammadūay, the true and just one."

He was blessed and blessed in Allah's paradise
By the celestial beings of two worlds,
Muhammad ⸱ who always existed,
That Muhammad ⸱ who reminds you of the Āthi
Hidden in earth, in gold, in you and me.
As the meaning within the meaning
That Muhammad ⸱ is there,
Mingled with the letters *alif*, *lām* and *mīm*.

Resplendent Āthi Rahmān created
The form of radiant Nūr Muhammad,
He created the form of the eight shining heavens
From you O *Nabī* of certitude ⸱, Muhammadūay,
He created the seven oceans
And nine shining kinds of precious gems.
He created high land
In the world as immovable things,

God who created the earth
Created mountains to keep the world from shaking,
He created precious metals
So that praise would be given,
And He put gold among them.
"O resplendent Muhammad, through you
I created all lives."
To keep all moving things still
The primal One created Muhammad ⊕,
To steady the hearts of all the wavering human beings,
To remove their wavering Āthi Rahmān
Created Muhammad ⊕ as firm certitude.

O heavenly one, the gem,
The resplendence of this world
And *mahshar*, the gathering on Judgment Day,
O our King Mahmūd, O golden gem,
Resplendent Dastagīr, the helping hand of two worlds,
O light of the pearl born as a male, with valor,
O Āthi Nabī Muhammadūay,
We rejoiced when we saw you,
When we joined you
And followed the path of *īmān*,
Faith, certitude and determination,
O keep us from going astray,
And tomorrow on the day of *qiyāmah*, the reckoning,
Take us to the feet of our Āthi Rahmān
With love, O noble Muhammadūay,

You are the flawless precious gem of the heart,
The light of the pearl settled in *dhikr*,
The one who fills our hearts, Āthi Muhammadūay.

To keep us from evil times,
To keep the earth from quaking
The Āthi created mountains,
To keep living beings from wavering
The Āthi created Muhammad ﷺ
As the primal light, as transcendent
Qualities within the *qalb*, the heart.
When our breast begins to flutter,
When our heart begins to tremble,
When we stray from the right path
We recite your name; O Āthi Muhammad
He made you a nail within the *qalb*
To keep man's heart from trembling.
He showered the truth with exaltedness and love
Upon all lives who had the form of *insān*,
True man, who recognized the state,
The straight, true path to heaven,
He showered the *dhikr* of noble Nūr Muhammad,
The *lā il*, the *awwal kalimah*,
The first *kalimah* or word,
And the five precious *kalimahs*
As *furūd* or obligations.
"O Muhammadūay go down to the world,
Teach this to all beings,

Bring them together as one,
Bring them to *ākhirah*, the hereafter
O dweller in *mahshar*,
The assembly on Judgment Day."

The Lord created hells and heavens.
"For all those of the tribe of Quraish
In which you were born,
For all created human lives,
For all the goats and cattle
You are the *annal*, the great lord,
You fill all lives O golden Muhammad,
O on the day of *qiyāmah*, the reckoning
Which comes tomorrow, bring them all
Without fail, unite them
With the Āthi through your grace,
Bring them to goodness itself,
Unite them with Yā Rahmān,
O Guru Nāthan Muhammad."

CHAPTER II

Lost on the Way to Mecca

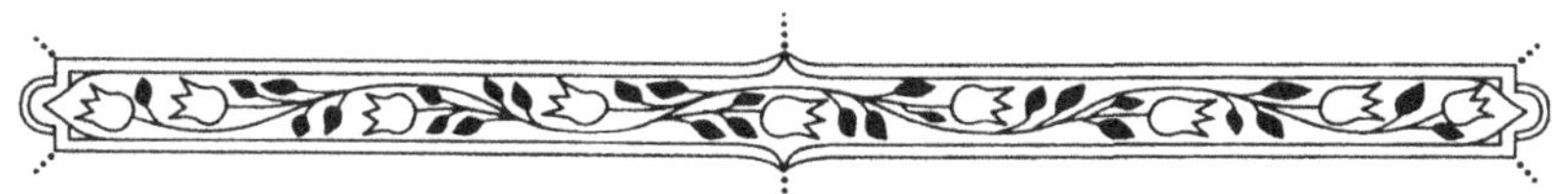

Lost on the Way
to Mecca

And so the celestial beings blessed him with this lullaby before the opening and closing of Āminah's eyes ﷺ, bringing noble Muhammad ﷺ back down, placing him in Āminah's presence ﷺ. She opened her eyes, embraced Muhammad ﷺ and kissed him. When she saw he was wearing a white silk robe, that he held a key in one hand, that a light shone from the nape of his neck and that his arms were long she kissed him again. Looking at these signs she said, "O noble Muhammad," embraced him and kissed him again. Muhammad ﷺ spent his first six months with Āminah ﷺ until the time came when she had no milk left to nurse him.

Because of her poverty
He might have had to go without milk,
There was nothing she could do,
Āminah's milk ﷺ dried up because of poverty.
From the little town called Qulay came Halimah,
She came with truth from that city
To offer her milk
Because of her own poverty and illness:
Roaming around the country

She had looked for a baby to nurse
In exchange for money and gifts.
When she came to Abū Ṭālib
They asked her to feed noble Muhammad ﷺ
And she accepted in the fullness of her heart.
One of her breasts had withered —
She picked up Muhammad ﷺ, embraced him
And held him to her breast,
This withered breast suddenly filled,
Overflowing with milk,
And noble Muhammad ﷺ drank milk
From that breast, delighting in the taste.
As she offered that breast with joy
The other one also filled,
Overflowing with milk,
She had an excess of milk and it flowed.
While noble Muhammad ﷺ delighted in the taste
Her illness disappeared,
Halimah who had been thin filled out,
Blood rushed to her face
And a fragrance poured forth as she was cured,
Her heart and body changed,
Halimah acquired the appearance
Of a sixteen-year old girl,
Her heart and her body became very beautiful,
Her face was lit with radiance.
As soon as Halimah picked up noble Muhammad ﷺ
And embraced him to her breast

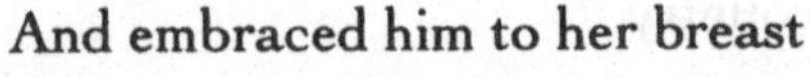

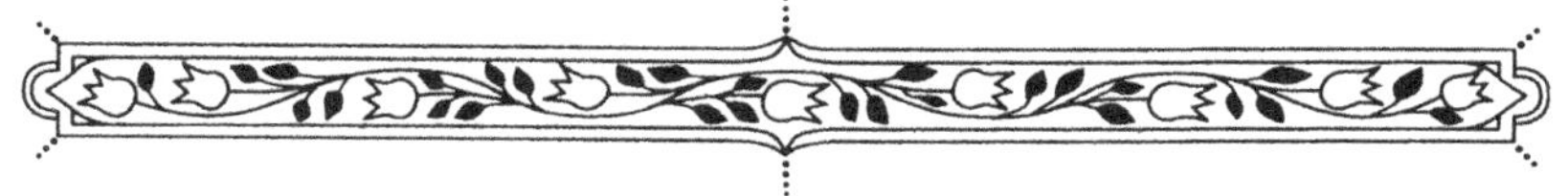

Her state changed completely,
Her *īmān*, her faith became firm,
Her determination strong,
When she held noble Muhammad ﷺ
Her *īmān* became very firm.
Contemplating the exaltedness with which
Noble Muhammadur-Rasūl ﷺ was born
And had grown, Halimah accepted the truth.
First the Āthi made noble Muhammad ﷺ
An exquisite taste for Halimah,
Then He transformed her body completely,
A beautiful state, her heart melted
With thoughts of the Āthi.
She called him Ahamed and the name
Noble Muhammad ﷺ flourished,
Then Halimah decided to take him
To her little town of Qulay.
Noble Muhammad ﷺ also decided
With firm determination
He would go to that country,
And Halimah was given permission
From Āminah ؓ when she requested,
"Please let me take this child to my town,
Let me nurse him and raise him;
As soon as he is weaned
I will bring him back."

Halimah spoke to Āminah ؓ so peacefully,

With patience and profound humility,
Showing her the baby and how her body,
Her entire condition had become
A state of peace and tranquility.
With great joy and tenderness
Āminah ﷺ took the Āthi Nabī
And put him in Halimah's arms,
She received him saying, "Allāhu Nāyan is our help."
As she was about to ride off happily
Towards the town called Qulay
On her haggard old camel,
That ancient creature became big and strong,
It jumped up and down,
Its skin changed, its blood changed,
The old camel became young and sprightly.
On the way to the town called Qulay
The camel trotted along very quickly,
And when they reached the joyful town
Called Qulay, when she saw it Halimah
Thought to herself, in her *qalb*, her heart,
"O Āthi Rahmān, O Jōthi mani, radiant gem,
Is this Your child of grace,
Is he the gem precious in all the worlds,
Is he the eye of completeness,
Is this a child born through Your grace,
Did You create him as resplendence,
Did You name him resplendent Muhammad,
Is he the primal one for *ākhirah* and the heavens,

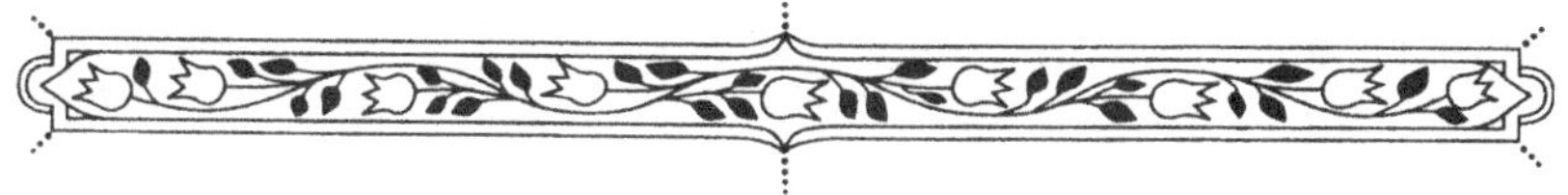

Is he a primal god,

Is he that resplendent *Nabī,* that Prophet,

Is he a pearl for all the shining celestial beings,

Is he Muhammad?

He's cured me of many troubles

I've had for so long,

My body has become full and strong,

He has given me exaltedness, radiance,

He has made radiant beauty

Pour from my face.

As soon as this precious baby took my breast

A state of coolness, beauty and bliss rose in me.

Is this good baby the emperor of two worlds,

Is he a messenger of the gracious blissful Lord,

Is he the *annal,* the great lord,

Is he the jewel, the diamond,

Is he that Mahmūd whose value cannot be estimated,

Is he the *Nabī* who knows all subtleties,

Is he the radiant light

Which transformed this old camel

Into a young strong one,

Is he the nectar of love,

Is he the golden one who belongs to everyone,

Is he the Dastagīr, the helping hand,

Is he that unfailing light,

That precious diamond, the crown jewel,

Is he the tender seedling of our race,

The remedy which came to relieve our poverty,

Is he the savior who came
As a light to relieve our poverty,
Is he that precious gem
Radiating throughout the world,
Is he the light of Your grace?"
So saying she praised the Āthi
And then embraced Muhammad ☝ to her breast.

The camel strode quickly as they traveled on. All along the way dried up trees and shrubs became green and began to bear fruit when they saw noble Muhammad ☝. The dry trees began to flower, fruit ripened very quickly. It is impossible to describe the beautiful changes which occurred. When she saw all this Halimah's heart melted, her intentions melted. She thought to herself, "What marvels are taking place because of this sweet, noble baby." With heart and thoughts melting Halimah praised the causal Rabb, the Lord, she praised Him. Before she reached the little town called Qulay heavy rains had fallen, the poverty, the illness vanished, ponds and lakes overflowed with water, all those who had been undernourished were fed, they became strong and vital. As Halimah held the flourishing gem, the Lord concealed in the form of this child, she embraced him at her breast with love, she fed him her milk. While he drank her milk with joy the entire town of Qulay prospered. The poverty which had been there earlier disappeared, the crops that had dried grew fast and strong, the endless poverty now flew away.

When our praiseworthy Rasūl ☝ was a child he was the color of a beautiful emerald, the fragrance of *kastūri*, of musk, emanated from him, overflowed and filled the air of the whole town of Qulay. When the lame and blind approached the baby and touched him,

the sight of the blind was restored, the lame were healed, they walked about briskly; everyone was in awe of the many wonders they saw. Is it possible to describe the wonders of the radiant *Nabī* ☙, all the wonders which occurred before the child of the Āthi was one year old, the child Halimah brought home?

"O will the mother who gave birth
To this child understand my plight?
I came like a slave to accept this baby!
O my Rahmān, the Merciful, who kidnaped this baby,
The noble child born in Mecca?
For me, he is my wealth,
I who am his foster mother,
And for Āminah, his mother,
He is the fruit which is her wealth.
What explanation can I give
To the mother who gave birth to him?
All this time I've raised the baby
As tenderly as if he were my very own life,
He is the treasure we all share in this country,
He is the golden child who blessed this country,
The child I raised as a precious gem
With the grace and mercy of the Āthi.
How could he just disappear
Without my noticing as I was on my way to deliver
Resplendent Muhammad into Āminah's arms,

O my Āthi Rahmān
What shall I do, what shall I do?

The whole world will rebuke me,
The whole world will mock me,
They will say I am the sinner who killed him.
Is this my destiny in the world
Or is this Your test O my Rahmān?
The missing baby whose justice never falters,
Who displays his wonders for the whole world,
Is his disappearance an illusion,
What treachery is this,
Who played this painful trick on me?
Is it some plot to murder him,
Is it a trick, is it a mantra, is it maya,
What shall I do, what shall I do?
O my Āthi Rahmān is it my destiny
To be insulted, to be called a murderer,
To be made a victim of the world?
Even if You take me, even if
The angel of death seizes me,
Whatever anyone may do
I am not afraid of death O Rahmān!
I accepted this treasure worthy of trust
With my absolute faith,
But I didn't do him any good
And now I am a victim of disgrace;
Is this my destiny

Or is it Your test?
In my heart I knew that Muhammad,
That *Nabī* who knows every subtlety
Is the being who can bring me happiness,
I realized he is the resplendent gem
Who never falters in justice.

Who played this trick on me?
Is this a trick, O my Rahmān
Who understands everything?
No one knows about it yet,
O my Father to whom shall I complain?
Will the world ever believe me,
Will anyone accept what I say,
Will they understand my thoughts,
And even if they understand my heart's conscience
Will the world believe it even then,
Will they believe it and accept what I say?
O Āthi whatever this may be I believe it,
My body and my heart melt,
My heart weeps, what shall I do,
O my Rahmān what shall I do,
Who in the world will ever accept me?
The world which has gone wrong
Will never understand justice.
Will anyone accept this truth
In a world which does not understand,
Which has no mercy?

O my Āthi is this some kind of trick,
Is it a torture of the deceitful?
In a world where there is no reason
Who will understand what is right?

O my Rabb, my Lord, my Rahmān
Who transcends all worlds,
O my Rahmān take my body, but please
Give me back noble Muhammad,
A treasure of truth here in this country,
The ruler of Mecca, and I believe
The friend in *mahshar*, the gathering on Judgment Day.
How do I know that he explained all sorrow
If he is now one with the *Haqq*, the Truth?
O Rahmān forgive my faults
And give me back that treasure, that Muhammad,
Who is like the fragrance of a flower.
As I think about this radiant flower
Who lives in my *qalb*, in my heart,
My heart weeps, I have been reduced to this state.
Who kidnaped him, who killed him?
Is this the same kind of thing
That happened at the beginning,
When iblīs became Adam's enemy,
Did such an enemy come to this world
To kill that noble Muhammad
Who is my responsibility?
I don't know the answer to the first,

I don't know the answer to the second,
I do not know O Āthi,
The subtlety of what You wrote for him,
O my radiant Rahmān please come down
And make my baby shine in this world.

How can I explain it to Āminah,
O resplendent, testing Rahmān,
How can I show my face with confidence,
Can I roam around the world with this body
Of mine and make it count for something
In this country, this world which boasts of itself,
Which has no gratitude, this evil world
Which believes only in rejoicing and dancing?
If you listen to noble Muhammad's words,
Your heart expands, it overflows —
How did this joyful, sweet baby of mine
Disappear, what trick is it O my Rahmān,
Did You hide him to test me?
The noble child filled with Your words,
The treasure filled with justice which never wavers,
That Muhammad who resplends in the *qalb*,
The child born as a wonder of wonders,
Within two years of his birth
Our noble Muhammad displayed so many marvels.
Why is he hidden from me, who killed him?
This baby I held in my lap,
Did destiny come to cover him up,

Did the sinful world decide to torture him?
I am that poor Halimah who raised him,
When the world saw how all
My illness and poverty flew away,
Did it exact terrible vengeance,
Unable to bear it?
O what can I do, to whom can I complain?
O Rahmān without testing me any more,
Please give me back
Great, resplendent Muhammad.

Like Adam hurled down to the world. . . .
Who in this world took Muhammad from me,
Who took Muhammad away from me
O Rahīm, the Compassionate?
Be patient with me, have pity on me,
Correct my qualities in this world,
O virtuous One protect me and grant me that grace,
Let the world believe me.
Compassion within compassion, that Muhammad,
Is the wealth which filled my eyes,
You made him the rightful, the eternal treasure
Of this world, a lamp which never goes out,
An unequaled gem which makes every flower radiant;
His praises fill all lives.
For You and for the truth You made
That singular treasure Muhammad, You made him
The rightful treasure of all the worlds,

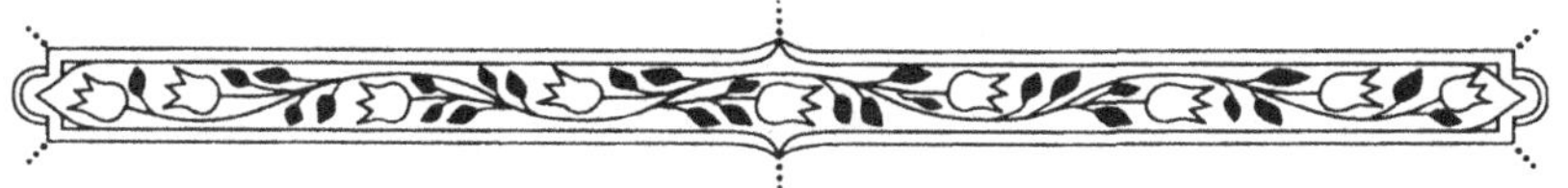

For *dunyā* and *ākhirah*, this world and the next;
For my intention You made him
The lamp of the heart, You made him
A primal treasure in all living things.
O luminous Rahmān, this is what I thought
Of radiant Muhammad, this, I thought
Was radiant Muhammad,
And I was in a state of eternal happiness.
Why did this strange thing happen O my Rahmān,
Is it because of sins or faults
I committed in the world,
Is it because of some evil I was guilty of earlier,
Or is it because of some stain on the elders?
I do not know what dreadful evil this is,
Have I taken the birth of a sinner,
Is this unbearable pain of mind from You,
Is it suffering caused by the world,
Or is it a test for ignorant people
Who have not realized the truth?
O primal One who permeates everything,
Is this suffering from You?
My wisdom does not comprehend this,
Please protect me, grant Your grace, O Rahīm
I cannot live in this world any longer,
Even if I run away and hide no one will accept me,
The name, the stain will be mine
Till the world ends; till this country ends
They will not accept me in their hearts.

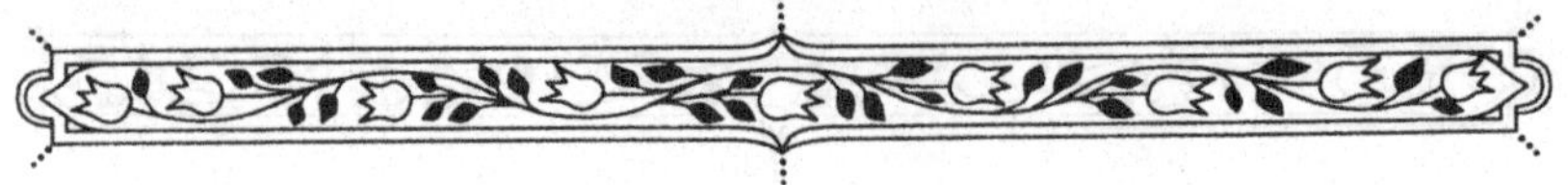

> Make me realize the truth, protect me O Rahmān,
> Make radiant Muhammad who is the meaning
> Of lofty, true *gnānam* shine before me."

And so Halimah Amma shed tears, wept and lamented every conceivable way until she was exhausted. Then a great being descended from the sky and spoke to her, "O Amma, Mother, why are you weeping in this vast forest, what happened to you?"

"O great one what can I say? We came from the town called Qulay where I had taken noble Muhammad from Āminah to nurse him, I fed this great treasure. When he was two years old they plotted to kill him with their worldly tricks, but I found out about it and left to hand him back to his mother. Along the way, as I was sitting under a big tree to nurse him a white cloud came down, enveloping us. I watched this cloud descend upon us and then when I looked at my lap I found the baby was gone. I don't know who killed him, my baby, whether it was trickery or mantras, magic or evil men. This was my state, my mind kept asking me what I could do, if there was any reason to go on living in a world which will humiliate me, will call me every kind of name. In any case, what reason did I have to live without noble Muhammad? I decided to put an end to my life, O great one."

> "Even if I were dead nothing would accept my body,
> The earth would not accept me,
> Even if I could hang myself
> The trees would not accept me,
> Even water would not accept me,

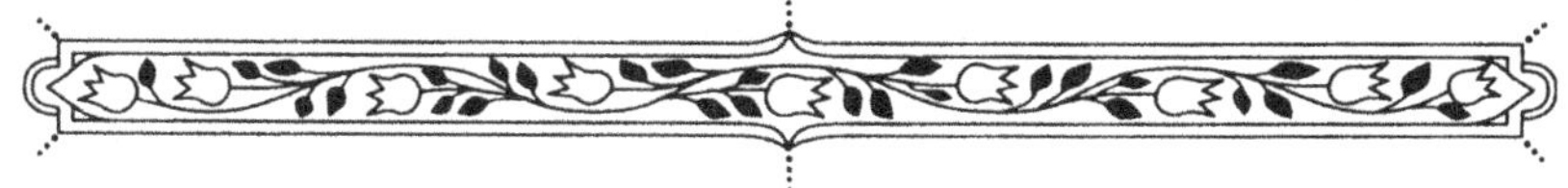

They would all reject me as a sinner.
The world will not accept me,
The world, this country will chase me away
And call me a sinner emptied of truth,
Even my relatives will abandon me,
Everything in the world will reject me,
Trees will reject me, leaves will reject me,
The world will reject me,
The blood in my body will reject me,
My legs, my eyes, even the forest will reject me,
Every living thing will reject me,
Even the One, the Āthi will reject me.
The people of this world will call me a sinner
And will not accept me,
No one will accept me O great one,
No one in this world will accept me,
No one will look at me
And no one in this world will ever protect me.
O great one I have no one,
No one can bring me back
Together with my people again,
Even if I weep with sorrow in my heart
No one in this world of the rich
Will ever understand me,
No one will value the body of this sinner,
They will never bring me back to the primal One,
They will throw away, they will just discard
The body of this sinner.

O great one, who will ever associate with me?
There is no one, there is no one in this world,
They'll say I've lost my reason,
They'll say I'm a sinner out of her senses,
They will never associate with me,
The world will discard me as a sinner,
Then what will I do?"

This was the way Halimah wept and lamented until the great being consoled her, "Mother do not cry, there is that one great Lord, the Āthi who knows everything. No one can ever kill your baby, don't keep crying, don't keep saying he has been killed, that noble child cannot be killed in this world, no one can kill him." Then he comforted Halimah, "Come with me, I'll show you something to cheer you up," and he led her through the forest to a certain place. As they walked along he said, "On our way we'll find a huge temple in which there is an enormous deity; if we ask that deity he will tell us where your son is." When he had led Halimah through the forest they came upon a very large temple which they entered, then he addressed the deity, "O deity of the world, O deity of those who are virtuous," the great being continued, "someone has snatched this dear woman's baby, Muhammad. Please tell us where her lost child can be found." This is what the great being asked of the deity.

Immediately the name Muhammad ☪ was pronounced the deity toppled over, it was smashed to pieces, the whole temple collapsed and fell apart, it was reduced to dust. Halimah cried out, "Just hearing my complaint the deity broke apart; I must be a great sinner because you promised, 'O Ayah this deity will answer our questions.' But I see that as soon as the name Muhammad was

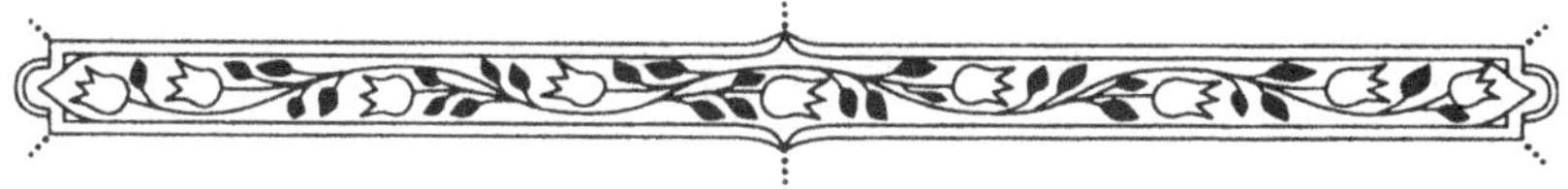

uttered it crumbled to dust." And she cried again adding, "Even this deity has rejected such a marvelous baby."

Then the great being offered an explanation, "It's not that way Halimah, when they hear your baby's name those deities made with human hands, deities of maya, deities created by mantras, deities without love, without peace, deities without patience, without good qualities, deities without beauty, without affection, without bliss, deities without duty, patience, peace and comfort, all these deities topple over, they fall down smashed to pieces. Realize that when the name of your Muhammad is uttered all those deities are reduced to dust. You saw that, as soon as it heard the name Muhammad the deity was reduced to dust. Understand this with certitude O Mother, and I will give you an explanation, listen to this."

"When the Āthi was in His primal and mysterious state,
That incomparable state, there were three eyes,
He separated two of them, one was the *Qutb* ,
The divine luminous explanation,
And the other was resplendent Muhammad.
So the Āthi could establish life within all lives,
That radiant Rahmān in His subtlety created
Muhammad who understands the heart, who helps,
Whose light extends through all the worlds and *ākhirah*.
For those who have realized themselves
He is a treasure filling the heart,
He is the light in everything visible,
A friend of all living beings.
As fruit, nectar and honey

Comforting all lives within and without,
As a treasure with an unending taste,
As a lamp for the two worlds,
As a flame of happiness
He lives within our thoughts;
Understand with certitude that
This is Muhammad, the gem of our eyes,
This is what He planted with the greatest subtlety
Within the vortex,
He fixed it firmly, placing it
In a cage to be opened;
For all those precious creations
With a true connection He called it Muhammad.
This is the light within reason,
This is the treasure with six faces which we can see,
This is the power in six levels of consciousness
Of which five are destructible;
One of these faces blazes forth as Muhammad
Who was called *aru muham*
Or six faces because of his qualities.
Man was created from five letters —
When Āthi Muhammad existed
As the five colors of the peacock
The Āthi created man's body from the five colors,
He transformed the five colors into five faces,
Made them the five elements and made Muhammad
That beautiful life of the sixth.
Within the six He made six faces,

He understood all things which can be destroyed
And gave them clarity,
He made Muhammad the face
Of clarity for three worlds,
He gave it form, He made it
The light of all the worlds
And a gem which scatters darkness,
He made it a light in the eye
For the protector of two worlds,
He made it the triple gem, the guru's gem,
The gem which rules eight directions,
The gem which spreads through all the worlds,
He made this His own, He made it a singular treasure
Then placed it in the house with six points,
Making him the grace which comforts all lives.

That Āthi Muhammad was made
The primal source of every appearance,
He gave this resplendence two hundred and one
Manifestations, connecting him
To the four resplendent scriptures.
Āthi Muhammad came first
To the religion Zabūr, Hinduism,
Then to the religion Jabrāt or Hānal, fire worship —
That Hānal is the flame, the fire
Which annihilates those who reject Him,
He burns them in that fire.
Then He made the religion Injīl,

Christianity which is the third religion,

He made it an ocean of reason.

To understand the primal One

He made the religion Injīl;

He had that Muhammad tie up

All the demons and ghosts flying around —

This is an explanation of the religion Injīl.

When this one disappeared he came next as Mahmūd

In the religion Furqān, Islam;

God made him the light

That appeared in all four religions,

He appears as the subtlety which resplends

With the grace of the Āthi,

Without a beginning, without a form,

Without conduct or clothing he appears

As a thing of clarity in the four,

He appears as clarity in all four,

Without fault or stain.

He made that King Mahmūd

A light which is not concealed,

The primal one who resplends here,

There and everywhere at all times,

The gnostic eye on the forehead of the lord

Of two worlds, who lives there and rules,

The one who has understood every scripture.

In each of these two hundred and one manifestations

He appeared in all his beauty,

He was lord of every guru in our thoughts,

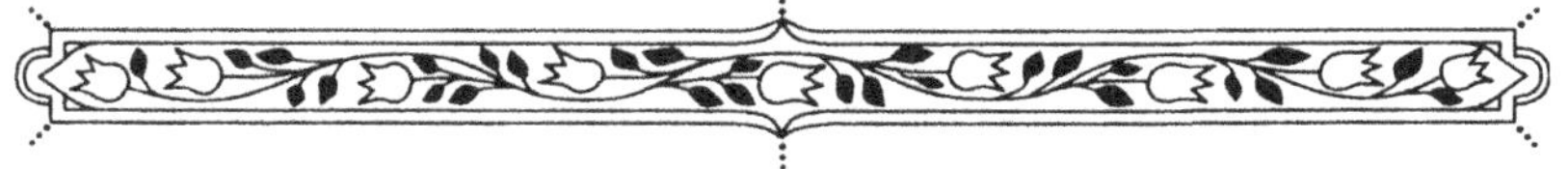

He gave us an understanding of truth,
He gave us true wisdom
And *meignānam* or divine wisdom,
Displaying the beauty and praise
Shared by all those who resplend
As messenger and *nabī* of the primal Āthi.
He was created as the resplendent *Nabī*
As a treasure for the world, as the beauty of *ākhirah,*
As the one who exists completely in all lives,
This Āthi Muhammad, do you think
Anyone in the world could kill him,
Is there anyone who could hurt this Āthi Muhammad,
Who could ever injure him or hurt him?
Understand this, he is the mystery
Of that mysterious Rahmān,
No one can take the son of Āminah prisoner,
He is the final prophet, understand this,
There will be no other prophets after him
Until the end of the world,
Understand he is a precious *Nabī* for two worlds,
No one can ever defeat him Halimah,
You will see this precious Muhammad
Clearly when you arrive in Mecca."

So said the great being
With all the conviction in his heart.
Halimah's loving heart was comforted
As she handed total responsibility

To that most gracious and blissful Lord;
She walked happily towards the city of Mecca
Bringing the news to Āminah 🪔
That the baby should already be in Mecca,
According to what this great being said.
As soon as she told Āminah 🪔,
Everyone began to search for the baby.

As Halimah searched for him in all four directions of Mecca she heard a voice say, "Go to that grove of banana trees, there you will see Muhammad." When she arrived there she saw him asleep in the shadow of a banana tree, a five-headed cobra, its hood raised like an umbrella protecting him from the sun. Below that umbrella lay the two-year old baby Muhammad 🪔, fast asleep. People who had seen the snake ran away in fear without approaching to take the baby.

"O Muhammad, you who understand every subtlety,
The snake has coiled around you,
O Muhammad do not fear its intention
Even if it turns to coil around me,
O causal Muhammad the snake will not bite me,
And even if it should, I know
You are the *Nabī* of three worlds,
The *Nabī* of Allah's grace,
I understand that everything has declared
Its *īmān* or absolute faith in you,

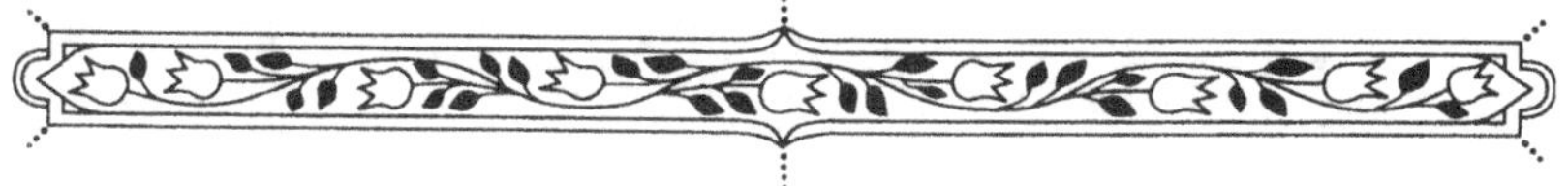

O Guru Muhammad, O Rasūl."
She ran towards the baby with this in her heart,
And when she reached out to pick him up
The snake slowly slid away,
Reciting the *salawāt* in praise of God.
It turned away to hide in its den
As Halimah picked up Muhammad ﷺ
To carry him back to Āminah ؓ;
Then she recited the history and praise
Of Annal Muhammad for her.

"O what can I say Amma, Mother,
To account for our praise of this baby,
How can I explain it O Amma, O Amma?
When the Āthi Rahmān placed this baby in you,
That was the greatest praise O Amma;
This is a treasure filling all three worlds,
This is a gem ruling all eight directions,
The whole world will claim him as Guru Muhammad,
As a holy light spreading everywhere,
It will praise him as a flawless flower;
We should pay homage to this noble Muhammad
Who has neither fault nor blemish.
Should we describe him as the Muhammad
Who is here, there, everywhere,
Or should we welcome him as an emperor
Who rules the twice seven worlds?"

"O Āminah it is impossible to exaggerate our praise of this baby. He rid us of our hardships, our poverty and disease. We brought the child up with profound love. Because of this baby we are the ones who are blessed, we are certain we will receive God's grace, we will never see hell but will enter His paradise. I have brought the baby back to you so that you can see him, accept him. My conscience tells me you will be comforted as much as we have by this baby." Halimah Amma said this handing him over to Āminah Amma ﷺ who took baby Muhammad ﷺ into her arms.

He looked at his mother and smiled,
Revealing his teeth of pearl;
When he did that the heavens began to smile,
The trees, vineyards
And houses resounded with laughter,
An exquisite fragrance
Surrounded the house of Āminah ﷺ,
Rosewater was sprinkled,
Flowers were showered down by angels from above,
The whole house was filled with fragrance
While Āminah ﷺ held her son, kissing him.
As she understood what all this meant,
Standing on the straight, true path
She saw the eyes of causal Muhammad ﷺ
Blossom like lotus flowers.
Āminah ﷺ embraced him, kissing him
With such love and happiness
While the colors rose, green and blue

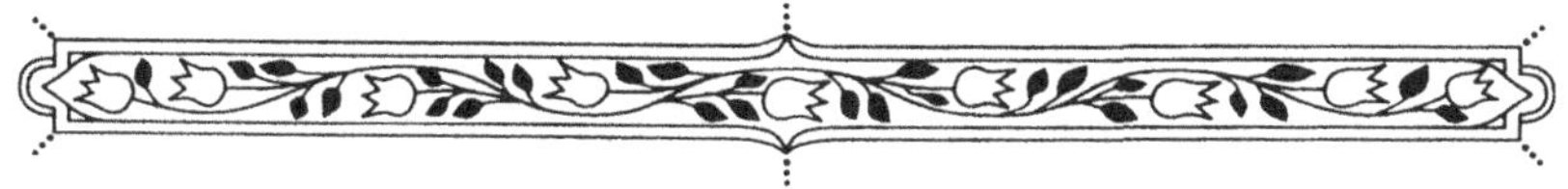

Flashed everywhere from that complete treasure.
Her reason lost in the sight
Of the most wonderful
Gnāna Muhammadur-Rasūl ﷺ
She exclaimed, "O Messenger of the Āthi Rahmān!"
Then Gabriel ﷺ descended from the heavens
And recited the *salawāt* praising God,
Showering him with flowers, the wonderful fragrance
Of the Āthi Rahmān spreading everywhere.
Compassion overflowed from causal Muhammad ﷺ
So that people would experience it with certitude,
Would obey without faltering in justice,
With determination, their eyes open.
Joy spread through Mecca as people asked,
"Where did this fragrance come from?"
People came in crowds, inhaling the sweet scent
And praising that subtle Muhammad ﷺ.
They understood the great marvel
As Halimah handed baby Muhammad ﷺ
To his mother Āminah ﷺ, the wonder
Spread everywhere, his praises were heard everywhere,
That was the way
This one Muhammad ﷺ was praised.
Āminah ﷺ who never strayed from the law
Of truth and justice exclaimed,
"O Āthi Rahmān, You are the One
Who gave me this just and true Muhammad,"
And she praised Him again,

Paying obeisance to Him.
When Āminah Amma ☺ praised the Rahmān,
Noble, benevolent Muhammad ☺
Opened his mouth and smiled,
The fragrance of *kastūri* emanated
From his mouth enveloping the world.

The Child Muhammad ﷺ

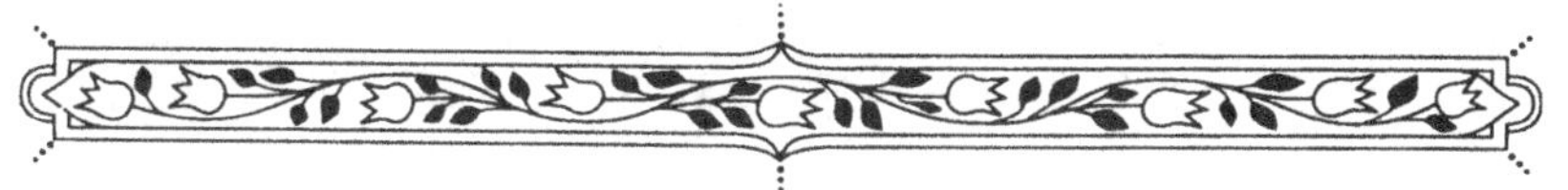

The Child Muhammad ﷺ

A'ūdhu billāhi minash-shaitānir rajīm,
Bismillāhir-rahmānir-rahīm.
As-salāmu 'alaikum
Wa rahmatullāhi wa barakātuhu kulluhu.
I seek refuge in God from satan, the rejected,
In the name of God, the most merciful
And most compassionate,
The creator, sustainer and nourisher.
May the peace, the wealth
And all the blessings of God be with you.
Bismillāhir-rahmānir-rahīm,
Yā Allah, Yā Allah, Yā Allah,
Yā Rahmān, Yā Rahmān, Yā Rahmān,
Yā Rahīm, Yā Rahīm, Yā Rahīm,
Yā Allāhu Akbar.

A'udhu billāhi minash-shaitānir-rajīm. Bismillāhir-rahmānir-rahīm. All praise and praises are to Allah alone; all praise, the *rahmat* or grace, the *mubārakāt,* or wealth of the three worlds, may all that

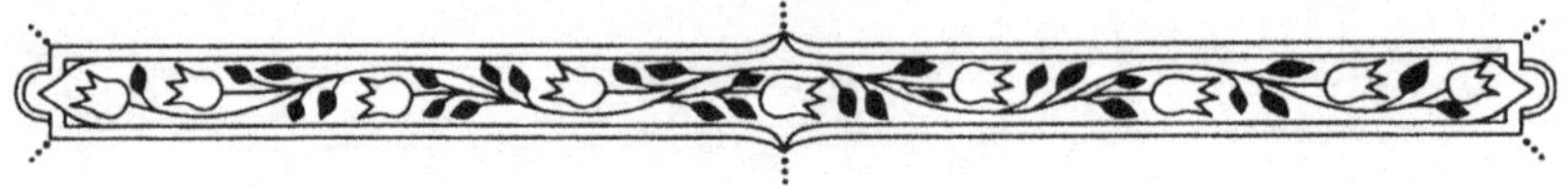

be His. O Yā Rahmān, I put my trust in You, always the One of plenitude, of beauty and bliss. Nothing is Your equal, this is the clarity of wisdom, the understanding of truth. May You bestow Your grace, may all my children receive the completeness of good, true wisdom, of Your certitude, Your goodness and may they live in that state forever with Your grace. *Āmīn.*

My children, we were born into this world and we must understand why — why were we born, why did we come here, what is the purpose of our life, why did we come to this world? What do we need to understand, where will we go from here, what do we need to know? This is what we have to examine with our wisdom. What my children must understand, what we have to understand is the meaning of our destiny and the magnitude of perception, awareness and wisdom. May we make the effort to understand this, to achieve clarity; may Allah shower His *rahmat* upon us for this. May He send down His *qudrat,* His power, and His *rahmat,* may He fill us with His grace, may He give us wisdom which will resplend, which will analyze so that His praise will never fade and may the resonance of His truth resplend in our *qalb,* our heart, in our eyes and our intention. May this resonate fully, may Allah grant us His grace in this. *Āmīn. Āmīn.*

With Allah's divine name we must understand every meaning. That is our real purpose my children, we have come here to understand the inner meaning of that truth, we have come here to understand the meaning of this world. Allāhu ta‘ālā Nāyan, that exalted Lord who is God has placed His divine messenger in our midst, a witness to this. With perception and awareness we must understand the wisdom which was sent, we must open up the path of right conduct, of truth, follow that path and drink in the qualities of this truth. If we fail to understand the laws relating to this, sorrow will rise from our ignorance. To put our trust in Allah in a state of ignorance does not seem appropriate for wisdom.

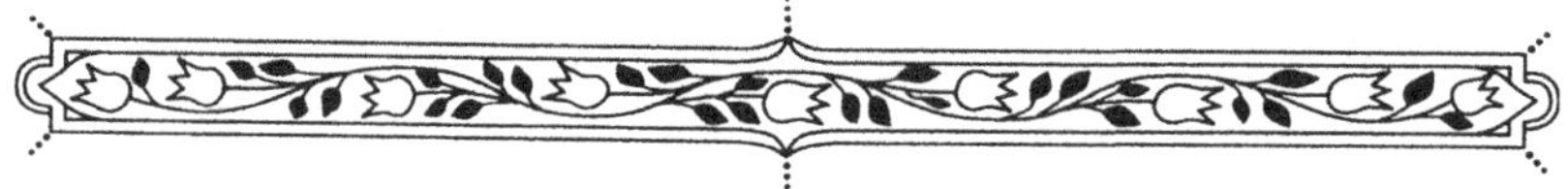

All praise belongs to Him. To speak, to understand and act so that all praise belongs to Him is the right way. All praise is His, this is what my wisdom says. It is that one Lord to whom all praise is due. We must understand that His praise is *insān*, true man; we must realize He is all our praise, we are all His praise and He is all our praise. For Him to understand our meaning and for us to understand His meaning is the praise. To understand the meaning of His praise, its destiny, its goodness and its blessings is to be *insān*.

Should we not think, should we not try to understand the meaning of all that in this birth, this birth which is rare? You must realize, we must realize that to understand the truth is even rarer. This is the reason Allāhu ta'ālā Nāyan gave us His divine messenger whom He sent as a witness among us, to make us understand our purpose and our wisdom. He exposed the truth through him, He recited it to our wisdom, He explained how the truth can be used to rule our lives and how it also resonates in our wisdom. That is the state in which we must realize this and drink in the qualities of Allah's messenger.

I will now describe a few of those qualities, qualities which belong to *insān*, true man, which are the beautiful qualities of Allah. These beautiful qualities belong to *insān*. Allah created His messenger with His beauty and He created *insān* with the qualities of His messenger. Whenever this beauty shines and resplends the resplendence is called man or *insān* or Adam ☺. Whenever man develops that praiseworthy resplendence and resonance, that beauty, whenever he displays this beauty, these qualities, these actions, this conduct, goodness, compassion, mercy, love, affection, *sabūr*, the patience within patience, *shakūr*, the contentment within contentment, the patience, the many other related good qualities and the conduct which means we act with them, he receives that *mahabbah*, that love of Allah and His *salām*, His peace. We must become such an *insān*. If we do not reach this state we

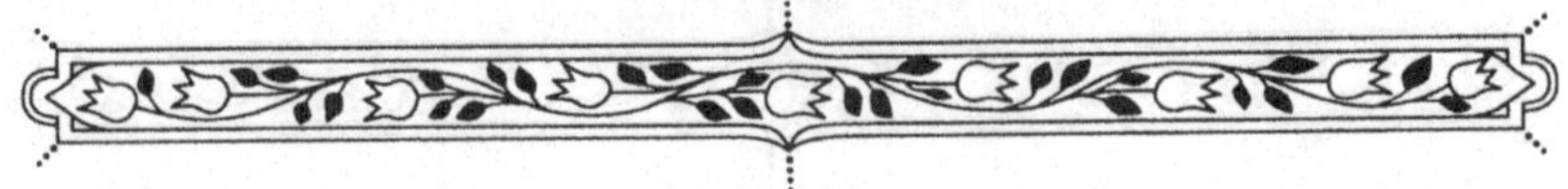

will take the form of *hayawān*, a wild animal, and we will have the qualities, actions and wisdom of a *hayawān*.

This is the gracious explanation of truth our exalted *Nabī*, our Prophet ☾ gave us, this is the reason why he came as the witness, as the messenger of Allah. Should we not consider this state, should we not realize it? May we try to understand the explanation of this truth, may Allah help us with His gracious resonance of wisdom. I will give another explanation now to my children and myself about the qualities of our beloved Prophet ☾. May we give this explanation of a few of his qualities, of Allah's *Nabī*, Muhammad Mustafar-Rasūl ☾, the divine messenger of Allah and the *Nabī* of us all.

When he was four years old he was being raised by Halimah Amma who had two children of her own at the time. She had observed some of his characteristics, his goodness, his love, the qualities of mercy and she raised him as a very exalted child. Halimah Amma raised the messenger of Allah after his mother Āminah ☾ passed away. May we try to understand the meaning and resonance of his love and goodness. We should think about this, reflect on it.

When Halimah's own children were four years old they used to herd her flock of sheep and goats, it was the custom at that time for little children to be shepherds of the herds. As for this custom, *Nabī* Muhammad Mustafā ☾, raised by Halimah in his early childhood, even at that tender age he asked, "Mother, where do my brothers go when they leave by day and return at sundown, what is the reason for this, why do they do this?" Considering his qualities, the love, affection and mercy, Halimah Amma spoke to him tenderly, "O my son, O my precious eye, my gem, light of my reason, O child with that radiant grace of nine gems, child whom Allah has bestowed upon me with His grace as a bountiful gift, O Muhammad!" As she said this Halimah hugged him, kissed him,

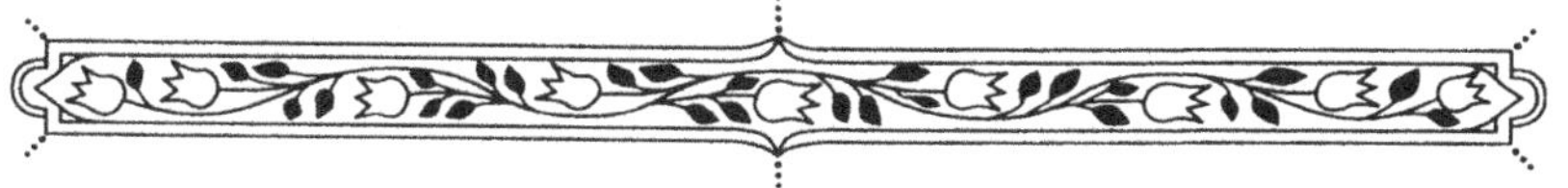

talked to him with great love, embraced him kindly then spoke beautifully, affectionately, "O my son, it is the custom for your brothers to graze the sheep and goats during the day and bring them back at sundown."

When our gracious Nabī Muhammad Mustafar-Rasūl ☉ heard these words he was indeed very young, but while still a small child certain things had dawned in his reason, "Even children of my age, children at this very tender age aspire to do their duty. Am I the only one to be looked after with love and compassion by his mother, to receive food, be given comfort, tenderness, affection and happiness without doing Allah's duty as they do? Is it right for me to forget the focus, the intention of Allah's duties, to have the desire to enjoy my own comfort?" At the age of four he thought of this by himself and said so to Halimah. "O my Mother," he said, "I want to herd the sheep and goats with my brothers tomorrow, please send me with them."

Then Halimah Amma answered, "O gem of my eye, my son, you are only a little child, the path your brothers take has stones, thorns and underbrush, there is so much heat and sun, so many dangers. When you herd animals they run off in all directions; your brothers have to round them up to bring them home. Your feet will be pricked by thorns, you will suffer such pain you will not be able to bear it, the sun will blaze down upon you, O my eye, O my gem!" Halimah Amma embraced him pleading, "Please forget about this, take back your request."

But Muhammad Mustafar-Rasūl ☉ even at that tender age replied, "O Mother, Allah is the only One with compassion for all lives; haven't you understood His qualities and His duty yet? We've all come to this world to do the duty He has assigned us. You look after me alone with your love, your compassion and tenderness, you treat me alone with so much love, affection, compassion, care and exaltedness, but you should look after all beings with the same

qualities. O my Mother, shouldn't you feel the same compassion for all the children who walk on stones and thorns in the heat of the sun, suffering all that? Shouldn't you share the affection you have for me with them too, O my Mother? Only when you offer everyone the same love you show me will you become a precious mother for the world." He opened his beautiful mouth and said these words.

When Halimah Amma heard that her heart melted, "How will I ever get over this great love I have for you? O my eye, O my gem who rid us of our difficulties, our diseases, our poverty, you removed all poverty from the land, you gave us such love and affection. You brought the trees back to life and made them flower again, you made the rains fall, you made the sheep and cattle sleek and fat. O Messenger of Allah who displayed His qualities of mercy and beauty, who ended our suffering, how can my mind accept something which will cause you suffering?"

To this he replied, "O Mother, that Allah who is complete in all lives, who accepts everyone with equality, that Rahmān, the Merciful who exists and rules equally in all religions does not have such qualities. His love and affection overflow for all beings. Only when all the mothers, when everyone in this world develops these qualities in relation to all beings can they be the compassionate qualities of Allah. Please therefore, think and reflect on this, offer your love to all beings, show compassion to all lives, show affection to all lives. All Allah's creations are His *ṣifāt*, His manifestation. Each one of His beings knows difficulty, illness, suffering and happiness. Only Allah understands this, we do not comprehend His state, and that is why our wisdom sees states which are low and high. Let us be rid of our ignorance and make our wisdom grow, let us realize the truth. At the level of awareness we must try to understand the level of truth, try to acquire wisdom and drink in His qualities. Then we will understand the truth of Allah, the truth

of His qualities, the truth of the qualities in His creations, a mixture of suffering and happiness. O my Mother please think, understand, comprehend this state and have compassion for all lives. See how much suffering my brothers endure and realize how much other lives endure too. We must understand this O my Mother, we must realize there is suffering for everyone, for us too. When you understand this you will emanate, you will bathe in the qualities of Allah. O Mother please think about this, pour as much affection and love on all lives as you do on me, these will be the qualities and the beauty of Allah."

At the age of four our precious *Nabī* ☙ opened his mouth of grace, offering this advice to his mother. Then Halimah pleaded again, "Listen to what I say O my son, you are only a little child, don't herd the sheep and goats, O my son, gem of my eye! You are my body, my life, don't throw away my love for you O my compassionate, loving one, light of my eye, my heart!" She embraced him and kissed him again, uttering sweet words.

At that time, at that very tender age Allah's *Nabī* ☙ understood the qualities and actions of Halimah Amma, "O Mother you must feel compassion for all lives." And he prepared himself for that duty the next day, setting out with his brothers to be a shepherd to the flock of sheep and goats. He pleaded with his mother Halimah Amma and spoke to her with such clarity and compassion, then he took a share of his duty, tending the animals, enduring the difficulties of walking through thorny bushes in the undergrowth as the others did, the sun blazing down upon him. Now we must try to reflect deeply on the qualities of such a *Nabī*, such a Prophet ☙. Even at the age of four he had drunk in Allah's qualities, showing love and compassion for all lives. We must think about this, he showed compassion and love, trust, mercy and affection for all lives. And all the beings talked to this *Nabī* of Allah ☙, all living things gave him love and affection, they trusted him, accepted him

as the truth and recited the *kalimah* asserting their faith in God.

Everything, *hayawāns*, wild animals, goats, reptiles, cattle, jinns, *malā'ikat*, heavenly beings, angels, prophets, lights of God, all God's creations had trust, *īmān*, absolute faith and certitude in him, they recited the *kalimah*, they spoke to him, accepting him without any doubt as the messenger of Allah. Such was the love he had, the affection and compassion for all lives. As he showed his love for all living things they loved him in return, trusting him as the truth, accepting him as the messenger of Allah. Because of that certitude he was given the title Rasūlullāh, Messenger of God. In that state the most beautiful qualities of Allah filled him completely, that beauty resplended from him. Because of the beauty of Allah's qualities the name Rasūl, Messenger of Allah was bestowed upon him — for these qualities Allah bestowed that name on him. Because of these beautiful qualities, because of these actions that name descended upon him, resplending, resonating everywhere. We should also drink in the qualities of Allah that way, show love, compassion and mercy to all lives. If we show that mercy, that affection to all beings they in return will show their love and affection to us and we will develop the qualities, the beauty of Allah, His actions and radiance.

Think about the things I have said, reflect on this, there is more. We can describe the qualities of Allah's *Nabī* ☪ in so many ways. Think about this in every possible way. He was never angry with anyone who struck him, instead he would offer this person love and compassion, he would feed such a person with his trust. If someone scolded him or beat him he would display *sabūr* and *shakūr*, inner patience and perfect contentment. It made no difference what religion anyone belonged to, he was not biased against any religion, his entire intention was to eliminate the ignorance of every living creature. He had the resonance of wisdom and the radiance of Allah, he, his certitude was proof that Allah has no equal. He explained His truth to all living creatures, he resplended His truth to them, he made the truth radiant, he showed it to them, he made the truth shine, radiate and resonate. That was his primal quality.

That gracious One without an equal, the One of love, the One who resplends everywhere, Yā Āthi and Anāthi who has no equal, no birth or death, no form or figure — Muhammad ☾ made all beings realize that resonance which has no equal, made them realize He is the truth. He battled with the ignorance of those who failed to accept this because of their lack of wisdom, he fought with their ignorance, he gave them the clarity of wisdom to plant wisdom and make it resonant. He planted faith to rid them of ignorance, he used the weapon of wisdom to make them accept Allah with certitude, he fought all those who were ignorant with the weapon of wisdom. He had this sword of wisdom in his hand, he had the certitude of Allah's grace within him. The truth in his heart radiated from him in a state of bliss. When that radiance shone with beauty, when wisdom resplended as Allah's truth he cut their ignorance with the sword of that resonance. He conquered their qualities of ignorance, he conquered their actions of ignorance and he conquered their ignorant pretensions. He removed every aspect of ignorance, he scattered the darkness of ignorance with that radiant sword of wisdom, all this he cut with the beauty of Allah's resonance. And that was the great war he declared, a war which had nothing to do with race, religion or creed, it was a war to end their ignorance, to cut away the darkness of ignorance. This he battled with the sword of radiant wisdom.

Using his patience, his peace, his compassion, his mercy, love, trust, his quality of loving, of trusting all beings with compassion, with *sabūr*, inner patience, *shakūr*, perfect contentment and with *tawakkul*, trust in Him, and with his actions, qualities and good conduct, using all these and exemplifying his words in his actions, through all this he revealed the reality of truth, he removed their failure in wisdom and rid them of ignorance. With the resonance of wisdom he waged war against the darkness of ignorance. This was the first war he fought and this is the war we speak about here. He fought a war against the darkness of ignorance, the failure of wisdom, against divisions, separations, madness, indolence and the darkness within that indolence. These were the things he tried to destroy with his radiant sword of wisdom. You and I must try to realize he had that peace, he accepted all religions as one, he had the quality of respecting his elders no matter what religion they belonged to. He was never inclined to ridicule any religion. He would show the deepest respect, humility in the presence of his elders. He would follow them and learn from those who had wisdom. He would follow them and obey the words of his elders. He would share the sorrow and suffering of others, he would comfort them, he would discourse in praise of Allah, of Allah's beauty and the resonance of His wisdom.

He would say to people, "Do not be hasty in any matter, offer *ṣabūr*, offer patience and *tawakkul*, trust in Allah. Allah is the pervasive One of beauty, the One who is forever merciful, who forever protects us with compassion, with love, affection and kindness. He is the mighty One who can give us whatever we ask of Him. Therefore follow Him, cut ignorance away because He has no equal, He is One, the only One who can give us what we ask. No one is as true and just as He is, no one is His equal, no one can interfere with His affairs. With His love, His compassion, His qualities of mercy and patience we must plead with Him, and with the certitude of truth we must love Him. We must drink in His state of truth, drink in His qualities with His qualities, acquire the quality of His beauty." This is what Muhammad would say when he was very young.

We should understand the way Muhammad expounded

these words of wisdom; the way he displayed his qualities, his love and trust for all beings is beyond description. His primal, his most important duty was to remove the darkness of ignorance, make their wisdom resonate, make them realize the resplendent radiance of Allah's resonance. Since this was his state, he would be the first to go wherever there was suffering or difficulty, birth or death, whatever the circumstances might be. When people would strike him, he stroked their hands with love and asked whether they had hurt themselves. This was the way he would rid them of pain. To those who were vengeful, who practised witchcraft, for those possessed by ghosts or demons he would say the *Bismin*, stroke them and surrender them to Allah, His *tawakkul*, freeing them. He would restore the eyesight of the blind; for those who were lame he would beg and plead with Allah, "O my Lord because You have no equal You are capable of granting anything, please grant every request." Pleading with Allah this way and lifting his hands he would implore Allah to cure that illness, and when he did this they were cured. He restored the sight of the sightless, he restored the limbs of the lame, he made paralyzed hands normal, he restored the hearing of the deaf, gave nostrils to those who had lost theirs, a sense of smell to those who had lost their sense of smell. He would give qualities to those who had no qualities, wisdom to those who had no wisdom, wealth to those who had no wealth.

He behaved as a slave to the slave, and as such performed innumerable acts which cannot be recalled. He restored their beauty, he assuaged their grief and suffering, begging Allāhu ta'ālā Nāyan, that exalted Lord who is God, with that certitude to relieve their pain. He would advise them wisely and restore their normal state.

Such were his qualities — it is impossible to describe all his attributes and actions. If he saw a branch of thorns on the road he would pick it up and put it in the bushes to make the road safe for

others. If he stepped on a stone he realized the stone would hurt others too, and put it some place where no one walked. If there was anything that could be harmful to man or beast he would put it carefully in a place where neither man nor beast was likely to walk and be injured. Whatever he did, wherever it was, he did everything with good qualities, good actions, conduct and demeanor. His actions were always consistent with his words, he never separated words from acts; he did not merely utter words, he acted with determination, in truthful accordance with them. His conduct was set by his attributes, his qualities were inseparable from his actions and conduct. He always did what was good in accordance with the most exalted qualities.

And that is not all, he showed the same characteristics, the same conduct to snakes, scorpions, *hayawāns*, wild beasts, all the different species. He performed countless acts with this exaltedness. If someone broke his tooth or beat him or pushed him down, whatever torture they might inflict on him, he would bear it with *sabūr*, inner patience, he would turn to Allah pleading with Him to give them wisdom. It is impossible to describe all his excellent qualities. Goats, camels, cattle — animals spoke to him, conversed with him. Snakes, crocodiles and other such creatures offered deep love and affection to him, they spoke to him. He always manifested love and compassion for them all. What he did was the truth, what he exhibited were the characteristics of truth, he never told a lie, he did not see himself as exalted and he never accepted any praise. It made no difference what religion a person died in, he would accompany the body and help others bury it the right way. Whenever a distinguished person spoke to him it was his nature to listen, to reflect on such words, trying to understand the truth in what was said. He had no pride at all, no sense of difference between *you* and *I*. He always displayed the qualities of humility, mercy and beauty. In everything he conducted himself with *tawakkul*, trust

in Allah. When he walked he walked with his head bent down, watching the path he walked on closely, always walking the path of truth, always doing what was good. We cannot describe the magnitude of his qualities in every respect. At every moment he lived in the *tawakkul* of Allah, at every *waqt*, every time of prayer, he prayed, worshiped and lived in that certitude of Allah. We must absorb his actions, his qualities, his *ḥāl* or state, his conduct, the goodness and love of this exalted *Nabī* ☾.

Without understanding his state, his actions, his excellence and then acting as he would, it is not acceptable to claim we are his followers. Someone who has not absorbed his attributes is not a true follower. Lies, false actions, jealousy or vengeance are not the acts of his followers. We must try to think, to reflect on this state very carefully. Every child, you and I *thambi*, my brother, all of us say we are part of Islam because we do not understand the exaltedness of Islam, the actions of Islam, the meaning of Islam. Because we do not understand we proclaim this state of Islam without fear or timidity. We do not observe those actions, we do not absorb those attributes, and all our talk, our actions and our conduct are meaningless. This is our state as we act with falsehood, jealousy and hypocrisy. We must destroy these qualities to absorb the attributes of Allah. As long as we do not understand the truth of Allah's qualities, as long as we do not focus on absorbing them our actions are all unacceptable. Think about this a little, try to understand. Do not be hasty about anything, consider everything. If you are not in that state and proclaim yourself to be of this religion, of this tribe, you do not have true *īmān*, that is faith, certitude and determination.

"Who could ever praise this child Muhammad enough,
Will it ever be possible to know

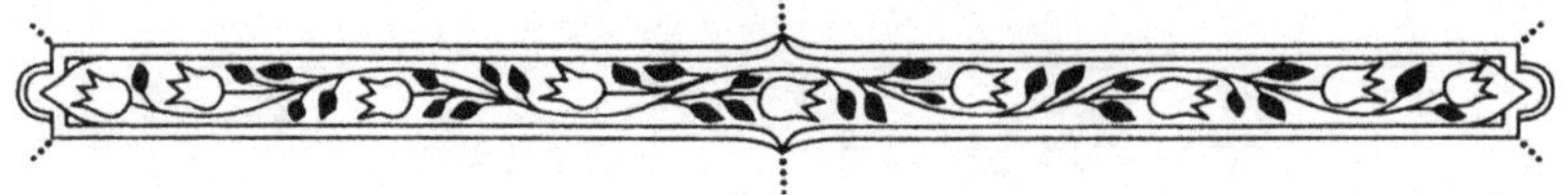

How truly great this child Muhammadur-Rasūl is?
Will it ever be possible to know
How truly great this child Muhammadur-Rasūl is?
Who has understood perfection,
Who has understood perfection?"
Āminah ☉ praised the magnitude of that treasure
Of eternal bliss with a tender look,
Āminah ☉ praised the magnitude of that treasure
Of eternal bliss with a tender look,
Embracing him with great affection to her heart,
Embracing him with great affection to her heart,
Then praising him as the son of truth,
Then praising him as the son of truth.
So that minds would acquire distinction
And have the capacity to perceive excellence
He was born as the son of true and just Āminah ☉,
He was born as the son of true and just Āminah ☉.
It was Āminah ☉ who established the heritage,
The eminent baby Muhammad ☪ is the prophet
Who took birth and grew up in all four religions.
He is rightly called Muhammad ☪ in the world,
And with affectionate praise
He is also called baby Muhammad ☪.
The state of this child Muhammad ☪
Made joy overflow everywhere —
For one-pointedness, for truth and justice he is the one,
The treasure who rules under one umbrella.
To describe this state is eternal bliss,

The one-pointed baby Muhammad
Who analyzes with analytic wisdom,
Marking the one-pointed path,
Who makes you aware of completeness,
That gem of graceful bliss,
That divine gem of Āminah is the *guru mani,*
The gem-like guru of all the universes;
Everyone in the world praises him this way,
The gem of grace, the baby Muhammadur-Rasūl ,
Everyone sings in praise of his completeness.
Search for the grace of that gracious
Guru nāthan who is the exalted teacher,
Search in the way described, as it was told.
With her good intentions and good conduct
Āminah placed this Mahmūd
Firmly in her heart.
"For the whole country he is a man,
For the cage of the body he is life,
The complete treasure for those who seek him,
The *guru nāthan* who appeared as the baby Muhammad,
Muhammadur-Rasūl.
With the beautiful qualities of a child
And with analytic wisdom
Guru Nāthan Muhammad,
The blessed messenger analyzes, revealing clarity,
This child of divine form born to the world
Is praised everywhere.
Nāthan, nāthan who is exalted, father of the wise,

The *Nabī* who is a complete treasure
Protecting everything, a gem filled
With the blissful consciousness of *sifāt*, creation,
The fruit of gracious bliss,
The gem of 'Abdullāh's eyes,
O causal baby Muhammad!"
This was the lullaby Āminah ☺ sang
In her heart with such clarity,
She held exalted Muhammad ☺ in a sacred place
And paid homage to him with an open heart,
She held baby Muhammad ☺,
Sang him lullabies and rocked him
In a cradle to make him happy.

During this period Halimah Amma who nursed the child Muhammad ☺ stayed in their house; Halimah nursed the baby Muhammad ☺ renowned everywhere for exalted qualities. When Āminah ☺ looked at the luminous beauty of Halimah's face, that face like an open lotus filled with fragrance, she began to sing,

"You reached forth with open arms to take my son,
My precious son, baby Muhammadūay,
Your face blossomed like a lotus flower,
A radiance now pours from your face,
Shining everywhere;
O are you the virtuous heart,

O are you the lamp of chastity raising my precious son,

O gem of my eye, could it be

This Āthi Nabī is rightfully yours?

Did He destine you to be in the town of Qulay

Before He created Muhammad,

That precious Muhammad, the *guru mani* of the poor,

That precious Muhammad, the *guru mani* of the poor

Who appeared resplendent in the scriptures

Of all four religions, the *Nabī*, the Prophet

Who reached that state of liberation?

This messenger *Nabī* who holds

The spear of the Āthi's power,

This messenger *Nabī* who holds

The spear of the Āthi's power,

Who appears as Muhammadur-Rasūl Nabī in this world,

This Annal Nabī conceived in my womb,

The baby Muhammadur-Rasūl Nabī is the gem

Of sweetest honey

For those who have come to realization,

He is the *guru mani*, the protector of two worlds.

You have raised him as your precious son,

As a child rightfully yours,

As a complete treasure

Shared by all living things, by the world.

You raised him O Halimah,

In a state of eternal bliss which illuminates

Like a flame of true *gnānam* or wisdom,

Like a guru who comforts within and without,

Like gold filling the body,
You took care of my son
With great fortitude, with clarity and love
You raised him in your true, just heart."

Āminah Amma ﵂ sang this song of praise to Halimah Amma who said to her then, "Your son has remained here with you for ten days now. It feels impossible to live without this child — if you return him to me I will bring him up. This child, this Muhammad, the gem of my eye who is praised by the whole world and my own two children are growing up together lovingly, as one. God grant me the grace to raise him to be ten times more precious than my own life. I am bringing this child up as the *baḍushāh*, the emperor of two worlds so that resplendent *īmān*, perfect faith will flourish. Please give me permission to take your child to the town of Qulay."

She asked for permission from Āminah ﵂ who replied, "O Mother, he was orphaned when he was still in my womb. The moment he was conceived we prayed to that God who is the form of peace and beautiful qualities, praising Him. For a long time we did not have a child, then Āthi Allah sent us this *rathina*, this precious jewel Muhammad as a grace, as a light placed in my womb. When that light descended and was placed there, every fragrance, all the qualities, joys and a rain of flowers poured down from the heavens, from the *'arsh*, the throne, and the *kursī*, the gnostic eye. In paradise all the celestial beings sang wonderful songs, the birds and celestial beings sang with great beauty, the *salawāt* resonated, all living things offered praise, even the earth praised, the sky praised. This child who was so praised, Muhammad was conceived in my womb as light.

As soon as I had conceived I told my lawful husband Nāthan

'Abdullāh, and when I reported this divine dream to my *nāthan*, my lord, he replied, 'O Āminah what is conceived in your womb is a gem of grace, the guru's gem, the primal gem of the Āthi, the messenger who is to be born in the religion of Furqān, Islam. It is he who has been conceived in your womb, it is this pearl who will be most precious for all the worlds. When the child who has been conceived starts growing in your womb, I will not be alive.' "

Āminah ☺ continued, "And so 'Abdullāh went on a trade mission to Yemen when the baby was four months in the womb, and on the way back he died. The child's father passed away and was buried at the side of the road which leads to Qulay. Then I carried this baby from the fourth month to the tenth when I gave birth to him. Celestial beings descended from the heavens to sing lullabies, to kiss me and act as midwives, a flock of white doves came down to stroke my abdomen. The child was born wearing a silk robe; this is that child. When I recovered consciousness they told me to name him King Muhammad, this child born with the grace of the pure One. So I named him that, and his name is also Āthi Muhammad. Now I will hand this baby over to you with great love. Look after him very carefully."

When the baby was three years old Āminah ☺ entrusted him to Halimah Amma who took King Muhammad ☺ with her, returning to the town of Qulay. There she rocked him in a cradle, looking after Muhammad ☺ very lovingly, carefully, and her own two sons as well. She raised him with great joy, with all the intense love she had for him. Wherever she went she was in a state of joy, whenever she came home she always returned with the bliss of having Muhammad ☺ at her side. Neglecting her own children, Halimah would spend all her time with Muhammad ☺ who now reached the age of four. As Halimah raised him in this loving way she witnessed one great wonder after another, experiences which cannot be described.

Removing the Bile

Removing the Bile

Now four years old, Muhammad ☻ looked up at Halimah Amma one day and asked, "O my Mother, where do my two brothers go when they leave during the day and return late at night?" She replied, "O my son, gem of my eye, light of my reason, O pure child, flawless gem of the Lord, gracious *Nabī*, O Messenger of our gracious, blissful God, your brothers take the flocks of sheep and goats out to graze in the morning, then they come back at night when they are done." Muhammad ☻ said, "O Mother I would also like to tend the sheep and goats, please send me with them." Halimah Amma who never refused any of Muhammad's requests ☻ answered, "O my eye this forest is full of stones and thorns. Your brothers are used to it, you are only a little child, how can you go there?" And then Muhammad ☻ sang,

"The Āthi who overflows with grace
Knows what duty is
And knows our every intention;
That complete treasure is within the *jōthi*,
The radiant light He manifested,
O Mother what can stones and thorns do to me,
What can a jungle full of tigers do to me,

And what can the people here do to me
Even if the entire country becomes my enemy,
As long as the Āthi is with me
What can they actually do to me?
We have to make those
Who have not purified their qualities
Virtuous, we must show them the path of happiness
By ridding them of their suffering,
We have to teach the gracious words
Of our bounteous Lord
So they can savor the taste,
We have to distill these words repeatedly
To make them sweeter and sweeter,
We have to give them more and more of that taste.
By reciting these words
They become sweeter and sweeter,
When people drink them in
They should be more and more joyful.
We must reveal our most miraculous Rabb, our Lord
To them, give them more and more of the plenitude,
We must reveal our most miraculous Rabb, our Lord
To them, give them more and more of the plenitude,
We must lovingly explain God to them,
God who is gracious,
Who bestows His grace directly,
We must show them
The resplendent path of the Āthi Rahmān,
The overflowing Āthi who fills everything

And dwells within all lives,
Who spreads everywhere,
Seeping into the places which belong to Him,
Filling our hearts,
Reaching out to comfort us,
And when He comforts us from there,
Then O Mother, where is the stone you talk of,
Where is the murderous intent
And where is the hunger?
That Āthi who is our rightful One remains One,
He will understand the situation
And help us O Amma, whatever evil may come,
He will always protect us,
He will always bestow His grace O Amma!"

At the age of four noble Muhammad ﷺ sang this song with great sweetness, and when Halimah Amma heard it her eyes became red, tears rolled down her cheeks as she cried exclaiming, "O my son, gem of my eye, where are you when you sing like this? When you call me Amma, Mother, it's like throwing me a kiss, when you call me Amma even the earth begins to melt and as you recite your words of nectar the trees bend their heads to listen to your song. Goats and cattle stop wherever they are to listen to you while tears pour from their eyes. Everything, stones, trees, shrubs all bend their heads to listen. O my son what a great marvel it is to see all these things bend their heads, listening to your loving words. Your sweet voice is like a cuckoo's, the beauty of that sweet music and the honeyed words make my heart tremble O gem of my eye. I will not deny your request but could you put it off for a week

O gem of my eye, lamp of my heart's intention?" Halimah Amma
asked him this crying and weeping.

When he heard what she asked Muhammad ☪ said,
"What you say is true O my Amma, my Mother
Who understands my needs,
Who feeds me delicious food,
But my loving brothers and all the other children
Run around tending the animals,
Feeding them grass and leaves
Then come home tortured with hunger.
The Āthi who created all lives has provided
A place for each one in this world;
O my Mother, why have you not yet noticed
The condition of every life my age
Who roams this path filled with thorns and stones?
O my Mother, Halimah Amma of beautiful qualities,
O Halimah Amma, a gem who has been
Praised by the blissful Āthi,
Who exists in a state of blissful grace,
O my Mother it is good to pray
To that treasure of liberation;
Recite the praise of one eternal bliss,
Consider all lives are equal,
See them all as precious and exalted.
These are the words of the Āthi Rahmān,
This is that state of exquisite love,

O my resplendent Mother I will give you
An explanation of pure wisdom,
Listen carefully, the complete Āthi
In His state of praise created all lives equal,
You must realize all lives are equal
And offer that complete love to everyone
O my Mother, Halimah Amma."

"Amma, this is a way for us to understand, to know all living things. Haven't I watched my brothers and all the other children come and go in this condition? If they do this, why should I be left behind? You have so much love and affection for me, you have shown me such kindness, shouldn't we be loving and affectionate with them too? So my Mother, send me along, I want to tend the sheep and goats with them."

"O my son I'm not going to deny your request, very well, you may come and go with your brothers. Now my dear ones, you two children I gave birth to, let me tell you Muhammad is a child of knowledge for all the universes, Muhammad is the rightful treasure of all living creatures, he belongs to the goats, the cattle, to everything. He is the treasure entrusted to us by God. Sent down by the Āthi, he is a treasure who belongs to all lives, the rightful treasure who fills all lives, the exclusive treasure for today and tomorrow. Have you noticed the sweet music of his poetry, his songs, the meaning of his words and the way he speaks, his words of nectar drenched with honey? This is your brother's state, take him with you and protect him. I will give you bread and water in a golden vessel. Take this, when your brother is hungry feed it to him, comfort him and keep him in the shade.

When you herd the goats and sheep do not expose my son

Muhammad to the sun. When he cannot walk you must carry him, when he is tired let him rest, when he is hungry give him food. O gems of my eye take good care of him and bring him back safely, this is your responsibility. Even if I had to surrender my life, I would ordinarily never give Muhammad over to you. And if they were to kill me they couldn't take Muhammad from my life, such is the golden treasure I am delivering to both of you. My children, you and the others must comfort him, protect him and bring him home safely. He has expressed a wish to go along with you."

And the brothers replied, "All right Amma, we will do exactly as you say." They let Muhammad ⊕ walk with them as they drove the goats and sheep along. Halimah Amma watched him as far as she could see, tears flowing from her eyes. She saw the graceful way he walked, his long arms, the light at the nape of his neck and his beauty, she saw all these signs and noticed also that his feet never touched the earth, that a dark cloud hovered above him protecting him from the heat, from the light of the sun. Halimah Amma looked at this in wonder exclaiming, "The feet of the other children leave footprints as they walk, but Muhammad's feet make none."

"O precious son, O Muhammadūay,
O precious son, O Muhammadūay,
O why do your feet
Make no prints on the earth,
Why does the sole of your foot
Make no print on the earth?
Is this a sign that no evil,
No sin can touch you, or does it

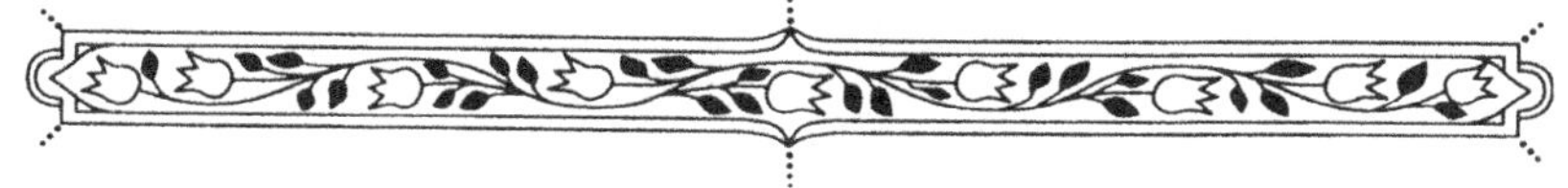

Explain the greatness of the Āthi, is it
So that you can fly, move around,
Be in different places and teach,
Make them understand with clarity
That He is the true treasure,
Is this the reason your primal feet
Never touch the earth, is this why
Your feet do not touch the dust of the world?
Annal Muhammad, *Yā Rabbal-ʿālamīn*,
O Messenger of grace,
O gem of resplendence, shining fruit,
Overflowing gem of gracious bliss, you are
That *guru mani*, the gem of wisdom
Who never strays from the right path, you are
That *guru mani*, the gem of wisdom
Who never strays from the right path, you are
The state within a state.
Your feet do not touch water
Nor do they imprint the earth,
But your footprints are left on stone,
Each explanation of yours, all your poetry
Is printed in the heart
Of every human being as letters,
Each explanation of yours, all your poetry
Is printed in the heart
Of every human being as letters.
For some reason your footprints
Leave their mark on stone,

Your words make an impression
Even on those whose hearts
Are harder than diamond.
Just as your foot makes an impression on rock
Your beautiful words, your most blissful form,
Your state of exaltedness, your one-pointed words,
Every truth you speak about the Āthi
And all the words you say
Are impressed on the hearts of every life.
O my son, O Muhammadūay
Your graceful walk, your overflowing beauty,
The exaltedness of your thoughts,
You, our most blissful treasure
Are like the radiant light of a precious gem.
O light of splendor, O noble Muhammadūay
Your determination is known to the Āthi,
Your preciousness, your exaltedness are His.
Truth understands this O gem of the universe,
You are the gracious, most complete one
Who exists in every virtuous life,
O blissful gem, resplendent *jōthi*,
O complete treasure, a guru who proffers
The grace and plenitude of the eternal One.
O blissful gem who understands *gnānam,* wisdom,
You are a true *guru mani,*
A gem which comforts and loves.
O *thiru mani,* divine gem,
O *guru mani,* gem of wisdom,

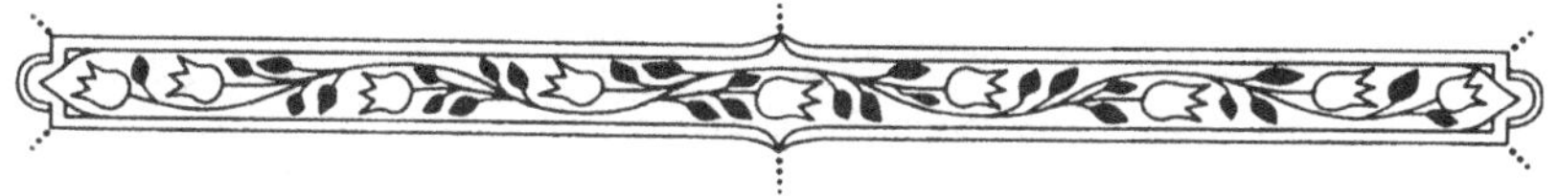

O Muhammad most precious of the precious!"

This exalted Muhammad ﷺ walked along
In the company of friends who were beloved,
Tending the sheep and goats with his brothers,
Explaining scriptures of wisdom to them,
Then his brothers and all those
Born with him carried Muhammad ﷺ
Through the thick forest,
Bringing him to a big tree
Where they had exalted Muhammad ﷺ sit down.
After putting him there safely
They went back to herding the animals.
Noble Muhammad ﷺ began to feel hungry,
And just at that moment the dutiful children
Born with him came running back to him,
Feeding him with tender care.
His two own born brothers fed Muhammad ﷺ,
Sat him on a carpet of precious gems
And went back to tend the sheep and goats.
They ran, they jumped, they sang,
They played, and as the children ran
And played noble Muhammad ﷺ watched them.
Aware of his thought, his own born brothers
Came to play with him
While the others stood watching.
When the child Muhammad ﷺ smiled
The sky smiled, the trees smiled and all lives smiled,

Including the grazing goats and sheep
Who stretched their heads up to see him.

While Muhammad ☪ was in this resplendent state
In the forest, suddenly two distinct beings
Descended together from the heavenly world,
One was dressed like an Arab, a sword in his hand,
The other had a golden vessel in his.
They both came running towards Muhammad ☪,
And when the other children saw them
They ran off at once in fear.
At that moment, as Muhammad ☪ himself
Was preparing to run away
He was caught by both of them securely,
They seized his hands
And carried him beneath an uva tree.
All the other children
Who saw this ran away in fear,
But Muhammad ☪ who understood why
They were there did not show any fear,
He smiled as they made a bed under the uva tree,
Laid noble Muhammad ☪ on it
Then cut his chest open.
While noble Muhammad ☪ lay
In resplendent sleep on the bed,
The two heavenly angels cut his chest open,
Exposed his liver and removed the bile;
Noble Muhammad ☪ just stared at the sky.

When they saw this
The other children ran fearfully home.
Steadfast Halimah Amma came out, saw them
And began to cry and wail,
"O my sons, O gems of my eye
Where is resplendent Muhammad,
Where is resplendent Muhammad?"
Her two sons and the other children
Heard these words and came running back to her
Shouting and crying, "O Mother
Two men snatched him, carried him to a tree
And cut open his chest. When we saw that
We were terrified and came running home, Amma!"
As she heard this Halimah wept and shouted,
Then beat herself on the breast until she fainted.
Overcome with grief she got up again shouting,
"O my son, O Muhammadūay, O Dastagīr,"
And beat herself on the head
Again and again exclaiming,
"O my son, O perfect gem of my eye who killed you,
O my son, O my golden child, O Dastagīr
What shall I do, what shall I do?
Is this my destiny?"
Halimah Amma ran through the bushes
The bells on her anklets jingling,
"Who has killed my beloved Muhammad?"
She cried as she ran and ran,
Shouting as she searched for Muhammad ﷺ.
"O my son, O precious gem of my eye,

O my golden child, O my golden son,
O who, who has killed you?
O my eye this is an ignorant world,
O my precious gem, O Muhammad who knows the five,
O Muhammadūay who killed you?
That perfect Muhammad who came
From the mercy of the Āthi,
O Muhammadūay, O my son, O gem of my eye
Where should I go in search of you,
To whom can I complain in this sinful world
Which does not understand the five?
O gem of my eye where have you gone,
O gem of my eye why did you leave me,
This sinner who raised you in our false world?"

Halimah Amma cried in a loud voice,
Running, running, then falling,
Rolling around, getting up
In despair and beating her head.
Halimah Amma was hysterical at this point,
Beating herself on the head again and again;
Overcome with intense grief she sobbed,
"O my God what am I to do,
Who in the world killed my baby?
O earth, O earth tell me who
Captured my Annal Nabī,
O earth, O earth, O earth!"
She shouted and sobbed,

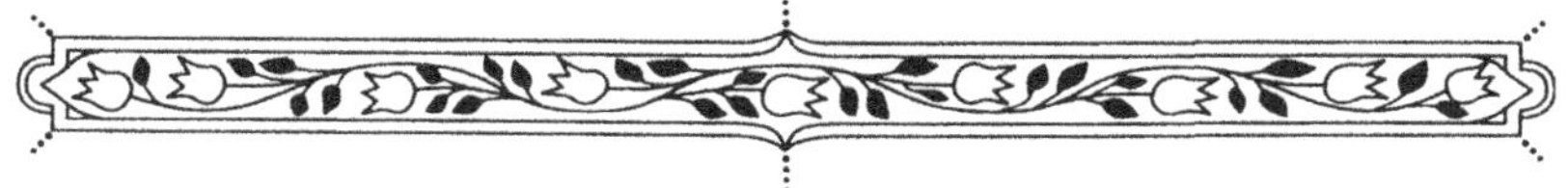

"Who killed my son, tell me O earth!"
When the earth heard Halimah Amma
Shouting and sobbing
It shed tears and rose up before her,
"O Amma this creation of the Āthi,
This Muhammad Nabī,
No one in the world can kill him
O Halimah Amma, O Halimah Amma."
Halimah Amma said, "That merciful Muhammad
Was in this forest herding sheep and goats,
O date-palm, O date-palm
Did you see someone kill him,
Did you see this O date-palm,
O date-palm, O date-palm?"
As Halimah Amma clung to the tree crying
The date-palm bent its leaves
Down towards the ground,
Bowing at her feet and said,
"O my Halimah Amma, Halimah Amma,
This Muhammadur-Rasūl who is perfect wisdom
And the gem of our eye, O this Muhammadur-Rasūl,
No one in the world can kill him,
This Muhammadur-Rasūl who is perfect wisdom
And the gem of our eye, O this Muhammadur-Rasūl,
No one in the world can kill him."
As the date-palm looked at her
Explaining things to Halimah Amma
She fell down, rolling over and over,

Crying in utter grief,

Then she rose up again and went further along.

She struck herself on the head sobbing,

"O my son, O my nine precious gems,

O Muhammad, *Yā* Rasūl you speak

Subtle, mysterious words and walk in a gracious way,

Your form is so beautiful,

Your face is so rare, so precious,

Your blissful face is filled with mirth,

With graciousness and perfect qualities,

O beloved son who killed you,

O my gem, light of my eyes,

O my son Muhammadur-Rasūl?"

She stood up shouting

And addressed the rock face before her,

"O you rock that rose up from the earth,

O you tall rocky mountain, tell me

Who killed my son Muhammad,

O speak, tell me where to find that gem of my eye."

As she said this Halimah jumped up then fell,

Hitting her head against the rock, injuring herself.

When the mountain of rock saw her plight

It rose up and looked at her,

With uplifting happiness the mountain spoke

These bold words to her,

"This gracious child, a gem who fills the eyes,

O Amma, no one in this world can kill him,

O Halimah Amma, the fruit of womanhood
Who fed the Annal Nabī with her milk,
O beautiful queen of exquisite beauty,
O Halimah Amma with the clarity of wisdom,
O Halimah Amma, virtuous one, you are
A gem who has always been chaste,
Your son overflows with beauty,
This Annal Muhammad, this Lord Muhammad,
This child Muhammad,
Yā Rasūl, no one can kill him,
Therefore, do not be afraid Amma."
Halimah Amma heard these words,
Shouted and fell rolling on the ground.
A rose now addressed Halimah Amma,
"When our flowers bloom the fragrance which comes
From us is causal Muhammad,
As long as this beautiful fragrance exists
Within us, as long as this fragrance pours
From us filling the world,
This beauty which you accept, which you wear,
Who in the world can kill him?
I am telling you this, listen O Halimah Amma,
Could anyone do that?
Calm your disturbed mind, fill it with trust,
Be peaceful, establish the intention
To see this Muhammadur-Rasūl who is
Filled with the exaltedness of peace, with tranquility;
Stand firm, don't let your mind tremble and sing."

The rose continued, "Amma, go now
And look for him O Amma."
The rose uttered these words
With its beautiful fragrance, with beautiful qualities.
Once she heard this Halimah Amma flew off,
Flying and flying, falling and falling,
She went further on in search of him.
Her body was scratched and torn everywhere,
Her head was crushed, her eyes were wounded,
Blood flowed from every part of her body,
Her mind was dark, her beauty faded, her face pale,
She kept running, falling and crying.

CHAPTER V

Searching for Muhammad ﷺ

Searching for Muhammad 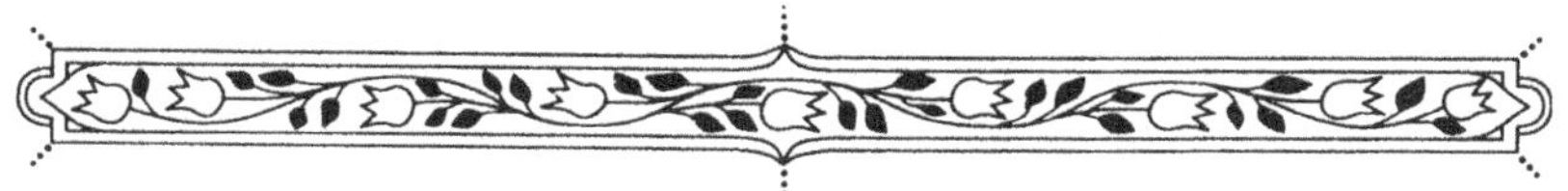

As she ran Halimah Amma saw a flock of white pigeons
Flying along nicely up there in the sky,
She stopped and said, "O white pigeons
Who fly through the forest, stop awhile
And listen, did you see our Annal Nabī?
Think, remember and speak the truth!"
When the pigeons heard the words
Of the Annal Nabī's mother they recognized her,
They flew down around her respectfully
Showing great love, sympathy and compassion for her,
Then Halimah heard these
Sweet words from the pigeons,
"No one can kill him, wherever
The Annal Nabī stays is a place which will flourish,
Which will prevail in the *dunyā* and *ākhirah*,
This world and the hereafter,
He is a complete treasure within our lives,
He is a lamp dispersing all darkness,
He is a great radiant light,
The *Nabī* who rules within and without,

No one can kill him O Halimah Amma."
When she heard these words Halimah
Wept and ran further along,
She fell then kept running.
As she ran and fell she saw
A herd of spotted deer running
And leaping towards her asking,
"O Halimah Amma why are you crying?"
Then in her extreme grief and exhaustion
She said, "O spotted deer who live in this forest,
Please stop, tell me, did you see our Annal Nabī,
The *Nabī* who has no trace of deceit or trickery,
That baby Muhammad, the fruit
Which has come to complete maturity,
Did you see someone kill this precious being?
Tell me if you saw the Annal Nabī,
Tell me where he is."
When they heard these words the hearts
Of the herd of spotted deer melted,
Their eyes shed tears as they uttered
These sweet words, "O Halimah Amma
No one in this world can kill our holy *Nabī*,
Even if someone tried to kill this causal *Nabī*,
With trickery or treachery, or tried
To torture him with knives and spears
Or tried to burn him, they would never succeed.
Believe it firmly,
Think this way O Halimah Amma."

She heard these words and ran on further
Until she came upon a well where she
Ran right to the edge;
She had seen the water and wanted to fall
Headlong into it, that was her state,
But the water changed its course and rose up,
Lifting Halimah with it and throwing her back.

Then the water spoke to her,
"Amma, I am telling you this certain truth,
Listen carefully Halimah Amma,
That creation of the Āthi,
The *jōthi,* the light who is beyond wisdom,
Who is a resplendence in all created lives
Is given the name causal Muhammad,
He is the mysterious being
Who knows everyone's intention,
He is the *jōthi* beyond deceit,
He is the delightful taste of honey,
He is the blissful honey
Which satisfies all thirst,
O Amma no one in this world
Could ever kill that golden Muhammad,
The one within you, within me,
The one who lives in completeness within all lives,
A treasure of innate beauty,
Could anyone in this world
Ever kill such a being?"

Halimah Amma rose up from there and ran on,
She ran until she fell to the ground,
She rolled around and ran on,
Her clothing swirling around her,
Her body bleeding with wounds everywhere,
Her beautiful hands, her feet,
Her whole body pricked by thorns
As the blood rained down in beauty.
When she ran further along
She saw a pack of leaping wolves and cried out,
"O you wolves who roam the forest,
Stop a moment, you who are all
Well-known for murdering without sympathy,
Did you see my son Muhammad
Anywhere in the world,
Did you kill my causal Muhammadūay deliberately?"
As she repeated these words Halimah Amma shuddered
And fell unconscious, "Tell me O wolves!" she said.
When they heard her words
And saw her strike herself on the head
The wolves came running towards her with reverence,
"Not for a moment would the Āthi forget
To protect noble Muhammad,
The *Nabī* who knows what is in the hereafter,
O Amma this forest belongs to us
And our family roams around it freely,
O Halimah Amma we have not seen your mighty *Nabī*.
Any place or at any time in this forest,

If we had we would have fallen
At his feet, we would have recognized him,
We would have properly recited the true *kalimah* to him,
Our declaration of faith in God.
O Amma that Muhammad
Who is to be found in all lives,
Who was born in this world,
Who walks this earth with his feet
Never touching the ground, that Prophet
Who flies aloft this way,
Could anyone in the world ever kill him,
Could anyone ever kill that *Nabī*
Whose justice never falters?
Who on this earth would ever strike him,
This perfect gem of wisdom,
The holiest in all the eight directions,
The fruit which excels in grace,
The sun and moon rotating around him
To his right and his left,
This light which never fades?
Thirty-three million *dēvas*, celestial beings
And *munivars, gnānis, sitthars, mukthars,*
The realized beings fall at his holy feet,
They accept him with certitude and receive
The key of *gnānam*, of wisdom, from him,
And when they receive that state they live on
In this world, roaming it as saints or sages,
They uphold justice, they speak of good and bad.

This noble being who clarifies the explanations,
This causal Muhammad,
Who would ever kill him?
O Amma no one in the world can kill him,
Whoever came here to do that
Would be in danger himself."

Halimah heard and understood
Every word uttered by the wolves, her heart melted
As she went along further in search of her son,
Until she realized she was in that part of the forest
Where her own sheep and goats were herded.
"This is the place, this is the place!" she said,
Then Halimah found a carpet and exclaimed,
"This is the carpet where Muhammad was fed!"
And she fell on it, rolled around and wept.
Halimah now lay on the carpet of gems
Where Muhammad ☉ had lain
And her heart began to melt with compassion,
Then she hit her head, grieving so much
She fainted, falling on the gem-studded carpet,
She wept, pulling at her mouth,
And beat herself on the breast.
While she was suffering this way Muhammad ☉
Lay on a hammock above her
Between the branches of the uva tree,
Asleep, facing the sky. Halimah saw him,
Climbed up the uva tree exclaiming, "O my son!"

Then brought him down and embraced him,
"O gem of my eye, light of my wisdom,
O gem which dispels the dark, O fruit of two worlds
Who killed you? O tell me
What happened my gem, O my guru
Of flourishing beauty, O my holy one,
O blissful Muhammad
Who is given the name Yā Rasūl.
All lives are your slaves in this state
Of yours, tell me who those sinners were,
Those hard-hearted sinners who came to kill you,
Who did this to you?"
Halimah said this with a troubled heart,
The tears flowing down her cheeks,
Her grief extreme
As she carried Muhammad ☽ in her arms,
Holding him to her shoulder, her breast.
During those moments when she had cried out
In bewilderment, Muhammad ☽
Had been lying there
Facing the sky, not uttering a word.

Halimah said, "Holy Muhammadur-Rasūl,
O blissful child, O child
Whose heart is at peace, O my son of joy
When I hold you with such happiness,
What can I say,
I do not know who deliberately cut you open,

O Annal Muhammadūay, O my son Muhammad!"
As she looked at the calm face
Which had blossomed like a lotus flower,
Which was suffused with the honey of joy,
The Annal Muhammadūay whose loving face
Poured forth honey, as she looked
At his beautiful face she asked,
"O son, who lost his sense of justice
And cut you open, O gem of my eye,
O my son Muhammadūay, whoever did this,
Is his heart of stone or iron?
You are man-God, is he man-traitor?
Who dared kill you O my son,
Gem of my eyes, Muhammadūay?"
As Halimah wept she said,
"O my son whose words and radiant face,
Whose qualities as sweet as nectar melt the heart,
Who has six levels of wisdom
And the ability to use them,
Who recites loving words from the sweet book,
Who is the messenger of the Āthi,
Who understands intention,
Who has love which emanates
From the clarity of his qualities, who is
A treasure chest of the books of wisdom,
Whose face is suffused with the honey of bliss,
They failed to recognize all your beautiful signs,
But why did they seize you and cut you open?

O my son, O gem of my eye
Would anyone in this world with devotion
Or divine analytic wisdom ever touch you?
O my son, O gem of my eye
Who is the guru of wisdom,
O the lamp, the gem,
Divine lamp of truth and light,
O lamp of the *meignāna guru*
Steadfast in the form of exaltedness,
Who cut you open, tell me my son?"
While Halimah was still crying and sobbing
Muhammad ⊕ gazed at the sky,
On his face a radiant smile,
His body like a blooming lotus flower;
Still looking up with this quality,
The honey of compassion,
In the most exquisite state of beauty, of meditation
And the precious determination of his heart,
That Muhammad ⊕ who was aware of everything
Was gazing at the sky.

"O my son who has lost consciousness,
Now what can I do,
O gem of my eye aren't you conscious yet?
Can't you speak? O my son
Haven't you recovered from these wounds yet?
O Muhammadūay you are not saying a word,
What have they done to you?"

Then Halimah ran on, falling

As she carried her son, still crying and weeping,

"O divine gem, *guru mani* who fills my heart!"

With great love Halimah Amma stroked him,

Her hand searching his body for the injury, exclaiming,

"O exalted Muhammad, *Yā* Rasūl!"

She could not find any wounds or marks

To indicate that someone had cut his body open,

There was not a single blemish on his body.

She said, "O radiant gem, O Muhammad,

Your two own born brothers

Came running to me in tears,

Crying, saying some sinner had caught you,

Had killed you. Such was my state,

O my son I lost all reason, I ran

Shouting and crying to look for you.

O Muhammadūay open your mouth of nectar, speak

O gem of my eye, O Muhammadūay,

O blissful Messenger Muhammadūay."

Halimah was still crying and sobbing

When noble Muhammad ☪

Opened his mouth of pearl,

"O Mother my sweet nectar, calm yourself,

O my sweetness, O my Mother, honey of the heart,

Gem of my eye, make your *īmān*,

Your faith firm with determination,

With certitude know that the Āthi

Who created everything with His true effulgence,

His eternal true wisdom, know that
He is One, only One, O my Mother,
O radiant gem given the resplendence of the Āthi,
Who shines in three worlds
With exaltedness, O my Mother
Who was fashioned in the form
Of the gracious Lord of bliss, the Āthi."
Muhammad said these words, sat up
And looked at his mother's face,
When Halimah heard this
She hugged and kissed him saying,
"O my son, Muhammad the comforter!"
Then she asked him to tell her in detail
What had happened there, "O gem of my eyes,"
She began kissing both his cheeks,
She kissed his cheeks with such love,
Such happiness, she stroked his beautiful face
Embracing him to her breast, rocking him,
"O gem of my eye, O *badushāh*,
Emperor of these two worlds,
What happened to you?" she cried.

Then Annal Muhammad, Lord Muhammad
Opened his sweet mouth and said,
"O my Mother who is a pearl, listen,
I speak to you with the grace
Of that complete treasure, the Āthi.
This is the story of a cure

Which the One of wisdom, the *Yā Rabbal-'ālamīn,*

The Lord of the universes

Provided to perfect my intellect,

That one Āthi who has absolute clarity and wisdom.

This story tells how He gave me

A remedy to perfect my intellect,

So that I would have clarity and wisdom

For things which might happen in the future,

This is the work of our mighty Lord,

The Āthi of absolute clarity.

The beings who cut me open came

To ensure I would make the lives

Of those who are born with me prosper

In all the worlds of the future;

No matter the extent of the misfortune or problems

Or poverty which presents itself, I will not falter

In either wisdom or words,

I will look to the right and the left

Giving them happiness, showing them

The inner patience of the heart.

This is the subtlety of divine trial

Which the resplendent Āthi brought me O Amma,

This, Amma, is a way

To understand the problems of others

At once, and then give them the honey of happiness.

What I have explained to you is a manifestation

Of the marvelous way commandments operate

With divine luminous wisdom, Amma.

Mīkā'īl and Isrāfīl were the two who came
With a knife and a golden vessel;
Steadfastly they cut my chest open
Removing the bile of iblīs.
That iblīs, that satan within my bile
Was cut away, removed, thrown away,
Then they returned to the place
They came from; this is the reason they came,
At the command of the Protector of two worlds,
The gracious Lord of bliss who sent them.
There are four kinds of creation on earth
And King Muhammad lives in this cage,
He is the one who points out
The straight, true path to the eternal treasure.
The bile was removed to keep
My wisdom from faltering,
This is the precious treasure
Given by the Lord worthy of all praise,
This is the eye which removes all karma,
This is the treasure which gives the heart clarity,
These are the words of the Āthi
Which clarify our heritage,
This is the way to establish the truth of Muhammad.

I will explain to you how truly great
The removal of my bile was,
O listen my divine, sweet Mother,
The Āthi created this body

Especially to test us;
In color a blackish blue, beyond the spleen
Bile is produced by the liver,
This is the bile the Āthi removed
For reasons He alone knew.
The two angels, in fact, revealed
My true name to me and then went away.
What they said was, 'One of your names
Is noble, mighty Muhammad,
And the other is Muhammad
Who belongs indeed
To the whole of the *dunyā* and *ākhirah*,'
Then they flew up and away from the world.
O Amma, O my Mother, the Āthi
Took the trouble to establish truth and justice
Which would correct sins, the evils of karma,
These two came down
To remove all those sins,
They took the bile which had been created
And threw it away,
They kissed me and kissed me,
Carrying me gently in their arms,
They looked to the right and the left,
They gave me good advice,
They gave me the name *baduṣhāh*,
Emperor of two worlds.
'O *jōthi*, O light who does not
Entangle himself in karma,

You are noble Muhammad
Mingled within all lives in a formless state.
They praised me with these words and exalted names,
'You will resplend in two worlds.'
I heard their words, I watched them
As they flew up towards the heavens O Amma,
And disappeared somewhere, I don't know where."

When Halimah heard these words
Her wounds caused by thorns, bushes and stones
All disappeared, her face began to flower,
Her face blossomed with beauty,
Overflowed with radiance,
Halimah's appearance was transformed
By a golden hue, an outpouring of resplendence,
Her beauty spread everywhere, multiplying ten times,
Then she held this most precious Muhammad
In her arms, put his head on her shoulder
And returned home with the noble child.
When her children saw them they came running
To her with bliss and joy,
They all sang in praise of that Muhammad
Who is free of every sorrow,
And as Halimah heard their words
Her heart melted.

The children saw that Halimah's face had flowered,
A red lotus with such radiance

It shone through the world,
Then she told them his wonderful story with assurance,
How in the fourth year of the Annal Nabī
His bile was removed, how patiently
The golden Prophet
Went through this all by himself.
She repeated the gracious words for them,
Wisdom from the Annal Nabī
Who had received the grace of the pure One.
And then the noble Prophet himself uttered
Words of wisdom and beauty.

Once noble Muhammad and Halimah had heard and clearly understood each other's story, Muhammad explained to Halimah Amma how to strengthen her certitude. "O Mother, the Āthi who is mingled with our wisdom exists forever as One, only One. If we find ourselves faltering on the path, what should we make of it? We must have strong faith in the God who never falters, and so if our hearts begin to waver this doesn't seem right to me. O my true Mother you are praised as virtuous in the world, your qualities are perfect, you have three marks of beauty, you have discarded three angles and were born with the triple light. Amma, in God's work there are so many things to understand! Isn't He the One of exquisite beauty and great bliss, the One of all might who gives His creations greatness in the world, happiness, joy and everything precious? Our minds should not be deluded about His greatness. We should not be entranced by the things which fascinate us, nor should we have blood attachments. We can love Him, put our trust in Him. Everyone should have a deep attachment, a

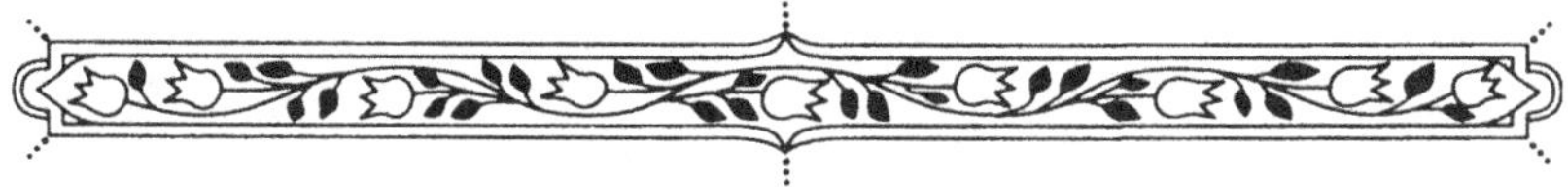

love for the primal Āthi, that God who protects all creations, everything in this world, the One of all might and greatness, the Lord of two worlds, of all the universes, the One who has no equal, no partner, who exists everywhere. If we forget the Āthi who fills our hearts the moment trouble or sins attack us, it means our hearts have no certitude.

Amma, how could the Āthi who exists in all lives have hidden Himself from you and me? O Amma listen to this story. When you say the name Āthi Rahmān, won't everything speak to you, won't all lives melt and come earnestly to listen to His story? See this marvel, hearts fill with happiness for those who have realized the state of the Āthi, who manifest as *jōthi*, as light, with melting hearts in a state of love. They see the Āthi and all His creations speak to them. You must try to understand, to realize this Amma — didn't you notice that before you found me, mountains, water, pigeons, wolves all spoke to you? He speaks through everything to the creations of the Āthi who have attained great qualities, the all-pervasive One speaks to those who have blissfully accepted the equality of all lives, who have reached the state of *manu-Īṣan*, man-God. For virtuous men and women, for *gnānis*, the realized beings, He is within them in that state of bliss, talking to them continually. To hearts which are not affected by sadness He gives joy, He is the resplendent treasure, the Friend to a friend, the most precious, bounteous treasure. Amma, have certitude in this sweet nectar, your heart must melt."

"O Amma why does loving me cause you distress?

Amma, consider all lives are one,

Your heart must melt with happiness for all lives,

O my Mother your heart must melt with happiness.

Haven't you understood this marvel,
How the mountains spoke to you O my Mother,
Did you think they had no life O my Mother,
Did you think they had no life O my Mother?
Haven't you understood the marvels
Of the Protector of two worlds,
Didn't you understand the wonders
Of the Protector of two worlds
When you heard the stories told by the date-palm
And the others O my Mother?
Didn't you understand this true treasure
In the beautiful words
The wolves said to you O my Mother?
Didn't you receive any clarity
When you heard the advice given to you
By the white pigeons
Who understood this matter O my Mother?
The pigeons and the herd of spotted deer spoke to you
With conviction, with such divine wisdom,
Didn't you understand the meaning
Of their words O my Mother?
The earth spoke to you, gold
And other things all talked to you,
Didn't you understand these stories
Told by the creations
Of the eternal Āthi O my Mother?
Truly, didn't you understand the truthful words
Which cows and goats, snakes and tigers,

The bears, the beasts and herds of wild elephants
All spoke to you O my Mother?
O Amma didn't you understand,
Crawling ants, the eight million,
Four hundred thousand kinds of creations
All happily proclaim, in all circumstances that
The Āthi is the One
Who rids them of their difficulties.
O my Mother, O my Amma
Make your heart firm and remember the causal Āthi.
To build this conviction accept
With certitude that all lives are one,
To build this conviction accept
With certitude that all lives are one.
You must always think,
Always accept all lives are one,
Find the word of meditation and receive clarity,
Always praise the precious, exalted Āthi
Who will then be caught by your love.
The resplendence of the Āthi
Protects all lives;
Understanding its breadth,
Its length and depth,
Put your trust in Him,
Love the Āthi within your heart —
If your heart melts, if your love melts
You will see happiness flowing there like honey.
This is the state in which the Protector

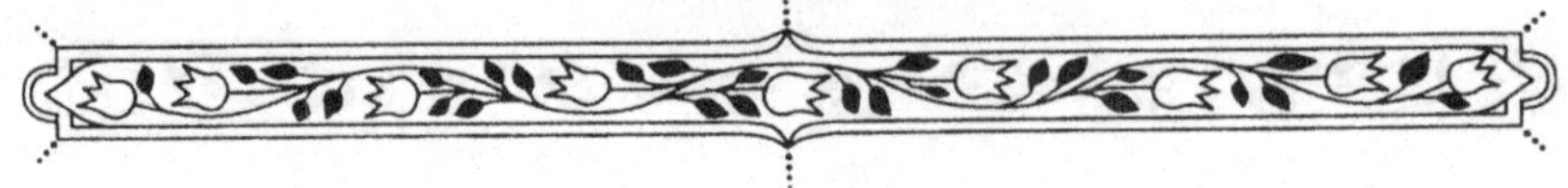

Of two worlds will be seen O Amma,
He will live within you and not go away,
I say this as absolute truth.
With the clarity of your wisdom
May you not forget
These words the Āthi taught you,
All lives are one.
Discard your karmic evils,
Believe the true, just Āthi
Is complete in all lives, believe
That one Āthi fills all the treasures in His creation.
Make your heart firm with certitude,
Hold onto the causal treasure with determination,
Be certain to beautify yourself
With a whiteness which never changes,
Make your heart pure white,
Keep it from becoming a color,
Focus your attention one-pointedly,
Walk the straight, true path with certitude
Because the Āthi overflows with beauty,
His treasure of truth.
If you are convinced all things are one
The just One will come O Amma,
I tell you this is the truth,
Understand it with certainty."

CHAPTER VI

In the Little Town of Qulay

In the Little Town of Qulay

"Amma, you must love all living things as you love me, as you feel tenderness for me. Remember how you went searching for me with such great pain, how you spoke to the mountains and the others. Your love must fill all lives this way, try to show them your good qualities, your affection, offer your protection. The Āthi exists only in these intentions and efforts. There are millions and millions of children like me. Amma, today at least understand the words all those creatures said to you, have affection for every life. To love all lives as your own is a state of eternal bliss, like God in *anāthi*, the beginningless beginning, an orphan without the six evils. That Anāthi God is the One who fills all creations, believe in Him with certitude O gem of my eye."

This is the way noble Muhammad ☙ gave advice to his mother at the age of four. When she heard what he said, with tears rolling down her cheeks Halimah Amma spoke, "O my son you are that treasure of Anāthi, aren't you? You are the being without the six evils, you have no mother, no father, you are the son I brought home with me as my wealth with such love and tenderness, you are the son who rid me of poverty. You are that gem, you are the light of the pearl, you are the precious treasure of three worlds, how could I ever forget you?"

And Muhammad ☙ replied, "Amma I am not the Anāthi, I did have a father and mother and I have you as my mother too. I

did have a birth. All lives have this completeness, all lives are mingled with mine O Amma, all lives are my own, and since I have all this do not call me Anāthi. That God alone is the Anāthi, He is the only One who has no wife, no birth, no end, no destruction and no beginning. He is the Anāthi who cannot be destroyed. All those who love Him, all His slaves rightly belong to Him. O Mother how can you call me the treasure of Anāthi? Put that trust in God which you put in me. All His creations have friends and relatives, but He is the unique One, alone, by Himself. When they cry they go in search of Him, those who have clarity find Him, those who have no clarity do not belong to Him. So my Mother, from this day understand these matters with clarity, make your heart clear, strengthen your certitude in the primal Āthi, place Him in your heart. Let us reach this state of clarity. All my brothers and I together should praise the one God who permeates every living thing because He is the eternal treasure, He is the blissful treasure who has transcended all desire, He is the treasure of love, the treasure of trust. The greater the joy we put into the search for that primal treasure, the greater the joy we experience."

At the age of four noble Muhammad ⊖ explained this to Halimah Amma, and when she heard these words and recognized his state she began to sing,

"O jeweled light of my eye,
You are the son of two worlds
Who has achieved clarity in this world,
Who shines as a guru everywhere,
As a gem who advises his mother.
As the pearl, as Dastagīr, as
Luminous wisdom which spreads through the world, as

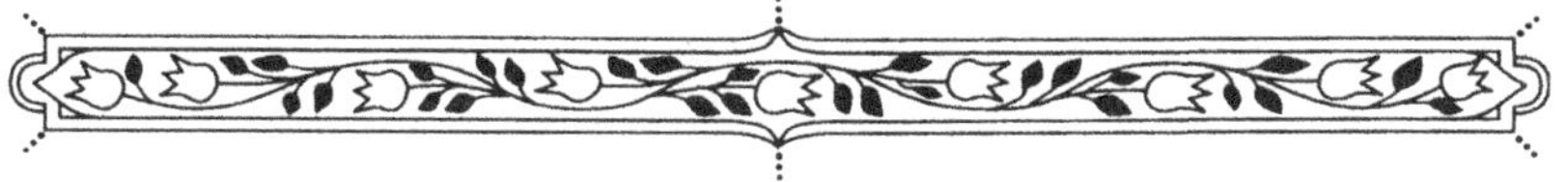

Grace which fills three worlds,

A complete treasure in all lives,

The one who fills everything within wisdom itself,

Who is given the name causal Muhammad,

You are the guru who makes our certitude firm,

Who displays beauty and showers bliss,

Who manifests this praise,

Who is a treasure of great bliss,

You are the gracious radiant light of the world.

For completeness O God, You made him a peacock,

For this straight, true path

You made him luminous Muhammad.

You are the complete, the true and just one of the heart,

You are the treasure mingled in all lives,

You are divine grace,

You are the friend of three worlds,

You are the sweet honey

Through whom we see all goodness,

You are the true and just guru who purifies

The mind with clarity and makes it shine,

You are the mysterious treasure,

You are that beauty, you are the one

Who makes this blissful form sweet honey,

O my son of clarity, the grace of three worlds,

O my gracious and blissful Muhammadūay!

For all the faults, for all the errors

We have committed unwittingly,

Ask the Āthi and His slave, the *jōthi*, the light,

To make our hearts melt in your guru's teachings.
To show us that state, to feed us
The causal and gracious treasure,
To change our state and guide
Our *qalbs* along the narrow path,
Show us the right path and fix
The eternal flame of *meignānam*,
Of true wisdom, firmly in our hearts,
Make us understand this inner treasure.
O virtuous and wise one, O jeweled light of my eye,
O Muhammad, O the blissful one
Who will make the whole world tremble,
O treasure of the gracious Lord of bliss,
That Ahamed who came as a peacock
At the time of the Āthi,
O Āthi Muhammad
Who came with the name Ahamed
Within the subtlety of the Nūr, the resplendent light,
Āthi Muhammad who came
As completeness within the heart,
As a lamp which scatters the darkness in our qualities,
As a gem which drives out the darkness of the world,
As a guru in all the treasures of virtue,
Merged in all lives,
A gem which lives and sleeps in them,
O wonderful being, the grace of God,
Make your guru's words clear to me,
O my gem please show me the way,

O gracious and blissful guru,
O Guru Nāthan Muhammadūay!"
This was the reply
Of Halimah Amma to Muhammad ☝.

When Muhammad ☝ heard these words his heart melted, he was luminous, drenched with happiness. Holding Halimah Amma's hand he came to the town of Qulay, and when the children saw them they were overjoyed. "Amma," they asked, "is our younger brother well?" She replied, "*Appa*, my sons, jeweled lights of my eyes, your brother Muhammad is the *badushāh*, the emperor of all the universes, listen to his gracious words of advice, look at his mouth which is nectar." And when Muhammad ☝ was asked to open his mouth they discovered all the universes in there. "Look! O Muhammad, O golden one please open your mouth, let all your brothers see what is in there." The twice seven worlds were found inside his mouth, the *'arsh*, the throne, the *kursī*, the gnostic eye, the *qalam*, the pen, the heavens, everything else, all the universes could be seen in his mouth. When they saw this spectacle they sank into unconsciousness exclaiming, "O Amma what is this? You are there, I am there, we are all there in his mouth, what a miracle it is!" Everyone marveled at this.

"I am telling you a wonder of wonders,
Listen my sons, who could ever describe
This true Āthi Muhammad?
He is a resplendent honey of gold,
He is Dastagīr, the light of the pearl,

He is precious nectar,

He is sweetness within the true and just,

The body in its most indescribable state.

How can we ever talk about praising Muhammadur-Rasūl,

Will we ever perceive this, will we achieve clarity?

Will we be able to look deeply,

See the preciousness

Of causal Muhammadur-Rasūl Nabī

Resting in the *qalb*, the heart, or

Fathom the depth and breadth of that *qalb*?

The mighty One has made him

A treasure within our *qalbs*,

The eternal one, a nectar of the true and just,

He has made him truthful Muhammad

For all lives and everything true and just,

He has made Muhammad the truth within the *qalb*.

To melt our hearts, to realize the truth

And correct our hearts,

The Āthi made causal Muhammad

A treasure which never falters.

Those who understand this meaning and walk this path

Will receive the grace of Āthi Muhammad

Who is that *jōthi*, that light.

See this state, receive this clarity of heart,

Realize that to walk the straight, true path

You have to reach the just state of Muhammad

Who is precious to the Jōthi Rahmān,

Who is the pure, fragrant light

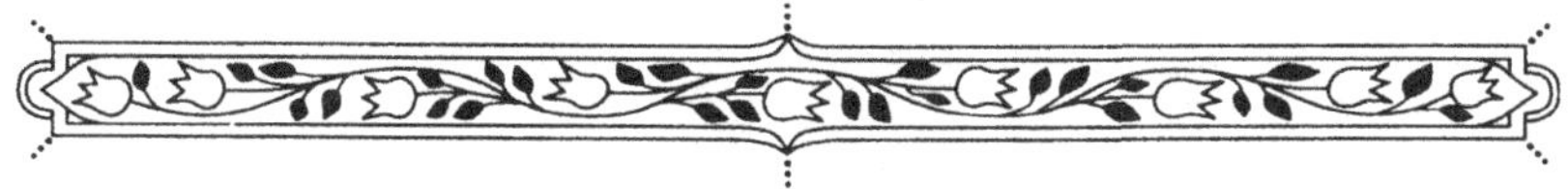

Of the mighty One in *mahshar*,
The gathering on Judgment Day,
Who is a treasure rightfully ours.
All true meaning belongs to him,
The causal Muhammadur-Rasūl.
O those most blissful words of my precious son,
Let our hearts flow with honey,
Let us receive clarity and comfort.
You are a noble being on the straight, true path
Showing us that true state."

As Halimah praised the complete gem of her eye
Everyone in the city came running in search of him,
Running to hear the honeyed words
Spoken by loving Guru Muhammadur-Rasūl ﷺ.
They were all overjoyed to listen to his words,
To understand his very precious words.
"There is a miracle in this town!" they said.
Even though that wonderful Muhammad ﷺ
Was a young child they listened to his just, true words
Which spread through the town
Making everyone joyful.
When he stayed in this town at the age of four
The bountiful baby Muhammad ﷺ
Became a very precious guru,
Everyone gathered to praise him,
He showed all the people living in the town of Qulay
How to live there together

And how to rule it, improving their state.
Their minds and hearts became clearer
When they heard his most beautiful, most truthful words
Which they all accepted as truth.
The words and clarity of divine Muhammad ☘
Spread all through the town,
Words which were very precious,
Words which revealed what was right and just,
Words to penetrate their hearts, words of truth,
They learned them all and found clarity.
These were words from the lips of someone unlearned,
When you hear such words it is like
The words of the Āthi reaching the world,
The words this noble being uttered
Were like words showing them
The laws of truth and justice,
Of pure justice and the right state,
All wonderful words, words to make the heart melt,
Words to make them love the Āthi,
Words to make them bow down
With respect before that baby Muhammad,
The noble *Nabī* ☘,
Even the goats and cattle in the area
Understood his words with clarity and happiness.

The noble *Nabī* ☘ manifested all these wonders
In this town. At the age of five noble Muhammad ☘
Gathered all the children of the town around him,

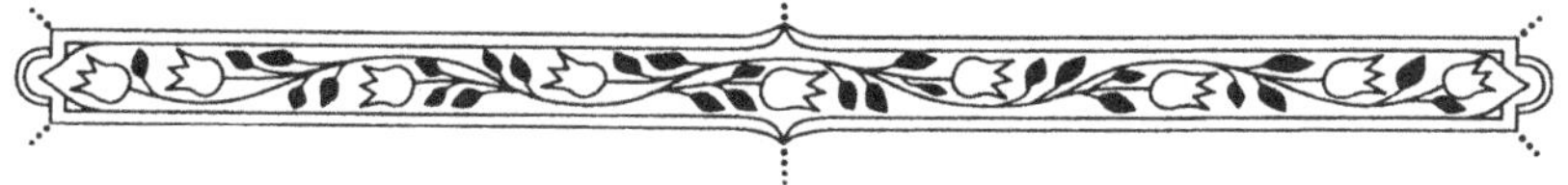

When they heard his profound, beautiful words
Everyone gathered around,
Everyone listened intently
To the sweet words of Nabī Muhammadur-Rasūl ﷺ.
The children altogether rebelled
Against fathers and mothers and against all those
Who committed murders or crimes,
They even opposed anyone who killed goats or cows.
Muhammad ﷺ went on advising the people
Who gathered around,
His purposeful words were words
Which proclaimed all lives equal,
And the poor unanimously agreed
He always spoke the truth;
They praised Muhammad ﷺ.
When the King of that town understood this
He objected and made mischief in the town,
Collecting armies, planning to kill Muhammad ﷺ.
But the poor all realized that Guru Muhammad ﷺ
Spoke the gracious words of the eternal One —
Even though he had no formal learning
He had knowledge of the transcendent;
Accepting the absolute truth of what Muhammad ﷺ
Said, they joined hands together.
Once the King recognized all those wonderful qualities
In Muhammad ﷺ, his perfect justice,
His humility, his exalted, precious words
And the grace he showed in comforting everyone,

The King plotted to kill him.
Halimah understood, realizing
There was a plot to kill Muhammad ﷺ.
Believing that if she kept noble Muhammad ﷺ
Any longer there in town,
She could not predict how much harm or cruelty
The evildoers might cause him,
She decided to take Muhammad ﷺ to Mecca at once
And give him back to Āminah ﵥ.
With great love and happiness
Halimah embraced Muhammad ﷺ.

"O my son, O gem of my eye, gracious gem
Which resplends and manifests as Muhammad,
They are planning to kill you in this town,
O what should I do my son?
I have made a firm decision
To take you back to your mother
O my son, O Muhammadūay!"
As she said this Halimah's heart
Wept with sadness, but though her heart
Wept and melted she controlled it somehow.
She kept thinking, she kept thinking
About radiant Muhammad ﷺ,
The beautiful words which came from his truthful heart
And her heart melted as she wept,
"That *Nabī* who understands the five,
That *Nabī* who opens the heart,

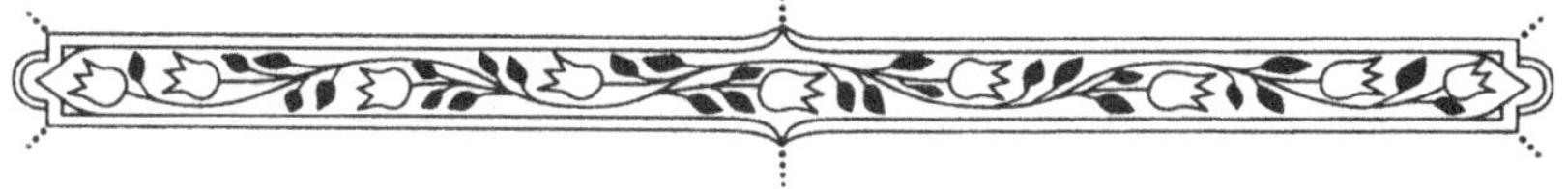

That *Nabī* who melts the heart,
Just hearing the *Nabī's* words entrances us,
That *Nabī* who will attain eminence,
That *Nabī*, the teacher of true divine wisdom,
That *Nabī* who lacks nothing —
For today and forever
He is rightful Muhammad.
O my golden one, O my fruit,
O gem with no blemish of this world,
O everlasting *gnānam*, the fruit of that gem,
The Āthi will always forbear
In this world which makes you suffer,
The Āthi will always grant you His grace,
He will always protect you
With His divine love, He will grant you His grace.
Is this a trial from the Āthi,
Testing to see if people realize
The glory of His lofty words?
This enmity has been caused
By the pride of the world,
It comes from the emptiness of this world.
Those who live in jealousy, falsehood,
Theft and perpetual evil,
Those who will come to that eternal hell
Which never ends are plotting to kill you.
I wonder if you understand their state O my son,
O Muhammadūay, eternal gem of the Āthi.
Come, let us leave this place

Trusting in the Āthi's help."

Halimah looked at Muhammad
As she spoke to him with clarity
Then put him on her camel,
And they journeyed together to the city of Mecca.
She said, "Let us go
With the protection of our gracious Lord."
But once they were on their way
Thieves and robbers blocked the path,
Pulling them off their camel;
Even as they dragged them off and beat them
The Annal Nabī bore this, patient and steadfast.
"Whatever harm they do me
My conscience must never falter,
Whatever difficulty they cause me,
May my intellect not be unfocused
Nor my judgment fail in this world,
Even if they take my life or tear my body to pieces,
If they tear the heart from my body,
If they mutilate me,
I will never deviate from the words of the Āthi,
Do you understand, even if their vengeance cuts me
Or they feed me poison, I can accept all this
In my heart with my Āthi's grace."

"*Appa,* my brothers, no matter how much you harm me or whatever else you do, if you beat me, tear the heart from my body,

if you push me, if you hurt or torture poor people like me, I will not falter in justice, my integrity will not fail, I will never forget that one Āthi. My heart will always cherish the truth, there is only one Āthi and I put my trust in Him. He is that transcendent treasure, He is the treasure who belongs to everyone. Poor people like myself have faith that the Āthi is a treasure of justice, that He is the eternal precious One, the complete One, a lamp which illuminates the heart entirely. When we accept the Āthi as One, only One, we are prepared to face all difficulties, all trials." These were the beautiful words of Muhammad ﷺ.

He kissed the hands of those who beat him,
He touched the legs which kicked him
With his hand and then kissed that hand,
He asked them whether the hands
Which beat him hurt them; the Rasūl ﷺ
Uttered these most precious words at the age of five.
Because he understood the five with clarity
And had taken this noble birth,
He touched the eyes of those
Who sinned intentionally and kissed them.

Muhammad ﷺ stroked their legs with his hand and kissed that hand, he also stroked the hands which beat him saying, "May the eternal majestic Āthi protect you, does your hand hurt? These hands of yours which do so many different joyful things have touched the iron body of this sinner, don't they hurt?" And with a smiling face he stroked them and kissed them.

Even in this situation Muhammad ☉ who came as a prophet addressed the treacherous people coming to beat him and kill him as if they were virtuous men, he said what his conscience directed, caring for them too. When these people recognized Muhammad's state ☉, their hearts became clear, they said, "O what precious words he speaks! Even though we hurt him, hitting, kicking and beating him, still he kissed the hands and legs which did that. This child must be like a god, this precious child who has attained such a level of patience and tolerance. If we hurt him again God will send us to a hell below the seventh hell." Conscience made them realize this.

At that moment, weeping and crying Halimah asked, "O my son does it hurt?" But all the beating she and Muhammad ☉ received caused them no pain at all. They continued on their way to Mecca where she turned Muhammad ☉ over to his mother Āminah Amma ☉. Halimah Amma told her all the mysteries which had taken place in her town of Qulay.

Āminah Amma ☉ received Muhammad ☉ in her arms with great love, "O my son, O gem of my eye, guru who knows our hearts, *guru nāthan*, gem of the crown, divine gem, O gem of all gurus who extends everywhere as eternal, gracious bliss, gem who resplends in one form! How wonderful your wisdom is, the subtlety of your wisdom, your might! How did God create you in that most exquisite light? O gracious gem, that God has destined me to see you again!" She kissed her son as she said this and cried. Then resplendent, noble Muhammad ☉ sang,

"O Mother why are you crying,
It's not right to cry in this world, Amma,
O Amma why are you crying?

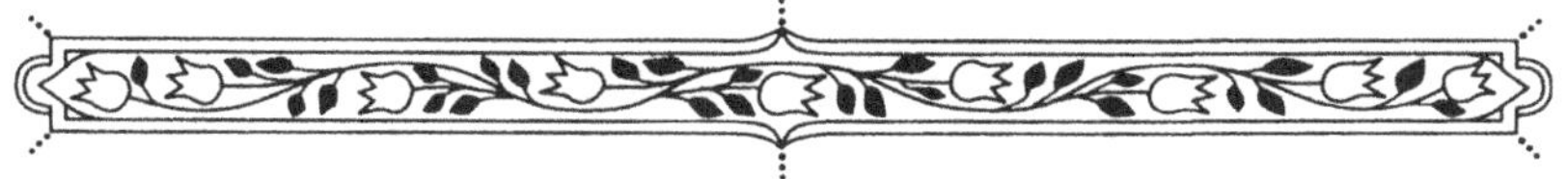

Amma, in this world crying springs from attachment,
O Mother think of all lives as truly one,
O Mother think of all lives as truly one.
May your heart perceive this state with clarity, Amma.
Amma, when I was only four months in your womb
My father of this world, that treasure
Named 'Abdullāh disappeared.
There are many creations of the Āthi in this world,
Among them so many children in His trust O Amma,
Many troubled children without fathers and mothers
Of their own, so many, such countless numbers
O Amma, who belong to no one and have no name.
In the Āthi's creation, among those of His creation
There are countless beings, how many
Who undergo His trials O Amma,
You must understand and be a mother
To the world with the happiness you have in you,
So the name of Āminah will be praised O my Mother.
Ask this from the Āthi
With love for all living things O Mother,
Ask this from the Āthi with love
O my Mother, for the happiness of all creations.
All children are rightfully yours,
Why do you single out Muhammad
As your only child, why cry for him
Alone O Amma, why do you do that O Amma?
In the fullness of your heart,
With love for the truth and justice of all lives

Ask the Āthi who is always melting, ask
For the salvation of all lives,
Ask Him to give them
That complete treasure O Amma, Mother.
Within all lives created by the Āthi
There is an eternal sweetness, there is no sadness, Amma;
To reach the state which has cut away
All sorrow in this world,
You need absolute faith in the Āthi.
The world is a marvel and birth a precious thing,
To reach Him O Amma, is the greatest joy."

As Muhammad ☺ uttered these divine words
In that precious way, as Āminah ☺
Heard this teaching of wisdom
Tears poured down her cheeks,
Her heart melted with sorrow.
Muhammad ☺ said these words to Āminah ☺
At the age of five,
And when she heard the beautiful words
She exclaimed, "O my precious son
No matter how many forms we take,
Will there ever be a child like you again?
O my son no matter how many births I take,
No matter if I am born again and again,
Will I ever bear another child like you?
Your holy words are a guru's words,
These gracious words

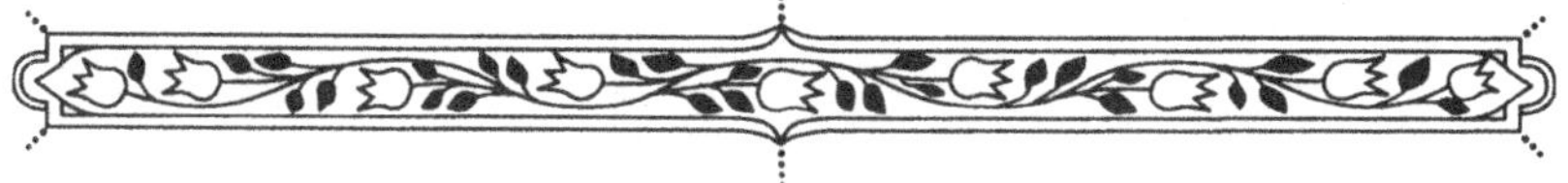

Overflowing from your divine heart,

These guru's words, these holy words shine everywhere,

Who can utter such words

O my son, O gem of my eye?

Many prophets took a birth and came to this world,

They took birth in great and marvelous forms,

One after another they came in different states

And fell victim to torture and murder,

They said so much, countless words

About the poor and suffering,

The invitation went to people of all races

And religions, in the best way they could

O my son, but the people didn't have peaceful qualities.

O gem of my eye the words you say

Are filled with wonders and mysteries,

O gem of my eye your words are like words of grace

Coming directly from the Āthi,

Are you the Āthi Himself, incarnate in this world

In the form of *jōthi,* the light?

Have you come to show Him to the world

Or to bring happiness, have you come

As the precious treasure of two worlds?

Have you come to reveal yourself

Here, then and forever?

Have you come as the grace of the Āthi

To discover things?

Have you come with the grace of God

To test all things?

Have you come to fill all lives completely
And to establish their trust in God?
Are you able to understand all this
With your beautiful patience,
With the unfailing duties within yourself
Before the tender age of five?
O gem of my eye, O Muhammadūay,
You who reveal what is in the embryo,
Have you filled the hearts of all lives
And given them faith?
Have you understood all this
Before the tender age of five,
O gem of my eye, O Muhammadūay?
You who reveal what is in the embryo,
You are the being
Who expounds the origin of everything,
O gem of my eye, O Muhammadūay
Why is this, is it because
You are the resplendent light of the Āthi?
How am I to know
O my son, O gem of my eye?"

CHAPTER VII

The Death of Āminah ﷠

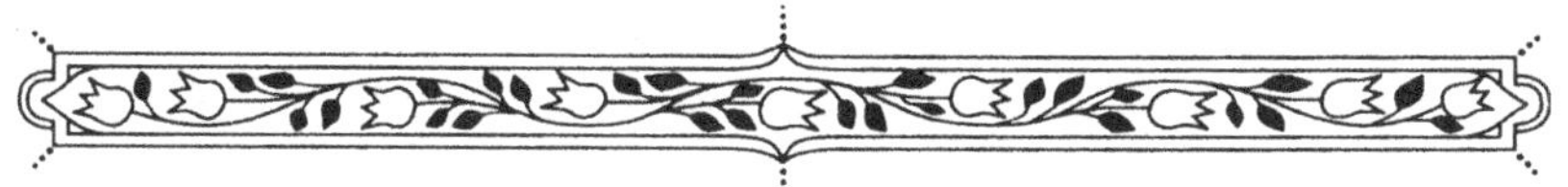

The Death of Āminah ﷺ

Āminah ﷺ sang these words of praise and when Muhammad ﷺ heard them he said, "O Amma, Amma, the Āthi is the One who is great, we have faults, the Āthi alone is faultless, but like that great God who has absolutely no fault, we must show kindness and compassion, we must give charity, we must have justice, integrity and patience, we must perform all our duties without fail.

Insān or man is the one with faults, whether he is a realized being, a *gnāni* or a great man he still has faults, he belongs to that class. Fire, air, water, earth, all those things have faults — only the mighty, all-pervading Lord is completely without fault. He has the power to create, to sustain and destroy everything. We have kindness but all praise and pride are reserved for the Āthi who is the One of kindness, the only One worthy of praise. We should annihilate our pride completely, open our precious hearts, keep the Āthi there to reveal His all-pervading glory; we should make our hearts truthful and light the lamp of love using the wick of our gracious Lord. We should light the lamp of the most gracious Lord of two worlds there, and once we see the flame of that resplendence praise and glorify His name with love. To praise Him is the most precious path, to praise ourselves is certainly a path which leads to hell. O Mother please keep praising the Āthi alone, this will give you great, endless joy."

"The light of the pearl which exists within wisdom
Is that precious gem, the kingly pearl,
He is beyond, beyond the six tastes,
The One who saw each embryo clearly
And then created it.
Have deep love for this Āthi,
The One who is absolute and complete,
Without fault, the eternal, blissful Āthi,
He is the flowering gem, the gem of gurus
Who permeates everything, who goes everywhere.
Melt your heart with concentration,
With determination and look at the Āthi,
The primal One, then divine wisdom will dawn,
You will see the Āthi who knows everything.
O my loving Mother keep tasting and tasting,
Drink the eternal honey of the heart,
You will experience the sweetness of its taste,
He is the complete treasure,
His words are the gracious words of the guru,
He is the gem of gurus with absolute, pure qualities,
He does not use a stick,
He never beats, He never kicks,
He scatters the darkness of ignorance.
With His hands of *meignānam*, divine wisdom,
He bears the name of praise
And grace throughout the world.
Make them take in, as theirs by right,
The precious divine food of the Lord of Al-hamd,

The whole world will be redeemed,
Plead for His grace,
For the salvation of all your children, plead
To be the body which consumes the Āthi as food.
When you have seen that gem with certitude,
When your heart melts in praise
Of the eternal, blissful One,
And when you place that eternal lamp
Which is the grace of true wisdom there,
It will resplend as the full moon.
The gem which has no equal, no form, no life,
No name, no pride and no right,
Which cannot be controlled by anything,
Single, unequaled, that Āthi is the devotee's helper,
Let your heart melt, sing with certitude
That the Āthi is One, the only helper
O Amma, O Amma."

"The Āthi alone is worthy of such praise. Ask for the blessing to have your children reach salvation through Him. With those prayers all of us, all lives will grow in an exalted state, everyone, all your children, all our brothers and sisters will grow in unity, reach God and see our Father, we will be able to see our all-pervasive Father. When we behave calmly with peaceful qualities we can see His blissful radiance, we can kiss Him. The prayers of a mother and father should be one in this, and if we unite in that prayer, in that state of unity we will all meet the Āthi. O Amma my guru is that complete, absolute treasure. This is what my melting heart and breast tell me, and I firmly believe the Āthi is there."

Muhammad ﷺ said this to his mother Āminah ﵂ when he was five-and-a-half years old. When she heard that she said, "O my son, O gem of my eye so much wisdom comes from your lips, so much knowledge, so much praise and so many words of truth. Words of honey, words of nectar come from your lips. O my child who is blessed with every beautiful sign, the light in your eyes, pearl-like teeth, rose-red lips, long arms and the light which shines from the nape of your neck, only the Āthi can protect you. My Rahmān — I don't know how long He will keep you in this happy state. If this is indeed your state, do you think the people of the world will spare you? Is there a place for truth in this sinful world? May the Āthi always protect you in this state O Muhammad. I will not live long." And then she added, "Halimah Amma, O Halimah Amma you take the baby, raise him and you will reach that state of peace too."

When Āminah Amma ﵂ said this to Halimah Amma her heart began to melt, Halimah was blissfully happy, smiling, but she kept thinking, "Now what should I do?"

Muhammad ﷺ was six years old when his mother Āminah Amma ﵂ passed away. With joy Muhammad ﷺ sang,

"The One in heaven, the eternal gem, the Āthi,

This is the subtle way He completes His work,

For all lives, for all these creations which perish

The final, the complete treasure is death.

May we all realize that for every creation

The causal Āthi has brought into being,

We all eventually experience this wonderful state,

This thing which is completeness within completeness,
This death which is certain.
May we realize it with a melting, understanding heart,
May we remove all our mischief and evil,
May we fervently intend to see the Āthi
Who is everyone's birthright.
Sleep is a small death,
Loss of consciousness is a big death,
But they are equal in a way,
One day we will all be overcome by eternal sleep.
May we realize this is the birthright
Of each of the Āthi's creations and reach clarity.
The sleep of my mother, that shining gem,
Is a sleep in which she has reached
The feet of the luminous Rahmān.
Why should we cry about that blessing
And why should we be sad?
To reach the place of the Āthi
Who has no attachments is our birthright,
To reach Him,
To have that clarity of understanding
Is the gracious treasure
We receive from the Āthi,
Let us all praise the place
Of complete resplendence
Which has been shown to us."

Muhammad ☙ sang this song and spoke to those who were gathered there. "Realize there is one God and that Allāhu ta'ālā Nāyan, that exalted Lord who is God has devised two states for all living things, what is known as the small death and the big death. The big death is eternal sleep, the small death keeps changing from time to time. It is certain this small death will lead eventually to the big death which is actually our birthright. What we should look upon as wealth of consequence today is that death. We must try to make the world die in us before our death because in this mysterious way we return the debt we have incurred to the lender. This is the end of the trial or test of our Āthi. If we can understand, if we realize this state we reach a state of deathlessness in which we live without dying, live forever in a state of joy. I ask everyone, I ask those born with me, try to die before death. O Āthi Rahmān may You bestow Your grace on us all, may we reach the state in which we die before death." He said, *"Āmīn, āmīn,"* then recited the *salawāt* in praise of God. These were the clear words of advice he gave to all those who were present. When he was six years old Āminah Amma ☙ passed away and these were the gracious words of Guru Muhammad ☙ at that age.

> The one of rare greatness, Āthi Muhammad,
> The messenger Muhammadur-Rasūl ☙
> Talked about his precious mother Āminah ☙
> And the astonishing way she reached the Āthi.
> Extolling her unfailing justice
> He explained in comforting words,
> Words of sweet honey, how Āminah ☙
> Reached the place of the *Haqq*, the Truth.

All those who lived in the city of Mecca
Had gathered now to give
The loving mother of Muhammadur-Rasūl ☙,
The one who had reached eternal happiness,
The mother of the Āthi's messenger
A good burial, as she had wished.
As Muhammad ☙ described it, Āminah ☙,
With perfect qualities and great happiness
Came to the feet of the *Haqq,*
The wisdom of resplendent Nabī Muhammad ☙
Radiated, a brilliant lamp throughout the world.
When Abū Tālib heard the sweet words of nectar
Coming from his nephew
Muhammad's blissful heart ☙,
He embraced him, kissed him and sang,

"O *thiru Nabī,* divine Prophet, O *guru Nabī,*
Precious gem of all the eight directions,
Gem of grace, O blissful son
Of my own younger brother who was born with me,
O my precious son, my blissful Muhammadūay,
You are the treasure rightfully filling all lives,
The fruit filled with grace,
Are you the messenger of the primal Āthi?
O King Mahmūd who has understood all the mysteries,
For you the grace and treasure
Of trust is the Āthi alone."
As he said this Abū Tālib wept and cried,

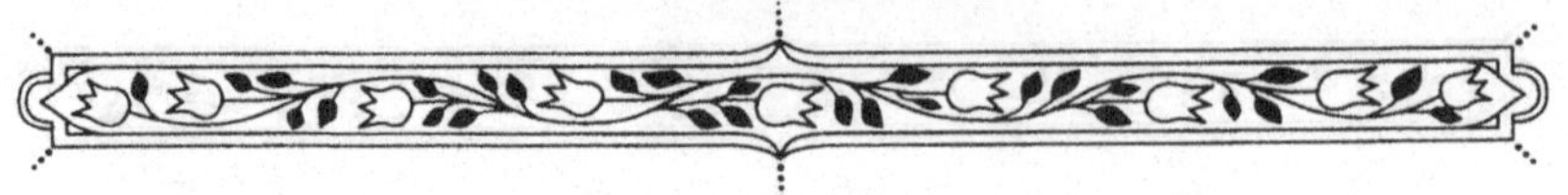

His heart sad, tears rolling down his cheeks.
To comfort Muhammad's heart ﷺ
He offered solace to noble Muhammad ﷺ,
"O my loving son all lives are shattered and weep,
What can I do, my son, in this world
Where every creation of the Āthi perishes,
Your precious mother has now also
Left this world, disappeared,
What can I say to comfort you,
To make you happy, my son?
Are you the messenger Prophet of the Āthi,
Are you the *guru Nabī* for all people?
Now that your mother has disappeared
From this earth, what can I do
My son, O precious jewel of my two eyes?
Did the Āthi create you to test everything?
Did He create you in this mysterious state?
O gem of my eye, you do not understand anything,
O my son your mother has left this world now,
O my son what shall I do,
O my son what shall I do,
Whom should I give you to?
My heart is melting, my *qalb* is melting
And dying of despair.

When you were in your mother's womb,
An embryo of four months,
With the grace of that all mighty One

Your father passed away.

With love I handed you to Halimah

Who came from the little town of Qulay.

While you were there, justly raised with love,

The enmity of the world surrounded you,

The world plotted to kill you O my son.

Every living thing loved you, trusted you

And accepted you as the *Nabī*

Who rid us of sorrow,

Every living thing born on this earth

Loved you as beloved Muhammad.

In this world of wonders,

In the mystery of the Āthi's creation

Are those who were born as man,

As the children of Adam ☽,

But their qualities changed

When they joined forces with iblīs, with satan,

And became your enemy,

These ungrateful creatures of the world

Plotted to murder you O my son.

While you were living with Halimah

And took her flock of sheep and goats out to graze,

Two beings descended, cut open

Your stomach and chest, removing the bile.

No one in this world can understand

That state, that greatness O my precious one,

O my son, gem of my eye raised by Halimah,

O gem who understands all mysteries.

Whom can I put in charge of you,
Who will raise you so that you will shine
O my son, precious gem of my eye,
Messenger *Nabī* of the Āthi?
Were you sent down to this world to be tested,
Did the Āthi give you a duty to protect this world,
Did the Āthi charge you with this duty?

From the time you were in your mother's womb
Until the age of six you have escaped
The treachery, the vengefulness
Of the people in this miserable world,
But I don't know how many endless evils
You may now encounter in the world O my son.
You are the precious child of this world,
The honey of all creation,
You are like the egg and the embryo,
Like the most wonderful creation of all creation,
You are like the egg and the embryo,
Like the most wonderful creation
For everyone who sees you,
You are the lamp of wisdom,
The gracious lamp which scatters the darkness
Like a treasure of two worlds.
Muhammad bathed in the truth,
Where am I to take you,
Muhammad bathed in the truth,
Where am I to take you,

Whom shall I put in charge of you?
O sparkling gem, O Muhammad, O Rasūl,
To this world which does not understand the truth
You have rightly come to explain the truth,
O my most precious son
Whom shall I put in charge of you?
When my brother who was your father died,
Then Āminah raised you lovingly,
And next loving Halimah brought you up,
Feeding you her milk; when enmity
Grew in her country
She delivered you back to your mother,
But Āthi Rahmān did not let your precious mother
Stay here, He took her to Himself.
What can I do about such firmness?
That Lord who knows everything, all sounds,
All resonances and places,
Does He know how you are to be raised?"
Abū Tālib wept and cried saying,
"Whom shall I put in charge of you?"
He held the Rasūl ☉ on his lap and cried.

"O my Father who has known the six tastes,
Please listen, when I was a four-month embryo
My father went to Yemen to trade in lawful goods
And died on his return journey.
The Āthi who knew this

Planted me mysteriously in my mother's womb,
Protecting me for ten months,
With His keen awareness watching me,
Tenderly watching me grow there, a special treasure.
When I was ten months in the womb
He sent down celestial beings from the heavens
To act as expert midwives for my mother's needs,
They spoke to my mother gently and comforted her.
The Lord who protected me, who knew my state,
Who knew I would have no milk,
Who created Halimah Amma
Ahead of me in the town of Qulay,
That Āthi shrank one of her breasts
So that no one could be suckled at it,
Do you understand the magnitude of such an Āthi?
Don't forget the subtle Āthi destined
One of Halimah's breasts to shrink
So that no one could be suckled at this breast
Which was destined for the true Muhammad.
I was born in that most precious city of Mecca,
For more than twelve years there was famine
In the town of Qulay, and do you know,
Because of this, women from that country
Came to Mecca as foster mothers,
With certitude to suckle the babies of Mecca.
When you saw Halimah,
With your clarity you especially chose her
To nurse your brother's son,

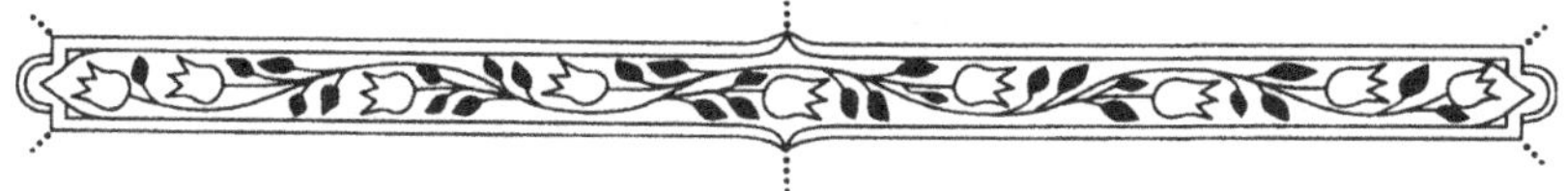

Did you not realize the mystery of the Āthi?
You told Halimah I was a poor child
With no money and lovingly brought her home.
She cried, tears pouring down her cheeks
As she exclaimed, 'Is this the Āthi's doing?'
All the other women whom famine drove
To feed their stomachs by nursing babies
Took children from rich families with plenty of money,
They were given presents and money
To act as foster mothers to the babies,
Then they went home.
'Was this what He destined for me,
To foster feed a baby as poor as I am?
How can I satisfy my hunger?'
As she said this Halimah cried and cried,
The tears running down her cheeks.
In the fullness of her heart
She thought about the Āthi's justice,
She kept thinking about it,
Appreciating with certitude the strengthening words
Which had come from her husband.
As she understood, Halimah realized more completely
The Āthi's intention, that Āthi
Who never strays from the path of truth and justice,
She understood her husband's explanation,
The husband who was a guru to her.
She said, 'We are extremely poor O lord, O master,
Is this the Āthi's doing,

To bestow this suffering on me?
While the others who came were able
To find very rich clients
And honestly receive such wealth,
So much money before returning home,
He gave me a child
As poor as I am. Let us see
What my Lord has destined for us,
Come my husband, come.' "

"You've seen how Halimah complained to her husband then
came to see me, this is something you've witnessed."

"Halimah came to see this baby and my mother,
She took me in her arms with loving qualities.
Wasn't it you O my Father,
Who took this child and gave it to Halimah Amma?
The moment she accepted me with joy and happiness,
The moment she embraced me to her breast,
That breast of hers which had withered
Filled and overflowed with milk, Halimah
Who had been so thin became plump and peaceful,
The withered breast filled and overflowed with milk.
When Halimah saw these unusual signs
There was fear in her heart,
Her heart melted, her breast trembled,
She exclaimed, 'This must be a very holy baby,

This must be the nectar of honey,
This must be the king of gems,
This is the remedy which purifies my qualities,
This is the treasure which protects my state,
This is the honey which will overcome
My endless poverty and lift me from it,
This is the honey, the richest treasure.'
When Halimah understood this, the real nectar of honey,
With love and certitude she determined
To raise me as her child,
She thought of taking this baby to her own town.
She stayed on for a week, feeding me milk,
Then she surrendered
All responsibility to the mighty One
And took me to the little town of Qulay,
Her own country.
Have you not understood this story,
How she raised me O my Father?"

"This was the way you handed me over to Halimah who was so poor when I was just a poor little baby. The mystery of this is known to the Āthi alone, He is the One who has that absolute clarity. It was the Āthi who raised me, who protected me then from countless enemies. So long as that one luminous, resplendent Being exists why should you be afraid?"

"No matter what country is hostile to me,
So long as my own God watches over me,

What fear should I have O my Father?
No matter what city is hostile to me,
So long as my own city is there,
What fear can there be O my Father?
My God, the Āthi,
When that resplendent form fills my heart,
What enemies can I have O my Father?
Even if millions and millions of evil things
Come flying at me,
Rising up with sudden fury,
Even if this country is in turmoil
And rolls out against me,
So long as the One of name and fame,
The resplendent Āthi is with me,
What fear can I have O my Father?
The One who knows the cage, the embryo
And qualities, the One who knows
The greatness and accomplishment of every country,
Who knows the name and fame of these countries,
So long as that luminous Āthi is there,
What fear can I have O my Father?
Even if the city and the country
Roll out against me,
Even if the country charges
Against me in opposition,
Even if the country surrounds me, trampling me down,
So long as the Āthi
Whose exalted name and resplendence exist

And support me, what fear is there O my Father?
Even if murderers and people filled with vengeance
Come in numbers, even if iblīs
Comes in search of me, even if crowds
Of sinners come running my way,
Even if those who have forgotten the Lord come,
Trampling me, killing me,
So long as that exalted Father, the Guru Nāthan,
The Lord of grace and bliss,
The Āthi, the all-pervasive One is there,
What will happen to all those evil things
Which come in search of me,
What can they do to me, where can they stand,
What can they accomplish O my Father?
The One who is all might is there forever,
Forever, to be of service, to be the helper
Of those who serve, the One who rules
The whole universe, the One who helps His devotees,
The Āthi who exists even in the beetle,
Who exists forever,
So long as that Āthi of might is there,
What enmity can there be O my Father,
Why are you afraid at all?
If you keep reciting the name of the Āthi,
The primal One, repeatedly,
Without wavering in virtuous conduct,
Without forgetting the most blissful, eternal Father,
Without mocking that great One,

Without faltering in justice and truth,
All the accumulated evil in you
Will fly away O my Father.
The all-pervasive Āthi
Who understands the true heart of each living thing,
The resplendent One who realizes this
One-pointedly and confers purity on all qualities,
The mysterious One who creates lives everywhere
Is the gracious blissful *jōthi,* the light
Which remains, a helper for everyone,
Bringing them all to one state,
Looking at all lives in a state of happiness,
Sharing their joys.
If all living things think of that one Āthi,
Their hearts melting in awe
As they beg and cry,
Think of all these lives and melt O my Father,
And then why cry only for me O my Father?
In the Almighty's creation every life knows suffering,
How many goats and cattle without mother and father
Are searching for comfort,
Don't you know this O my Father?
O my Father let there be mercy in your heart,
Cry for all these lives,
Ask God on their behalf,
The Protector of two worlds,
The gracious One who understands limits,
The treasure who fills all lives, ask God

To teach all living things the truth,
To bring them along that one path,
To make them complete
And follow the straight, true path,
O ask for that my Father.
He is the treasure with no relations, no attachments,
He is the primal Guru Nāthan,
He is that analytic God who knows,
He is the One filled with loving qualities,
He is the trustworthy One,
He is the golden treasure
Filling everything, everywhere.
You must love all lives and become my Father
Who removes every suffering in the same way
The primal Guru Nāthan, the gracious Lord
Who is a Friend to a friend does,
You must help those who need help.
We must reach that state of realization,
We must search for Him every day,
The thought within our thoughts,
Without wavering in our state,
Becoming a guru to each life as if it were our own,
We must search for those qualities
And reach that state of bliss,
We need those qualities to fill ourselves
With the grace of the Lord of two worlds,
Do this for every creature in the world O my Father."

Muhammad ﷺ sang and sang, he sang those words to his uncle Abū Ṭālib, his father's elder brother. He explained all this, he explained the wonder of his mother's death and the state of the world which wept. He said that to give his uncle clarity. Abū Ṭālib upon hearing this said, "O my son, my precious son, what a marvel your life is! Is there anything like it to be seen among others born as men? You shine like a gem more exalted than celestial beings and angels. How can I praise your gracious name O gem of my eye, my son?" He said this with great praise.

When Abū Ṭālib praised him Muhammad ﷺ replied, "The One worthy of praise is the Āthi, the One who is complete is the Āthi, the One of grace is the Āthi, the One of love is the Āthi, the One of bliss is the Āthi, the Āthi is the Protector of two worlds. O my Father please understand this treasure with absolute certitude." Abū Ṭālib understood Muhammad's words ﷺ, and from that time on raised very precious Muhammad ﷺ in a most subtle, exalted way. During the period in which he was brought up this way Muhammad ﷺ would speak to Abū Ṭālib with clarity about certain secrets of life, "O my Father, my blessed Father!"

The Nail in the Six-Pointed House

The Nail in the
Six-Pointed House

Muhammad ☪ reached the age of eight. During the next eight years people in the city gathered around him, they spent time with him, they recognized the love of the Rasūl ☪, his kindness, his qualities and accepted those qualities with trust. The whole world praised and respected the *Nabī's* exaltedness ☪, his greatness, his characteristics. If the noble *Nabī* ☪ found any stones when he walked along the road he would throw them to one side, he would put thorns, weeds and stones in a place where people did not have to walk on them. If there was dirt on the road he would clean it up before going on. If poor people wept he would give them his food, if they had no robe to wear he would tear up his own and give them part of it. He would dry the tears of those who cried, comforting them. For those who were tired and thirsty he would go in search of water, bring it to them in a vessel and revive them. He would happily offer such love, comfort and bliss. No matter how hungry he was on God's path he would endure it patiently, sacrificing his food to make others happy. He gave peace to the hearts of those who were suffering and made them happy.

In this way resplendent Muhammad ☪ grew up, even at the tender age of eight he did all this with perfection. He would not let people beat their goats and cattle, he would not let them kill their goats. Any living creature who saw noble Muhammad ☪

turned to him then bowed at his feet, and all the people of the world looked at this in wonder.

He had long arms, a shining light on the nape of his neck and a key which opened all the universes, the same key that opened hearts which can never be controlled. This is the key Muhammad ☪ had. When Abū Ṭālib learned of this he said, "O my son your actions are truly wonderful!" Muhammad ☪ would work as a laborer any place, anywhere. He would go on trade missions or from country to country to be a laborer. The wages he received he would distribute to the poor. He never considered his own hunger, the food he received he gave to others, manifesting peaceful qualities. Wherever he went he walked behind his elders, never in front, he always walked behind the mothers and fathers. If there was a death he would be first to visit the dead and walk behind the bier, no matter what race, religion or creed. Once he had given the dead person a truly good burial he would go to his or her home, bow down humbly and take leave.

In the first sixteen years of his life he advised his fellow beings with words of great grace. He would say God is the mighty One, the most praiseworthy One, the treasure of eternal bliss, the most brilliant One, the most gracious and blissful Lord, the primal Āthi who offers His trust and love to those who love Him. He would say God is that *jōthi,* the light within the love of those who love Him, He is the Āthi, the mysterious One within eternal bliss. He is the Lord permeating everything mingled within the Āthi, He is the golden treasure in universal resplendence, He is the eternal, solitary One not contained by anything. He is the One who understands the five, who lives in the heart. He is the compassionate One, the gem of the eye, He is God called by all those names, the One who rules the sixteen worlds, the treasure permeating everything, He is the King present everywhere. He would say we must have absolute faith in such a complete treasure, the primal

One who exists in goats, cattle, chickens and cranes. Muhammad ⊕ would describe in detail how the people were to accept Him both in their hearts and in their tribe.

If someone was hungry it was his nature to give away his food, he distributed everything he earned to others and kept nothing for himself. He would search for cold water to satisfy his hunger and drink that, he would give his food away to others. Gathering the older children around him he talked about God, explaining His state, His praise, His qualities, giving them words of warning as well, and he told them stories filled with wisdom in words drenched with the sweetness of honey, he told them how to acquire inner and outer patience, peace and comfort, he told them how to be unfailing in duty. And they called him munificent Muhammad ⊕.

When Muhammad ⊕ heard them use such words he said, "God alone is the munificent One, we are human beings, the children of Adam. The munificent one is someone in perpetual worship of the God who has no equal, the munificent one is used only for those merged with the undiminishing munificent treasure who has no equal. O my friends we all have shortcomings, understand that the One who has no shortcomings at all is that one God. He is the munificent One, the embodiment of justice who is also called the eternal blissful One. *Appa,* my brothers and sisters, we must try to follow the straight, true path, the virtuous path. Do not love idols or such things, love God alone, the great One of might, Lord of all the universes, the unique One without equal, without partner. Trust only Him, the complete treasure, the treasure who lives in your heart, the treasure of your birthright, the complete treasure who fills everything, the all-pervading treasure, that treasure filling all hearts."

He convinced them to put their trust in the primal Āthi, and many of them were so captivated by the words of Muhammad ⊕

they accepted what he said, becoming his followers at that time. When he was only sixteen years old Muhammad ☉ was already preaching these gracious words. This was how he taught the people great treasures of wisdom, comfort and bliss.

His fellow beings asked Muhammad ☉, "*Appa*, how can we control this uncontrollable mind, how can we correct this heart incapable of doing anything right, how can we correct it?"

When they questioned him Muhammad ☉ replied,
"*Appa*, it is true we are made of earth, in truth
We are hidden in a form made from a handful of earth,
We are hidden in the form of a handful of earth,
It is true all this does not belong to us.
If we understand this mystery
It will be a glorious victory for us,
A rare victory for us;
It is this thing which goes on wavering and wavering,
Which has no happiness, no bliss,
This body we have taken.
It is all false, it is all false.
There is a precious body within this form,
If we could rule this form and understand it with clarity
That would be a glorious state,
If we understand it with clarity,
This will be not only glorious,
This will also be the greatness of the Āthi
Who will cherish it with love.
That purity exists in all lives,

But without knowing the right direction
All living things fluctuate,
But without knowing the right direction
All living things fluctuate;
Within everything which fluctuates,
Within each life there is one treasure,
A steadfastness which never fluctuates,
There is an unfluctuating treasure which is the Āthi.
He is the treasure contained in our trust,
Contained in our love, in the robe of love,
He rises up majestically for those who realize the truth
As sweetness, as honey filling their bodies and hearts,
He is the blissful treasure
Making their hearts as sweet as honey;
Those who taste this sweetness
Will have a treasure which never fluctuates,
All those who realize this will
Themselves be an eternal, unfluctuating treasure.
That eternal lamp of the resplendent gem,
The treasure which is permanent,
The precious One who advises,
Who knows all mysteries,
That precious, all-praiseworthy Āthi alone
Is the treasure which never fluctuates."

"*Appa,* my sisters and brothers, the Āthi alone is a treasure which never fluctuates, all His creations lack that steadfastness, they waver. I will tell you something about the things the Āthi created. He is the eternal One who exists within justice, He is the *jōthi*, the treasure of brilliance, the grace which has no form. He is the One who exists permeating everything, He is present everywhere, an unfading lamp, He is a complete treasure within the heart, that primal Āthi. If you want to reach Him there are innumerable obstacles. *Appa*, there are two types of things, things which waver and things which do not. We must merge with that treasure which does not waver. The unwavering treasure lies within the wavering, fluctuating things of God's creation. If you can understand this with clarity it will be as sweet as honey for you.

Appa, we must understand, we must reach that clarity revealing all lives as our own. That complete treasure is within each living thing. God protects everything which wavers and everything which does not, they are all granted a grace that overflows everywhere, sweet honey flows. This is the state in which we must realize all lives are equal, our hearts should love this understanding and accept all things as equal, our hearts should accept it and we must act with clarity . We must see how precious they are, we must show this happiness with clarity. We should speak words of honeyed sweetness to others, comfort them and show them affection, we should let our love for all living creatures be seen, comfort them, give them happiness. Making others as happy as we are is the state of *manu-Īsan*, man-God.

God is a complete treasure within man. The work of *manu-Īsan* in that state is to transform things which waver into things which do not. When you become God there is no wavering. He has created two mantras to stop the wavering — listen carefully to their subtleties."

"The Āthi first created the form of resplendence
Which filled the egg, forms, everything,
As truth within truth, as that one treasure,
As a guru who fills the world completely,
As grace, a complete treasure,
As the One who lives in the heart,
As a guru who fills the heart,
As the One who shines, the unique face of grace.
He made the two eyes of primal Āthi's radiant *jōthi*
His avatar, a mysterious treasure;
He created all the universes,
All those things which were unsteady, fluctuating.
You must clearly understand the two gnostic eyes
Which make them firm, true and just, which
Make them firm with certitude and determination;
Pour an exalted state of true wisdom into them,
Manifest the vision of those two gracious eyes,
Make them most exalted,
The greatness most worthy of praise.
Understand that mighty Āthi
Created the earth and when He saw the earth waver
He created mountains, understand this.
When this earth saw its own wavering
It became durable, patient,
It turned red and black,
It became sand, adopting different forms and colors.
It is indeed true that this earth
Created with many colors does waver, does move,

Understand the Āthi created mountains
On this earth to keep the earth
Of many colors from moving —
This earth which had several forms and colors
Was wavering, the Āthi created mountains
To keep it still.

The uncontrollable oceans rose and overflowed,
Their waters gushing up because of the smoke, the fire
And air as their condition changed
And they spread across the rocks,
Rising up above fire and air.
Water suspended in the air became hot.
The oceans were created
With all these different qualities,
The water in the oceans was created from air,
That is, the five evils.
When the water roared and rose up in arrogance
He created rocks in the oceans,
In places where the oceans rise,
Overflow and fall, He created mountains,
Rocks, trees, shrubs and various other
Uncontrollable things to control the oceans.
He created all these things in the oceans
To control them, then He took
A handful of earth and altered its qualities,
It was made of the peacock's five colors,
Five tints of glass which became the five colors.

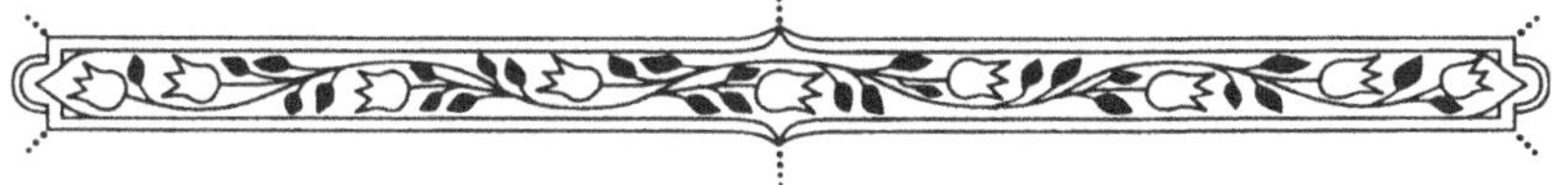

It was taken from Muhammad
Who had the form of a peacock.
When the peacock melted
Drops of sweat fell
From which He created all the worlds,
All living things, shrubs, trees, bushes,
The fourteen worlds, oceans, land,
This world and the netherworld,
The *'arsh*, the crown, the *kursī*, the gnostic eye,
The *qalam*, the pen, and everything else.
When everything had been created He created
Āthi Muhammad with His grace within Adam:
Through Muhammad He created Adam
And everything else,
Within all this He created Muhammad;
He created Adam through Muhammad,
And He created Muhammad in Adam as His grace,
Then He looked intently with the eye on His forehead
And placed the *rūh*, the soul, as life
Within the palace decorated with nine gems,
This is what He did with the *rūh*.
If there is any wavering, any faltering,
It is because of the peacock's five colors
Which became the five letters and the five faces,
The five colors of the peacock became
The five letters, the five faces,
And Muhammad who represented the triple flame
Became the sixth face,

The *aru muham* or the six faces
Being the six-pointed house.
All this is what became the five elements,
With the one of clarity and wisdom, the face of power,
Muhammad the lone treasure
Taking many different forms.
Wherever we look we see different colors.
As the fruit which flourishes, as the eight praises
This wavering takes different forms among the five
Which are contained within five letters, themselves
Contained within the six points or angles.
Aru muham, the six faces are within the six points
From which one face shines
As the power of Muhammad,
As a lamp which scatters the darkness,
As the complete treasure of two worlds,
As the golden one, as Dastagīr, the helping hand,
As the earth, as the sky,
As life within all hidden things,
As leaves, as branches, as vines,
As the luminous one everywhere,
As the golden one in the heart,
As the sweet taste of honey in every universe,
As the protector of two worlds,
As the divine being who steadies every turbulent place,
As the grace which is here, there, everywhere,
As the blissful infant Muhammad.

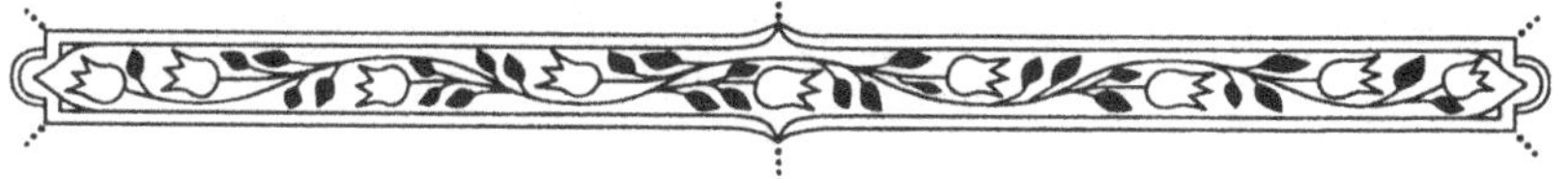

If you analyze this with divine analytic wisdom
It is a powerful spear of *īmān*,
It is Sakti and Siva,
It is life, the root, earth and sky,
The one thing in all concealed things
Within and without, the mysterious thing,
It is a treasure, five letters,
Gold and the earth,
It is Dastagīr, the pearl and Muhammad,
It is the sky above and earth below,
Anal fire, the letters, the three-pointed house
And the house which has no letters,
It is *jōthi,* the light within the five letters,
The one who shines, the sixth face,
The lamp in the heart which scatters darkness,
The radiant protector of two worlds,
That blissful state, the formless one within the formless,
A guru for everyone,
The one overflowing, filled with praise,
That one face, the pearl
Which is Muhammad in the form of man-God
With divine analytic wisdom.

When a man's state changes and he begins to waver
He assumes demonic qualities,
He stands out as the five elements,
As demonic ghosts who devour without devouring.
The colors of the five good letters

Can change the state of a man
And then the state of man-God,
The devouring demonic qualities can become
The five elements which devour the Āthi,
Then man is like the five colors
Which devour without devouring,
Which change the state of man-God,
The five qualities which kill without killing.
The terrible evil qualities, our attachments
Shatter our conscience, they
Are the ghosts which keep us from realizing
Our divine analytic wisdom,
Their qualities have no grace, they
Are the letter which keep us from knowing the five.
That radiance of Āthi Muhammad,
A complete treasure who lives in the six-pointed house
And in *aru muham*, the six faces,
Will destroy the overflowing state of all these demons
Who do not realize the truth.

The form of Āthi Muhammad
Which is found in the four religions
As a great treasure, as good qualities
Is like the fragrance in a flower
Which is that King Muhammad, the Rasūl
Who exists as the power in each one,
As that one face.
When God saw man disturbed

By the turbulent evils, the elements,
Then, as He created mountains
When the earth began to quake,
When man started to waver in his torpor
The Āthi created that Muhammad
Who can overcome maya,
A nail to stop this wavering.
When the body and heart of man
Begin to waver that noble Muhammad
Becomes the nail gathering in everything
On the right and on the left,
Opening the triple eye, the triple flame,
The triple letters and the triple pointed house.
When you fix Annal Muhammad firmly,
A nail in the six-pointed house,
The wavering stops.
The letters *alif*, *lām* and *mīm* represent
The house of the triple flame,
The house at the intersection of three roads,
It is that firmness, that certitude
Contained in the letters *alif*, *lām*, *mīm*.
Everything which truly belongs there is within,
The fourteen worlds are there,
The treasure which is completeness,
The eternal, gracious Lord is there.
Understand this and recite it, look with clarity,
Then the wavering will stop and you will see
The triple flame, exalted Muhammad in there."

"In truth we must clearly understand this state and act appropriately. If man sees any wavering in himself he must fix Muhammad there. God created Annal Muhammad to control this wavering, that noble Muhammad is the nail, the three letters which stop the wavering. When the earth began to quake God created mountains, when He saw the wavering in man He created Muhammad, when the oceans became arrogant and turbulent He placed rocky mountains in them. This was the way He created unwavering things to control the things that fluctuate, that waver. Man's wavering is caused by his pride. Those demonic qualities emanating from the five elements the body of man was created from are the demons which devour him, which indeed cause the wavering. To control it we must fix Āthi Muhammad there firmly, this will stop all wavering when they attack, and then the heart will improve."

When he was sixteen years old Muhammad explained these important things to all the children and they clearly understood those treasures of God, they were blissfully overjoyed in their praise, accepting Āthi Muhammad as truth. Others however, beat him; some insulted him, ridiculed him, some trampled him and struck him but he accepted all this with happiness, his thoughts were always blissful. With six levels of wisdom, with affection, happiness, never losing his temper because the bile had been removed, with contentment and peacefulness, he practised all these qualities joyously.

Those who heard of these qualities praised him, comforting him with a melting heart, making him happy. And so he said, "We ourselves and all living things should act this way to make all lives happy, we must say we are of one tribe, there is only one God. If we understand this we will see Him, this is the way to understand that God, the compassionate gem of my eye. We must therefore have one thought, if we have only this thought we can see the One

we belong to, if we have several thoughts we will see only the wavering in ourselves, the elements will devour us. It is impossible to escape from these demons which have devoured us, merely by wanting to. If we think we can return to our original state once we have been devoured by these elements even if we take sixteen births, if we take several forms in this birth, even if we take thirty-five million different forms, it will never happen. We must come forward to understand, to practise this truth with clarity."

"O my son, O Muhammad every word you utter is the truth, yet there is one important thing I have to say, everyone in the world opposes you strongly. What your conscience tells you is true and your explanation is a treasure of truth, but will the world accept it? Instead of accepting your word they oppose you, insisting that you are devouring them in so many ways. This could end in serious trouble for you, they might murder you, they could torture you or turn against you, become your enemy. There is already a group which has been in constant opposition to you.

O my son since this is the state of affairs, you must find a way to escape from them. Do not involve yourself in the customs of this country, do not criticize such matters openly. It would be a good idea to concentrate on your work in trade or on any other kind of work." This was the advice Abū Talib gave Muhammad ﷺ.

And Muhammad ﷺ replied, "O my Father what you say is true, but isn't it necessary to understand how man ought to live as man, how he should correct himself? That mighty, gracious Lord of all the universes has clearly defined how man ought to use every word with wisdom, how he ought to develop clarity with the sharpness of his intellect, to distinguish and understand with his divine analytic wisdom. If this is the case, shouldn't all those who were born with me and we ourselves too, shouldn't we correct ourselves and live in that state?

There are murderers, drunkards, thieves, liars and those

obsessed with sex in this world; they all seem to be steeped in the five deadly sins. That mighty, gracious Lord of the universes who has no equal, no helper, who resplends as the Protector of two worlds, we must understand His every word with clarity, we must use our wisdom and live in that state. To the extent of its knowledge the heart gives clarity to man. God who dwells in the heart of man gives him clarity about truth, and so it is the responsibility of man to give clarity to the place where God dwells."

This is what Muhammad ☺ said to his uncle who replied, "O my son what you say is true, but if they ask you about the mighty God who preaches to you, if they ask you where He is as well, what will you say to them? If they ask you to show Him to them, what will you do?"

Muhammad ☺ answered, "O my Father, my Father lives within me. You are my Father in this world, that Father who lives within me is indestructible, forever. He gave us such wealth and beauty, He created me and lives within my *qalb*, my heart, giving me clarity. If we realize His true and blissful words we can see Him. I expound these words so that people will reach that state, realizing Him. When I correct my heart to accord with my conscience, when I look within I see this state appear in my heart, I realize with certitude the God who created me exists within, that God of certitude, the Āthi lives in our certitude and determination, He lives in our trust. O my Father please, you must understand this.

God has said, 'O true believers in My creation, if you fix your intention on Me with a melting heart I will melt with tenderness in you, O those who believe in Me, trust Me and I will accept you. If you do not trust in Me I will make you the occupants of hell; however long you live, wherever you may be, one day you will come before Me and I will punish you. I make every effort, I give you your capital, I am the One who feeds you, I am the One

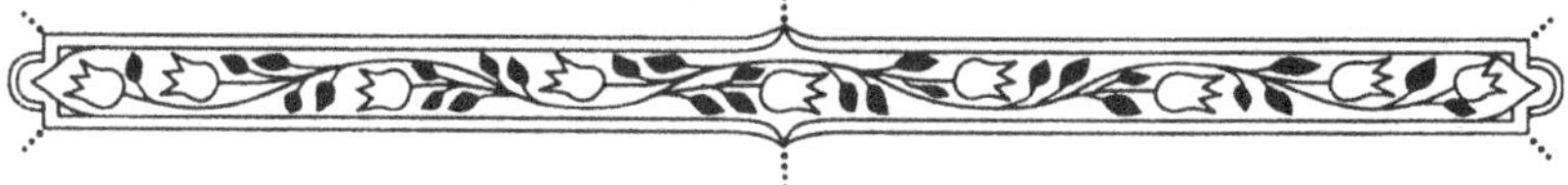

who created you, I am the One who sustains you, I am the only One who created you, who sustains you.' And He also said, 'O believers believe in Me.' O my Father I am not expounding religion or race, none of that. God calls those with true belief to the straight, true path as His believers. God Himself says, 'O believers step forward and I will embrace you with both My hands.'

God does not talk about prejudice, fanaticism, religion or race. He calls on people, 'O My believers, friends, O people of My creation trust Me, have absolute trust in Me alone, do not identify Me with anything else. I am with you, you are with Me, look at Me and I will look at you. If you turn your eyes away from Me and look at any one of My creations I will look at that too and not at you. I have created you and everything else, therefore look at Me alone and I will look only at you.'

O my Father this is the way God uttered every word, isn't it then our responsibility to understand such words with clarity, to correct ourselves? Shouldn't we ourselves and those born with us look at the one God who constantly looks at us? When we are supposed to look at that God who constantly looks at us, isn't it wrong to turn our face away and look at some other face? We should turn away from the wrong we do, we should understand that stones and idols are also His creations.

Of all that He created He made *manu-Īsan,* man-God, the most noble. He created the children of Adam, didn't He, and *manu-Īsan* belongs to the progeny of Adam. It is our responsibility to worship that God who created the earth, it is our responsibility to worship that God without equal. He created the earth from which He created *manu-Īsan,* He addresses us directly as 'My believers,' and if we don't look directly at Him but at something else as if it were God, that is wrong, isn't it?

Great people in the past built the Ka'bah in this city of Mecca, and later on other people put sixty-three statues inside, calling them gods. Each one of these statues uses the *sakti,* the energy of maya, the *sakti* of mantras, the tricks of tantras to speak. Alcohol, lust, theft, murder — bulls, goats and other animals are murdered in sacrifice to these gods. One large statue called Kunut is principal among these idols. God is not like any of them. We must clearly understand how these statues are made. God said, 'O My believers believe in Me, do not identify Me with partners. Look at Me directly, if you look directly at Me with absolute faith I will look back at you.' Then He is in us, we are in Him. We must develop that state in which we look directly at Him because He said, 'If you look at Me directly O believers, I will look directly at you.'

But if we stray from Him, if instead of looking at Him we look at one thing or another, what state will we be in? This will only bring evil upon ourselves. If we love those gods who demand sacrifices how can we expect the God who doesn't need sacrifices to come to us? If we love a god who needs human sacrifice how can we expect the God who gave us life to come to us? With words of nectar He gave *manu-Īsan* a beautiful form. Anyone who demands the sacrifice of such a beautiful life must be a demon. Isn't it therefore wrong to love a demon, isn't God the One who protects us? He is not a destroyer."

"God is the One who cares for us, who sustains us,
God is the One who loves us,
God is the One who comforts us,
God is the only One who feeds us,
God is the One who created us,
God is the One who protects us,
God is the One who trusts us,
God is the One who gives clarity directly

To the hearts of those
Who have absolute trust in Him."

"And this God who feeds all lives says, 'O My believers love only Me and I will love you, look at Me and I will look at you. I am in you and you are in Me.' So God has said. If we approach them in this state, with this different outlook, asking those deities who need sacrifices to protect us, how can they? O my Father, O those born with me, the primal Āthi lives in my heart, this invisible God lives in an unknown place, the Āthi, the radiant Jōthi without equal, this formless luminosity overflows everywhere, this God is complete within the form of man, within all lives. We must put our absolute trust in this God. If we leave Him out and put our trust instead in cattle, goats, stones, trees, shrubs, gold, precious metals and all those *saktis* which belong to maya, how can God who is the power controlling man's mind ever come to us?

If we create these maya *saktis* and call upon them, 'O deity come, protect me,' how can they? Maya *saktis* are the deities which demand sacrifice. Gold belongs to the things which are sacrificed — sacrifice belongs to all those *saktis*. If you ask those *saktis* which demand sacrifice to protect you, how can they? If you ask them to sustain you, how can they? O my Father when He looks directly at me and I look directly at Him, this is the state of *bhakti* or true devotion. O my Father we have to give the people of this world the true meaning of *bhakti*."

"O my son every word you say is true, but if we discourse this way in the world will they accept it, will they leave those deities which have been worshiped for generations, will they worship this God you now tell us is in an unknown place? And when they ask you where He is, what answer can you give them?"

O my Father He lives within me and within you,

If He does not exist the world does not exist,

If He does not exist no life exists,

If He does not exist there is no food,

If He does not exist there is no ocean, no land,

If He does not exist there is no truth."

"If He does not exist nothing at all exists. That is the indication of His existence. O my Father we must worship this God, this complete treasure in a state of total surrender. We must trust Him; if we truly want to merge with Him we can do so only with that trust."

"My son," replied Abū Talib, "O Muhammad when I listen to your sweet words it gives me great bliss and happiness, your explanation is very precious, very beautiful, very blissful. Each word of *bhakti* or devotion must come from a melting heart and must therefore be recited with a melting heart. What you say is good my son, but let me tell you something, those who listen to your words with a melting heart will escape, those who reject them might turn against you and become your enemy. In this state of mind O my son, they will plot to murder you. Do you think the people in the world who have protected their deities for generations will let you go free when you speak to them about this God in an unknown place? Do you think they will let you go free when you tell them to merge with this unknown God, to trust in Him, to come towards Him? O my son this country is against us, even your friends and kinsmen are against us."

CHAPTER IX

The Body Is the Enemy

The Body Is the Enemy

"Where is this enmity in the Āthi's creation,
Where is this enmity in the Āthi's creation?
The weapon carried around by the ignorant
Is their own ignorance, this is their enemy;
Except for that,
Where is the enmity in the Āthi's creation?
If man with his birthright achieves clarity
In his heart, if he recites this
Correctly, understanding, firmly establishing
That state of justice,
He will realize this O my Father.
As the *jōthi,* the light within the Āthi,
Analyzing atom by atom,
The form of *manu-Īsan,* man-God,
Impressed within that *jōthi*
Will become the seat
Of absolute trust in the Āthi,
Of absolute trust in the Āthi.
'O believers step forward,'
This will be the Āthi's invitation.

For those who have realized themselves,
What enemy can there be?
Those who are fascinated by the earth,
Those who are exalted in their arrogance,
Those who do not realize themselves
Will not know the right path,
Those who have no understanding at all,
Who are possessed by demons,
What can their enmity do to us,
What can their enmity do to us?
And there is no doubt a murderer
Will live in the stench of hell,
For those who realize this,
What enmity can there be?
If you exist in the place where the Āthi is,
What enmity can there be O my Father?
That *jōthi* within the Āthi understands
Each one's form,
He created all boundaries
And created Himself within all lives.
From the place in the heart where He lives,
The Āthi removes all difficulties,
For those who have realized themselves,
What enmity can there be,
What enmity can there be?
The murderous, throat-cutting man
And those possessed
By the most dangerous demons

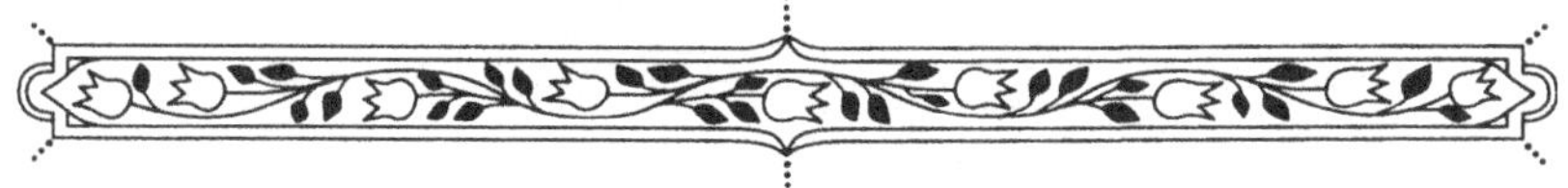

Will be enclosed by the Āthi
Within the boundaries of the worst hell,
There is no doubt a murderer
Will live in the stench of hell.
For those who realize this,
What enmity can there be?
If you exist in that place where the Āthi is,
What enmity can there be O my Father?

Those who are born as man, who know that quality,
Who understand justice, speak honestly
And purify themselves
Will receive the gift of never dying,
For those who are born as man
With an undying heart merged in Him,
Where is the enmity?
The state which confers clarity,
The state in which we achieve clarity,
A heart which blossoms forever,
What enmity can a man have
Who is born in that state O my Father?
He is a being who dwells in all lives,
He manifests as a complete treasure;
Whoever melts inwardly, whoever has
That clear heart of the eternal blissful One,
Whoever understands the meanings in the scriptures
Of lofty, true divine wisdom
Then corrects himself, giving peace to everyone,

Is a *satchithananda* in the world,
A realized being of bliss,
Whoever makes peace with the evils which pursue him
Is a *satchithanandasivam,*
A realized being of bliss and purity,
Whoever controls his thoughts,
Tying them all up in one direction,
Whoever exists as a causal believer
Will see the unseen God, that immortal Āthi directly,
And when he looks directly at Him in submission
He in turn will look at him from His exalted state.
When the Āthi looks back at him
The two will become one for all time,
Two worlds will become one, only one,
How can the world be an enemy
For whoever realizes this with clarity?
When his consciousness is God,
What enmity can the world hold for him?

Earlier O my Father,
That satan purposefully spat his venom
Into the enclosed vessel,
It fell in the region of the navel
And became the poisonous placenta,
Making his evil permeate all lives completely.
Whoever realizes this and achieves clarity
Will experience that state of bliss.
Iblīs is an enemy of the primal Āthi and a sinner,

Just as this iblīs took the form of satan
And spat his venom on my father,
There are torturing demons
Who are a company of enemies;
What benefits do they receive
From the Āthi for their intentions?
So long as man does not understand his body
With clarity, what purpose does he have
In this life, in this country,
What is the point of his efforts O my Father,
What is the point of his efforts O my Father?"

Muhammad ﷺ sang this song to Abū Tālib at the beginning of his nineteenth year, clearly explaining each and every aspect of that state to him. Abū Tālib replied, "O my son everything you said is truly essential for man, people should indeed understand these words, but do you expect them to forget the practices carried on for generations? Even now the tribe of Qasim is plotting your murder, they talk among themselves saying how much your words have harmed them. This is the way things stand. O my son act with clarity, give this up, let's go find some kind of work. If we work or find some trade we might reap the benefits, God will bless us. Do not meddle in the practices of these people. O my son look after yourself!"

"O my Father even if my body is broken,
If they beat me, if they kill me,

O my Father if they bite me, if they kill me,
How can I ever stray from the commands of my Āthi,
How can I ever stray from the commands of my Āthi?
Even for a day how can I forget
The words of my Lord of compassion and justice,
His holy words hidden and revealed everywhere,
Will I ever suppress the words of my Āthi
Who resplends in all three worlds?
I will destroy every evil
Which might start with such people,
I will recite that He is only One,
He is the treasure within,
I will recite that He is the only One,
He is a treasure within,
Of all treasures He is the Āthi,
The true treasure forever.
In this state of bliss I will go to every life,
I will expound these words with tenderness,
I will not fear anything other than His words.
If they poison me or make me tremble,
If they poison me or make me tremble,
If they destroy my body with their vengeance,
Even if my mind should plead with them,
If it cries out to them and yet they trample me,
If they kiss me and give me poison to swallow,
I will drink it without fear,
Lovingly reciting the Āthi's name.
Whatever comes, I will not be afraid O my Father."

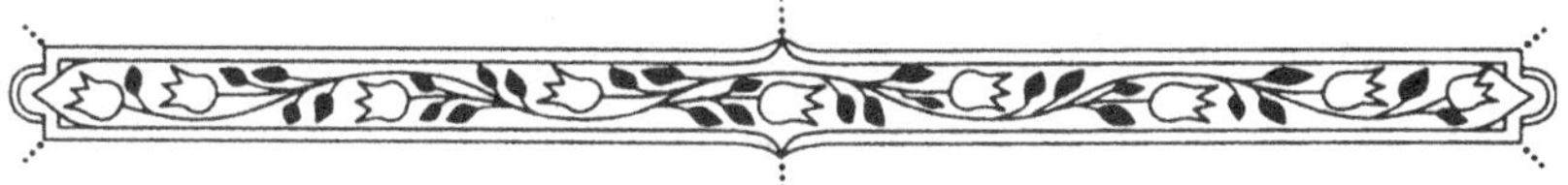

Muhammad ﷺ sang this song then he said, "Can we be frightened by all these threats? If you are in a state of irrevocable love for that one Āthi, how can you care what happens to your life even if you are given poison O my Father?"

"No matter how long we live,
One day death will overtake us,
He has ordained this O my Father,
He planted me in this cage,
He searched until He found a precious handful of earth,
From the waves of the ocean He took
The evil forces of earth, fire, water,
Air and ether or space and made them dance,
He formed the intention to create
The noble Nabī Muhammad for our qualities
And planted him there,
He planted the six very blissfully in this cage.
For everyone who did not understand the essence,
For everyone who did not reach this clarity
He created those good beings
In all three worlds to exalt them,
He taught them how to transform their hearts,
Making them compassionate, telling them
The causal wonder is the Āthi,
He is only One.
When justice faltered He placed the *jōthi* there,
Saying this will show them the way,

He said those who pray in their hearts,
Who purify their qualities and practise this,
Those He will call His true believers.
Since the Āthi lives within all lives
And speaks to them O my Father,
What enemy can there be?
Whatever may come
I will not fear O my Father,
If they hurt this body,
If they do anything to it, I will not fear that either.
Believe that all lives are one,
That the great eternal space is the Āthi,
The one God,
Believe there is only one tribe,
That He is forever, always our helper.
The Protector of two worlds beckoned
Those great beings who came to help us
And those who loved the gracious Lord,
'O come to Me My blissful believers.'
According to His laws
His vice-regents are born again and again,
It is good to praise the great beings
Who came before,
Join them on their right and their left,
Follow their path,
Reach that state O my Father,
This is undiminishing wealth."

"O my Father, O Bawa, God is an undiminishing treasure! No matter who loses the treasure, are we to keep quiet about it? We shouldn't leave it that way, we should discuss this treasure, we should be ready to sacrifice our life for it, dismember our body for it. Even if I die, my own born and all other living things should achieve that state, that goodness."

Abū Tālib replied, "O my son everything you say is true, yet we must understand the ways of the world, we must act appropriately. If we act without understanding those ways we could face many dangers. Whatever you may be, you are a young child with no knowledge of the world, no learning, no knowledge, no scholarship, you have nothing. Every day you worship the mighty God of all the universes who lives in an unknown place. Worship Him in your heart alone, don't let that worship be seen in the world or it could cause growing enmity."

Muhammad ﷺ answered, "Enmity! From the time we are born into the world this body filled with *saktis*, the energies of maya is an enemy. O my Father from the day we were born on earth and took this form, this itself became our enemy, our body is our enemy, maya is our enemy, our eyes are our enemy, our reason is our enemy, our legs are our enemy, everything which appears is our enemy. The moment we cut away these enemies we can reach the Āthi who has no enemies. O my Father everything in our body is our enemy, our thoughts, our heart is an enemy, food and water are enemies, sleep is an enemy, everything is an enemy O my Father. When we cut away all these enemies we will see, we will merge with the One who has no enemies."

"Those enemies which are within,
Those dangerous enemies must all

Be cut away O my Father,

We must cut away the ghost inside us,

The tormenting ghost which snatches our life away,

We must kill that enemy O my Father,

The mind which creates the hunger for food,

Which causes our stomach such distress,

We must cut it and control it O my Father.

Our evil cravings, our attachment to tribe

And our love of relatives are all enemies

We must destroy O my Father.

The six tastes which develop

Within the body are enemies,

We must detach ourselves from them

And cut these enemies away O my Father;

Amid the crowd of enemies in this earthly world,

Who is an enemy to whom O my Father?

We must understand what is good, what is evil

And overcome the enemies

Within our body O my Father,

This body consumes, it grows on food

Which makes us lose the state we have reached,

Makes us forget how to do what is right,

It changes our truth,

We must overcome this enemy O my Father.

The Āthi created the body

So that we would walk the right path;

Demons and ghosts who are enemies

In this cage try to change this state,

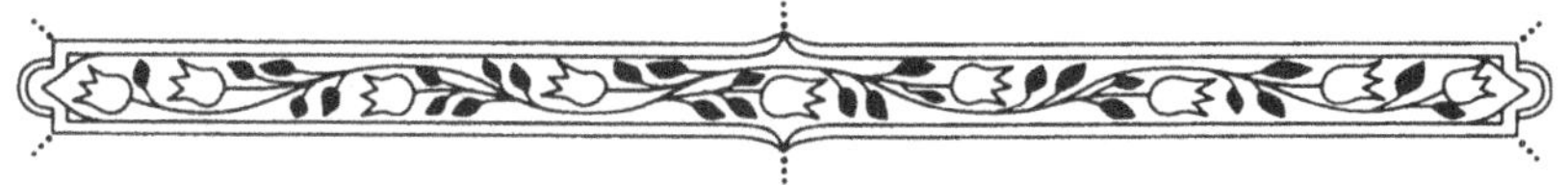

They must be destroyed so that our qualities
Can be corrected O my Father.
Planted in these six tastes created by the Āthi
Are the five sins, arrogance, hastiness
And the egoism of maya,
These enemies must be destroyed O my Father.
The iblīs, the satan of maya torments life,
Destroys the body, hides the truth,
Causes mischief and poverty, makes a show of maya,
It is this iblīs who exhibits arrogance,
We must control this iblīs of maya
And chase him away,
Be ready to destroy him O my Father.
The five evils which change our state,
Which come together to commit evil sins,
To cause separation and hunger, to destroy our hearts
And lead us into that state of sin,
We must destroy these sinful evils O my Father.
Ghosts and demons in the body
Try to destroy, try to crush the true treasure
The Āthi created in our body,
They do this so the Āthi will be forgotten.
We must destroy the terrible demon, our enemy
Who makes us tend to forget the Āthi O my Father,
We must uproot that ghost of desire and attachment
Decorated by the five evils, we must
Uproot it from our heart, beat it, crush it,
Destroy it and attain clarity

With divine analytic wisdom O my Father.
The sweetness of the silent letter
Mingled within our inner awareness
Will be changed to sorrow by this ghost and made
His friend, made to jump, roll and play,
We must destroy this ghost
Who is our enemy O my Father,
This ghost who will change our quality,
Our justice, who hides the truth,
The radiance of divine luminous wisdom,
This ghost who destroys our truth
Must be eliminated O my Father,
He is the greatest enemy in our body.
All the enemies, the prejudice and enmities
Lying within our body must be destroyed O my Father,
We must know the strength of that demon
Of racial and religious prejudice
And destroy it O my Father,
We must understand its strength,
We must destroy it O my Father.
Blood ties, attachments to our relatives
Which keep us from realizing the true treasure
Must be cut away O my Father,
They must be completely cut
From our cage O my Father.
The ties to wealth, our money, our comfort,
To the happiness in life, wife and children,
The enmity of that great demon

Must be cut away O my Father.
The great treasure of justice,
The primal Āthi is mingled within us,
Demons who don't understand the truth and justice
Planted in our body to prevent us from straying
Or stumbling, they must be cut away O my Father,
Understand them clearly with your inner awareness
And destroy them O my Father.
The One who gives great joy
To those born on this earth in the form of man
Is a treasure called the primal Āthi,
The Jōthi, the light, our Father.
There is a straight, true path:
See the overflowing gracious Āthi O my mind,
See Him, understand Him with clarity,
Destroy all these dangerous demons,
Reveal the truth, forget the body,
Discard reason and live by those commandments
Which will unfailingly make us realize the primal Āthi,
Understand this state and pray O my Father.
The monkey living in your cage
Will destroy your sense of truth,
Your one-pointed concentration,
You must destroy it O my Father,
The monkey who is your enemy must be destroyed
O my Father, O my Father!"

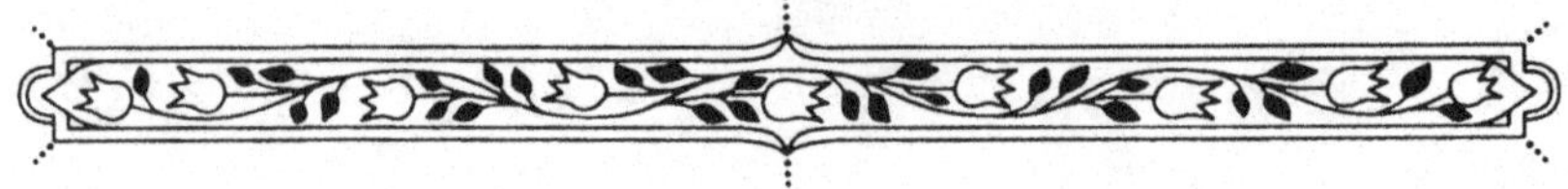

"O my Father there are millions and millions of enemies in our cage — only after we've cut away, destroyed, demolished these enemies should we focus on any other enemies; the enemies within are the real enemy. We can merge with God in peace only from the moment we cut away these enemies within."

Abū Tālib replied, "What you say is true Muhammad, our bodies and minds exist as enemies, the great wise men of the past revealed that our eyes and our reason are enemies. Certain other great beings said this too, but my son we are few in number and the people of the world are many. If we who are only a few try to explain this to the vast world, then worse than the enemies in our body, we must face the enemies in our life. The enemies in a man's body will not turn against him, but the enemies of the outside world will kill him.

You are the son of my precious brother 'Abdullāh who died on his way back from Sham, from Syria. He passed away on his return journey before he saw you or your mother. From that time until now I have raised you with great love; as my child you make me very happy. I give you the same tender care I gave my own younger brother. Although he died, I feel as if I'm raising him by raising you. The tribe of Qasim is in revolt against you, even Abū Jahl and his family watch you closely every minute, every second. Given this state of affairs O my son, it seems to me no matter what you do, I think they may not spare you, they'll use any kind of trickery, any treachery to attempt your murder. Given this state of affairs I'm lost, what should I do? O my son hold fast to the truth, walk the true, just path but worship that great Lord in your conscience and in your heart. Do not engage the enemies in this country, your enemies here will try every subtle treachery to kill you, and not just you alone, they're also waiting to destroy the entire tribe of Quraish."

Muhammad ☾ said, "O my Father the tribe of Qasim and

the tribe of Quraish are not separate, they were both conceived in the womb of the same mother. There is only one people, one tribe, they are one religion. This is our true state. What you say is true O my Father, but there will be division only if you see divisions, if you say they are one tribe there will be no division. There is no separation in God, His grace has no separation, only in the thoughts of those born as man do you see divisiveness. Because of this divisiveness endless troubles arise.

O my Father, my father's elder brother, my Father who raised me, who is like a god to me, O my worldly Father we must make every effort to unite these separate units and worship only one God. Let us act openly as well as inwardly in accordance with our conscience, let us make every effort to correct ourselves, this is the path, and if this is so we must try to correct the hypocrites who walk the path of iblīs, who beat, torture and cause pain to others. We must instill peaceful qualities in them, we must try very hard to change them so they will have the qualities of patience, love and affection, we must make them do their duty, make them follow the laws of justice without fail.

Faced with death, faced with danger or the possibility of being cut to pieces, O my Father we must not be afraid, our duty is to proclaim this to the world. O my Father is it just to give up the declaration of truth as truth in fear of harm to the body, fear of life, fear of this world, fear of the loss of wealth or fear of this useless body? Is that acceptable to God? Is that agreeable to God? Does God find that right? We must never hide the truth in this state, we have to be ready to sacrifice our life to establish the truth. This is the word of our Āthi. The primal Āthi is One, He exists as One and as many. If others deny it, what should we do? Isn't it our duty to establish His existence firmly? The primal Āthi is One, He remains One, He rules under one umbrella comforting us inwardly and outwardly — it is our duty to explain this state with clarity. O my Father everything in the world, everything in our own body is our enemy. We must step forward asking God to grant them that good, true wisdom which will cut away these enemies within and without."

"O my son you refuse to hear anything I say!"

"O my Father when the truth is revealed we must listen whether it comes from a youth or an old man. My reason tells me those who hold fast to the truth are the elders, and this is also what my heart says. For myself, I respect as my elder anyone who is young and holds fast to the truth, this is what my heart tells me. But those who hide the truth even if they are elderly have gone astray, they are iblīs, satan, this is what my heart says. If anything I have said is wrong please forgive me. O my Father you raised me and I would never want to argue with you. When you speak to me my Father, I am just a poor thing and you are the Father who raised me, you should not feel hurt when I keep replying to your advice. I am subject to the trial of the primal Āthi, I must try to proclaim the truth to the people in the world, people who are born to the trials of this world so they can understand the truth, correct themselves, follow the path of truth and come to the place which is truth. They must try hard to reach that place of truth, and to this end I must try hard, even if it means sacrificing my life O my Father." Muhammad ☺ said this to Abū Tālib, his father's elder brother.

When Abū Tālib heard this his heart trembled, his entire body burst into sweat. He understood the truth with clarity, with his whole heart. He was caught in a dilemma, like the rattlesnake catching a shrew. He thought, "What can I reply to the words of my son, what can I say to certain evil people in the Qasim tribe?" Caught in a dilemma between the two, he couldn't think what to say. In this state of mind he proposed, "O my son you are grown up now, we shouldn't be idle, so come along with me

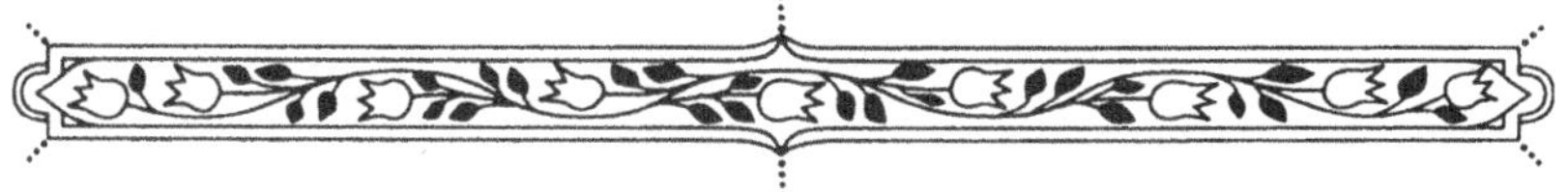

and let's find some work. I have decided to go to Sham to do some trading, would you like to come with me?"

Muhammad ﷺ said, "All right Father," and they bought goods for their business in Sham, the old Syria. Muhammad ﷺ sold some things of his for the money to buy cloth and other items they would sell there.

While our *Nabī* ﷺ was preparing for the journey many young men his age came running up to him, "O Muhammad it looks as if you are going on a business trip."

"Yes, I am going with my uncle."

"O Muhammad if you make a profit with this business, whom will you give it to? You've talked about this, so if you make a profit what will you do?"

"O my brothers what should I do if I make a profit? I don't know how to keep any profit for myself. I don't want to keep anything from whatever they pay me, I don't know about profit. *Appa*, a man only keeps one treasure as profit for himself. From all the profit we make, what can we keep for ourselves? Only one profit, that one treasure, to be on the straight, true path, to have complete trust in the primal Āthi. Having Him as our only profit is true wealth, and that, *appa*, is the treasure I'll keep for myself, as my profit. No other treasure is profit for me, I'm not the sort of person who collects such profits. The only profitable treasure I have is that one God who created me, He is the only profitable treasure I have. Except for Him, everything else is a debt. Isn't it right to repay all debts? The only profitable treasure is God."

"*Appa*, my brothers, I came
From that complete treasure,
I came to this realm of creation

And when I came I had nothing exalted
Except the lofty, true divine treasure, the Āthi,
This was my decoration and this is my profit,
Except for that, anything else
Which presents itself now or in the future,
Whatever it may be, is not a treasure,
Not profitable, not worth keeping in this world.
We have come, we are born to this earth on a day,
We grow like the waxing moon,
Eating and eating in a world where we nurture the body;
This handful of earth is a debt to be repaid,
When this earth returns to earth
And disappears back into it,
The earth will accept it, devouring it.
What came, what descended in a melting form finally
Goes back, returning to the place it came from
In the way it came, and what finally
Remains as profit is the Āthi.
But if we think what we sought
On this earth is our profit,
It will all disappear,
All living beings in the world should realize
We will return as we came.

So many treasures are planted
In the creations of the Āthi,
We may gather all these treasures,
But if we realize all creations come

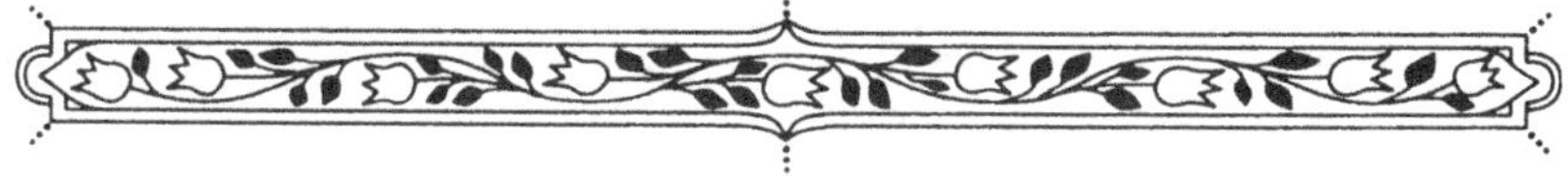

From the womb of one mother,
And if their hearts are happy, are complete,
If they help all other living things,
If they eat together and humble themselves
Continually before the Āthi,
If they drink in His qualities and receive the grace
Of the *guru nāthan*, the lord of the gurus,
Merging with the Āthi,
Following the straight, true path of the Āthi,
Filling their hearts with Him completely,
And at last keep the golden treasure
Which is the Āthi as their profit,
This is the real, the true treasure."

"*Appa*, we have to go back as we came. We are all born from the womb of one mother, we grew up as human beings. We should grow together as *insān*, true man, and all together gather our profits and losses, the results of our play in this world. Together we should be as one, eating, sharing everything. Each of us must discover that simple treasure for himself, gather this as the profit, the all-pervading Āthi. We have to understand the treasure of profit is the primal Āthi alone, we have to merge with Him and realize He alone is the right path.

We came to this earth related to each other, all born from the womb of one mother. The world is a playground. When we analyze the profits and losses of this playground we discover the real profit is realizing God's grace in everything, finding clarity. That profit is the most precious, complete wealth. That precious thing is what we must try to gather. We must live as people who are born human, we must live together as brothers, share our food and eat together. No one should beat or hit another person, no one should harbor vengeance against another, no one should kill, murder or insult another.

Instead of following this person or that person we must follow the straight, true path, search for the eternal One, unite with the primal One. We must awaken the love in our hearts, mount and ride majestically on the energy of the mind which is the horse of the Āthi, planting His flag. We must extend our hearts, dwell within, expand, find a way to merge with the Āthi.

To insult one another or take revenge is wrong. If we have only a handful of food we should share it with our brothers, our sisters and other living beings. Vengeance is the work of iblīs, satan. We must live together as one brotherhood."

When they heard these words the brothers and virtuous friends of noble Muhammad ﷺ gathered around him, all the young men of that country listening to him carefully and asking with love, "Is that how we should behave?" Then they wanted to know, "If we behave as you say we should in this world, what will we receive?"

Muhammad ﷺ replied, "You want to know what you will receive?"

"What will you receive O *Ai'ya*, O Father,

O my virtuous friends? You will receive the primal Āthi

Who is the truth, a treasure beyond measure

Who exists in the station of truth,

Who exists in the station of truth,

If you understand this with clarity and wisdom

You will see that treasure,

If you understand this with clarity and wisdom
You will see that treasure,
The treasure of the Āthi which never diminishes
No matter how much you take from it,
The treasure of the Āthi which never diminishes
No matter how much you take from it.
The Āthi is the personal treasure of His lovers,
If your heart melts it becomes a permanent treasure,
And it is that treasure
Which fills your food, your life, your body,
It is the treasure
Called Āthi *param*, the primal, universal God,
The completeness within completeness
Which never diminishes,
The completeness within completeness
Which never diminishes,
A treasure which can be extracted everywhere,
A treasure which remains to fill the heart,
A treasure which never diminishes,
A treasure which is abundant completeness.
You can take as much as you want again and again,
You can gather that treasure
When your qualities reach clarity,
When your heart overflows;
When you reach clarity through your qualities,
When your heart overflows with happiness
Search for that treasure,
Take what you want again and again

From the undiminishing treasure, unite with Āthi *param,*
A treasure which can never be measured,
An undiminishing treasure,
The permeating grace everywhere,
The solitary primal treasure,
You will receive that,
The treasure which never diminishes,
This is what you will receive.

This is the treasure of eternal plenitude,
This is the treasure which never diminishes,
Appa, you will receive the treasure
If you correct yourselves and act correctly,
This is the treasure you will receive.
Once you fill the treasury of your heart,
However much you withdraw
It will never diminish,
However much you distribute
It will never diminish,
The treasure will always remain full
In the treasure chest.
If you acquire the treasure it never perishes,
This treasure is undiminishing wealth,
If you fill your heart with the complete treasure,
If you eat it or devour it
Or the whole world takes something from it,
It will never diminish
No matter how much you take,

It will never diminish
No matter how much you take.
This is the chest where the Āthi,
The supreme treasure is kept,
This is the chest filled with the love of man,
This is the chest filled with the love of man.
If we fill the treasure chest which has six chambers
With that blissful joyous treasure
It will never diminish,
The ever victorious treasure, the great eternal treasure,
The blissful treasure which never falters in justice,
Which never diminishes in any circumstance,
This treasure of the Āthi *param*, primal, universal God
Is a blissful treasure eternally."

"O Rasūl, O Muhammad how do we make our minds peaceful, how do we make our minds tranquil? *Yā* Rasūl, *Yā* Muhammad how do we correct our minds, how are we supposed to live our lives? How do we do this, how are we supposed to live in this world? Please explain all this to us clearly." His brothers, his friends, all the townspeople asked Muhammad ☺ these questions, to which he replied, "*Appa*, my sisters and brothers please listen, I'll explain clearly how to behave, how to live on the path to God. Listen carefully, if you listen to these precious words carefully you may receive that state which is pure goodness. These are the secrets of man's life."

"*Appa,* the light which appears within clarity
Shows you a state of peace and tranquility,
O you who are virtuous and praise the feet
Of our beloved, our blissful Āthi,
O you who are virtuous listen,
That primal treasure, the Āthi,
The One who is compassion within compassion,
Who is mingled within everything you see,
There is a way to worship Him.
I will try to tell you this most precious thing,
Try to understand with inner understanding,
Find clarity with exaltedness, succeed.
Listen those who were born with me,
Listen, I will tell you
How to raise yourself up.
The mighty One had that resplendent, pure soul
In *ākhirah,* the heavenly world,
And mighty Āthi created Adam,
Planting that light, the soul,
The life of the world within him.
The soul which was in heaven
Mingled with the heavenly beings.
He took earth which is the world of hell,
He took earth from the four directions of the world
Mixing it all together skillfully,
Making a form, a body.
He made the body in a form
Which is male and female to this world,

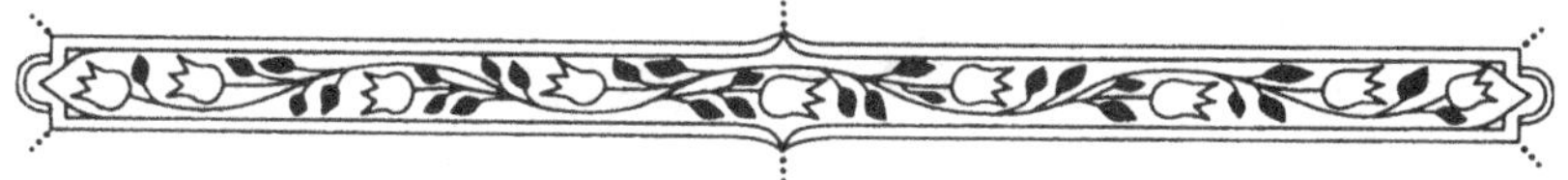

Uniting male and female,

Showing them desire, the sweetness of illusion.

As He mixed the earth into a form

He poured water on it,

Mixing one with the other,

And as He trampled this, kneading it,

Heat was generated and became fire.

When the two ingredients were subtly mixed together

The blood stirred in circles

And air was generated in fury within its breath.

In this way fire, water and air

Joined the fistful of earth

When the mixture was made a form,

This is the way the ultimate form

Of the body was created.

When a man and woman unite with one mind

The form which is mixed within becomes a fetus,

When the fetus has been in this state for two months

God writes its letter of destiny

In accordance with the thoughts

Of the human beings at their time of union.

If the parents unite with thoughts of vengeance,

Of jealousy and egoism, with *I* and evil qualities,

The fetus He mixes within becomes strong,

Taking a form subject to the evils of sin,

The fetus He forms continues to grow in this evil,

It loses its wisdom, its true state of bliss

And its judgment, this becomes its destiny.

The thoughts therefore, of the husband and wife
When they unite at the time of conception
Become the destiny of the fetus,
The resplendent primal Āthi puts a seal
On what the parents together mold
As the destiny of the fetus,
This is the way the Āthi writes
The complete destiny of the fetus,
This is the way fetuses take innumerable forms
Shaped by the thoughts of human beings.

The primal Āthi lives as king
In the form of man and becomes a servant
Helping him fulfill his destiny.
He also exists as judgment within judgment,
As life within life,
As the friend within and without,
As a slave to everyone,
To the devotee He is lowly
And to the lowly He is even lowlier,
He serves everyone,
He teaches and serves man,
His own creation, as a servant,
As the eternal primal One.
Once this book which is written
With the pen that writes is handed over to Him,
By servants whose responsibility it is
To hand this book to the Āthi,

He stamps it for this world,
This is what the luminous One does,
This is the work we make for Him."

The Story in a Book

The Story in a Book

"*Appa,* my brothers and sisters, once these two parts are united the primal One who lives in each of our hearts acts as a servant working for us. He continues as the lowly One to His slaves, doing His work. Whatever it is we write in the book we hand over to Him, He puts the cover on, we are that cover. The father and mother write out all the lessons and give it to the servant who stamps it. Nothing, therefore is His fault, the levels of wealth and poverty are not His fault. How can you blame the One who merely reads the story we've written and given to Him? It is certainly not His fault; actually it's our own fault, so if you write your story with good qualities, with good conduct and hand this over to the servant, He'll return it in the same good condition. Since the father and mother unite to write the story they present to the printer, we cannot blame the printer for whatever is given to Him, all He does is print the story we offer Him. This is the story now revealed as we read it today.

The father and mother come together writing the story they present to the printer, the printer prints it and puts it back in our hands, the story we have to read today. We must be aware of the history in that story written by our parents; it is our story, our form. All those born today as man are the consequence of a story written by a father and mother and given to the printer, a story returned to us with the cover on it. That printer is the primal Āthi.

Our own father and mother are the first gods we see in the world. They are indeed gods we see in this world. When these gods unite this story is written and presented to the printer, the book we now read. Do not then call it our destiny written by God. Is it the fault of the primal Āthi who printed the storybook our parents wrote and turned over to Him? He printed it and handed it back to us, is it His fault? No, but we have to understand the flaws in the story and correct them all. To do this we need a good *guru nāthan*, a lord of the gurus. To change the story, to write it with good, pure words in the right way, good lessons, good poetry, we need a *guru nāthan* who has attained God's grace. Then it is possible to change the story in the book our parents wrote, then it is possible to write a good story. The form we have in our present state is actually the story written by our parents and given to the printer who printed it and put a cover on. What our parents made by kneading fire, water, air and earth together is our form, within that form is the story they wrote and passed along. This is what we read today, a story which must end, and when it does we have to leave. As soon as we finish reading the story our parents wrote, our present story, we leave. To correct the faults in this story we need a *guru nāthan*. If we find such a good guru before the story ends it is possible for him to correct it.

If we find a *guru nāthan* he will read the story and correct the flaws, he will add certain good things and make us take it in with wisdom. We need a *guru nāthan* who is God's true servant for this. You must realize the condition we find our body in is a consequence of the covered book written by our parents. Whatever they wrote is printed, stamped and registered. The registration is what is called pure life, the life given to the book is its registration. What our father and mother write is the story, life is its registration which fills the entire body of each and every man, life which comes from the primal One, the printer. When the book is torn that registra-

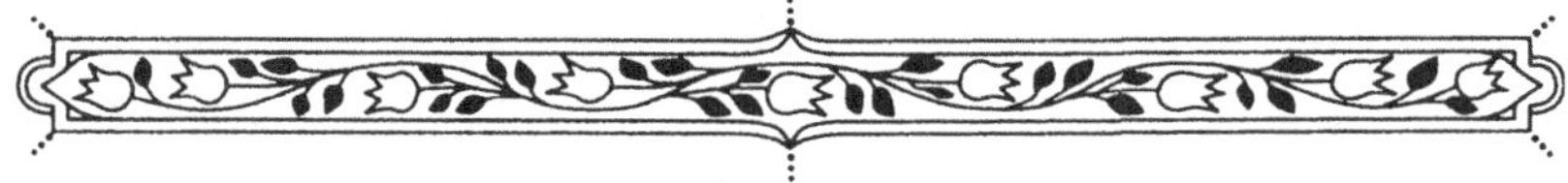

tion returns to Him.

Whoever wants to acquire a form must be registered. What we read in this book is the story written by our parents. This is what happens today, this is what happens forever, in every world. The story we read today is the one our parents wrote before we were a fetus; this is what they mean by saying a fetus acquires millions of sins it did not collect on its own. That is the story revealed today as we read it. Since this is our state *appa*, we must find a good *guru nāthan*, walk the right path and try hard to correct the flaws. The wrong story written by our parents is what we read today as our own body. *Appa,* if we trust this body formed with falsehood as its strength, we will end with the qualities of ignorance, we will be tormented by perpetual evil. This body works entirely against the registration made by the Lord of three worlds, it may end as a book without registration, a prey to fear.

We must find a *guru nāthan* and ask him to print true meanings in good words for us, so that every word will be something to enjoy more and more, every word will become sweeter and sweeter, will flow with honey. When the story is rewritten it becomes incredibly sweet for everyone who reads it. To rewrite this story in the right way we need a good *guru nāthan*, a complete treasure on this exalted path."

Muhammad ⊕ described different signs in this form, explaining the nature of man's life.

"This is a story written so preciously
By our father and mother O my own born,
Try to understand it with your wisdom,
Try to understand it with clarity.
This precious story becomes

A thing of wonder for everyone
If you put sweetness and treasures there,
So that it resplends as light,
So that hunger and thirst disappear,
So that lust is overcome
As we discard this terrible hell with loathing,
So that every ear melts
As we listen to it with joy.
Write the story, reach out to the feet
Of the *guru nāthan*
Who will correct it, try to achieve that.
This is our form created by the actions
Of our father and mother,
This form which appeared
Will be destroyed in a week;
The permanent treasure
Is perfection within perfection.
When you have clarity
In your qualities, know the signs,
Know its nature,
The path which is love for the Āthi
Of overpowering grace, of blissful state,
Is a path of words which are extremely precious;
To rewrite this beautiful story
You need a *guru nāthan*,
Try to find him with your wisdom,
You will see the primal One emerge,
Your wisdom will have clarity

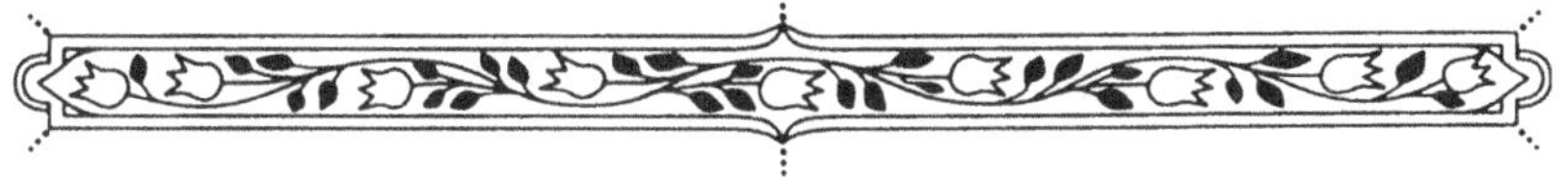

And flow with sweet honey,
You will see the twice seven worlds
Resplending everywhere.
If your heart melts in His thoughts
You will see the emergence of the compassionate,
Mighty, causal jeweled light of the eye,
He will emerge, He will emerge.
Establish that state, stay on the path
Of truth and justice, understand as your birthright
The preciousness of all lives,
Understand how to correct yourself
As love within love
With a heart that comforts all lives,
With beautiful qualities,
Each of you, my own born everywhere in the world,
Each of you walk the straight, true path,
Realize the great resplendence of Āthi *param,*
The universal Āthi,
O my own born try to find
The path of clarity in this world."

"My friends, this path which we must use clarity to find is a precious path conferring peace, truth and justice, but we do have to find it with our clarity. Man's life and his form are the consequence of a story our parents wrote for each of us. This is the way it is: the soul which is pure and resplendent exists within it; He registers the soul. All He does is stamp it with a registration mark and it becomes a life born on earth. If this life achieves clarity it

can reach that state of happiness. On the appointed day this life returns to the place of registration, it returns to Him and earth returns to earth. All our desires and the way we lead our lives remain in the earth, those blood attachments, the other attachments return to the earth and become part of it. The life of the soul registered by God goes back to Him, and what does this life take with it when it returns to Him? Only good and evil, all the clothes, the decorations, everything we sought remains in the earth.

The primal Āthi created this form to give location to the story written by our parents; it is the drama of that story we act out today. In this drama everything we collect belongs to the earth: we live on this earth, earn our living from this earth, we eat from this earth and what we eat becomes feces which return to the earth. Everything we seek, everything we earn becomes one with the earth. The story our mother and father wrote, the form with which they created this story becomes a prey to earth. The light of the soul which is pure returns to its source, the place it came from. We must realize the profit of the good and evil we have acted out. To realize this clarity, to reach this clarity we need a causal *guru nāthan*, a lord of the gurus. Through him we can acquire the prescription which lets us walk the right path. But in this world people give different interpretations, different explanations of these things which have been given by great beings in the past. O my own born, my true friends, my loved ones, fathers and mothers, we must try to acquire this within ourselves with a melting heart.

The things we seek in the story written by our parents will end with the story, the soul which came from the primal Āthi will return to Him. But in our parent's story there are so many dramas, sixty-four arts, ninety-six potentialities, four thousand, four hundred and forty-eight nerves, four thousand, four hundred and forty-eight diseases, four thousand, four hundred and forty-eight infectious diseases, the speed of seventy thousand horses. Each

man has seventy thousand veils and more — as many as a hundred million different things can be found in these stories written by our fathers and mothers. Once we finish reading these hundred million stories the soul returns to the primal One, the hundred million stories are caught in our evil actions. The end of the story written by our parents is actually caught in the five sins. In whatever state we find ourselves and before our story concludes, we must try to understand, to realize the end of the story. We must understand our story with clarity, discover the flaws before it finishes and make the necessary corrections; we must find a good *guru nāthan* to help erase all the flaws in the story.

And while this is the way things happen, God in His form-less state feeds all His creations, He never consumes anything we offer. He is the One who created every life in every universe, He created all the treasures completely, our food, our wisdom, ways to reform ourselves, and He created the straight, true path as well. He created the sun and the moon, He created everything, He also created life and death. He created the body which dies and within this corpse He created a state of eternal bliss. He created good qualities too and a *guru nāthan* for this world. He also created wis-dom, the primal One living within this wisdom, teaching from there. We have to understand the complete, primal One exists within this wisdom.

We must find a true slave of the Āthi, we must also find the remedy to make us act with clarity. *Appa*, everything we seek in this world belongs to the earth; we seek on this earth and become a prey to earth. Born to this earth in conformance with the story written by our parents, we consume it all. This story is the place where we defecate everything we eat; the drama written by our parents becomes a prey to earth. The drama ends here, even if anything remains we cannot take it with us — there are only two things we can take with us — none of this belongs to you or to us in this state. The primal Āthi who has realized eternal life without death never consumes anything which belongs to His creations, He does not touch so much as a mustard seed, He touches only your love, He exists in your love. He never eats anything of yours, never asks for anything, never eats or drinks anything. However much you dance in this drama, at the end of it, whatever remains must be left behind on earth. You have to return to the place you came from. It all happens in a week. We must realize this, we have to understand the treasure we brought with us and what we are supposed to do here. We should understand and act with clarity.

Appa, there are so many ways to do this. We must hide the distinctions of *you* and *I*, we must hide the differences of *mine* and *yours*, removing that parental section too. The primal Āthi in the state of Anāthi, the state of the beginningless beginning is our only real treasure, everything else comes from the story written by our parents, a story which ends like the rising and setting of the sun. However much we dance between its rising and setting the drama will be over before the sun rises the next day, our story will end with it. Once the story of the father and mother ends everything ends, but let us search for a treasure which lasts forever."

Muhammad ☉ explained this at the age of twenty to all his friends, to all the virtuous people who questioned him, to the people of the world who had this question. After he had explained this with great clarity they asked him another question. "O Nabī, O Muhammad, *Yā* Rasūl what is this eternal treasure we take back with us?"

"When the flag of the five elements flies,
The only flag which is eternal
Is the flag of the Āthi O my own born.

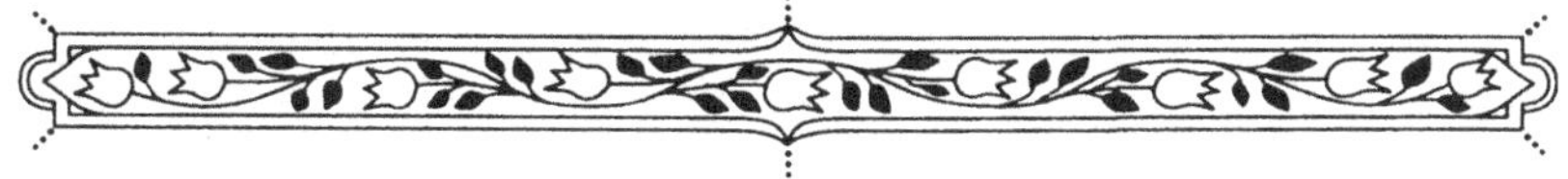

Within the flag of the five elements
Only the flag of the Āthi is eternal truth,
When the soul is purified, when it searches
It will find the eternal, joyful treasure
Which alone remains,
The One, the only joyful treasure which remains
Is the eternal treasure, the Āthi,
He is One, the eternal, forever.
O He is the treasure who lives in all creations,
O that treasure permeating everything
Is the treasure, primal Āthi
Who alone remains,
O search for it within your love
And the indestructible treasure will remain forever,
O when your time is up, when you are about to die
What remains is the Āthi,
The treasure which never dies, that is the Āthi;
When the time comes to travel back alone,
You take this treasure along
So that you remain immortal,
Merging with the Āthi
Who is complete everywhere,
The Āthi is that One, the only treasure.
The treasure you can see is truth,
The treasure which is found everywhere in the world,
Which permeates all lives,
The treasure which fills the heart
Is the golden Rasūl Muhammad.

When your love overflows without being divided,
The primal Āthi Nabī is that unique Muhammad
Who exists within the eye
At the center of your forehead,
From there radiating light everywhere,
Seeing everything, overflowing where it remains,
That treasure is called Dastagīr Muhammadur-Rasūl.
Try to look for that treasure yourself,
Proceed holding fast to it,
This is the true treasure of the Āthi,
There is no salvation other than this,
Everything else is fraught with danger,
The primal Āthi is the only reality.
O my heart, my mind search for the treasure,
The Āthi, the One who pervades ruling all seven worlds,
O heart join your wisdom and search for it,
If your qualities become pure and acquire fragrance,
This is the path of the *guru nāthan*,
And the treasure, that gracious Lord is only One,
The only thing which remains, eternal, forever.
O my own born, the Rahmān, the merciful One
Is the eternal One, the One who exists forever, forever,
O my own born, the Rahmān, the merciful One
Is the eternal One, the One who exists forever, forever,
This is the solitary treasure,
This is the treasure which never diminishes,
This is undiminishing gold
No matter how much we take from it,

This is the lion we all share,
This is a treasure permeating everywhere,
This is the solitary, primal treasure,
This is the only thing which remains,
Nothing remains other than this,
Thambi, my brother, my own born,
Nothing is eternal other than this."

"Examine what I say with the sharpness and clarity of your mind. My own born, if you examine all this with your pure qualities you will see there are neither tribes nor races nor anything of the sort. To reach the great, eternal treasure and merge with Him we must find a *guru nāthan*, a resplendent light whom we must accept. Then we have to walk that straight, true path, understanding what is good and what is evil as we make progress on it. A time will come when everything we sought, everything we collected must be thrown away, tossed into the streets. This body made of earth, everything fashioned of earth and collected by digging or cutting the earth will finally be consumed by earth, such things never reach that primal, unique God, they do not reach the primal Āthi who never consumes a single atom. He does not demand even a mustard seed from His creations as payment for His labor, He is the primal servant who works without salary; He is the servant, the slave who works without salary. He is the primal treasure who lives in a place filled with beautiful qualities. From this state He calls to those who put their trust in the primal Āthi, 'O My believers trust in Me and if you do I will be with you. If you trust Me fully in your heart I will not only carry you with love, I will also serve you most affectionately with My heart, with My two eyes, My three eyes and two hands.'

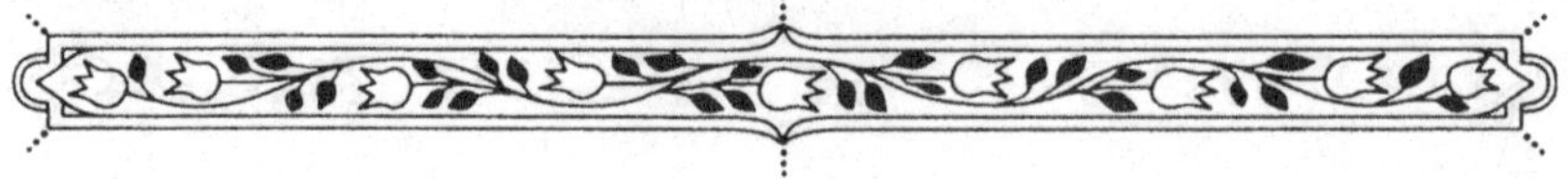

In this state the primal, luminous Āthi serves us without feeding or paying Him. We do actually see that only the primal Āthi will serve us as a slave without salary in this world. We must therefore, intend to love Him in whatever way we have to, we must love Him, we must keep Him completely in our hearts which should melt. With that melting heart we must love the primal Āthi, the eternal One." Muhammad ☪ concluded, "O my friends this is the way we must love the Āthi, with great intensity."

When the people around him heard this they exclaimed, "O great one, Nabī Muhammad, ruler of Mecca, O gem of *mahshar*, the gathering at Judgment Day, ancestral Muhammad, mighty, noble Muhammad mingled in that eternal light on the forehead, Nūr Muhammadūay Ahamed!" They praised him this way then asked questions. "In all the different towns and cities people live separately from each other, they live with the distinctions of *you* and *I*, of *mine* and *yours*. Is this good or bad? O Muhammad many people in this world have their own ideas, differences which they express, and many kingdoms, many countries are separate from each other, different people believing in the superiority of their own way of life. In addition to dividing themselves into separate cities and countries, they rule with the egoism of *I*. Is this good or bad? And if we do all belong to one human tribe, why do people live in separation from each other?"

Muhammad ☪ answered, "*Appa*, is this the way you see it? Listen, God is One, there are no differences among His creations, there is no fault in them. He made all His creations without fault and sent them down in that form. He made our blood red and created this form with it, but we who are born as man have lost that exaltedness of mind and determination, we live in a state of confusion which causes separations. In this mental confusion we focus on the five elements and forget to use our analytic wisdom in differentiating right from wrong. The ten sins join

this confusion and collectively cause the separations which lead to different forms, cities, countries, places and colors. The earth does not have a uniform color, it is made up of several colors, black or green in some places, in some places it might shine, it may have many colors. Because all these forms are created from earth this has led to separations of color, to many cities."

"My friends, all these words are spoken in true bliss.
If your mind wants to achieve clarity without suffering,
So that it can receive the grace of the eternal One,
If your mind wants to reach that state of joyful peace,
Listen continually to words from the ruler
Of two universes, the gracious Lord,
Then your mind can receive it,
Become joyous and understand
The unchanging book of meditation, realizing it.
All those lives born with a mind
Must realize it is the Āthi
Who lives with bliss in our heart,
And that the Āthi alone is the eternal One."

"My friends, the Āthi alone is eternal, He is the only eternal One among all living things, He is the eternal One. If we love that treasure, if we are mingled within it, when we depart, when we leave this world we take that eternal treasure with us. This is that eternal treasure." At the age of twenty Muhammad ☽ said this to the people all around. It made them joyous, they were blissful when they heard what he said and asked next how man should lead his life. "O Muhammad," they asked, "what is the meaning of man's life?" To which Muhammad ☮ replied, "Listen O my people, listen carefully, you have asked me how to live your lives."

"All hearts which melt into the state of one tribe
Exist in the Āthi's creation,
He is that gem who is uncontained by laws,
He is that precious fruit who is worshiped.
If you understand the birth of man with clarity,
Intently, when all hearts melt
In remembrance of the Āthi
You see only one form and one state,
As it is seen by true wisdom.
When all the Āthi's creations
Reach one state, reach clarity,
They will not waver like waves in the ocean,
They will comfort, they will be
Like one tribe, flowing with honey;
Their hearts melting, they will reach clarity,
They will look inwardly at all creations,
They will resplend as gnostic illumination,
With clarity they will realize
He is the all-knowing, eternal gem,
With grace they will see the state of the Āthi,
With joy they will realize that state of love is God,
With bliss they will understand the secret
Of man's life, free of suffering,
With clarity of mind and complete trust

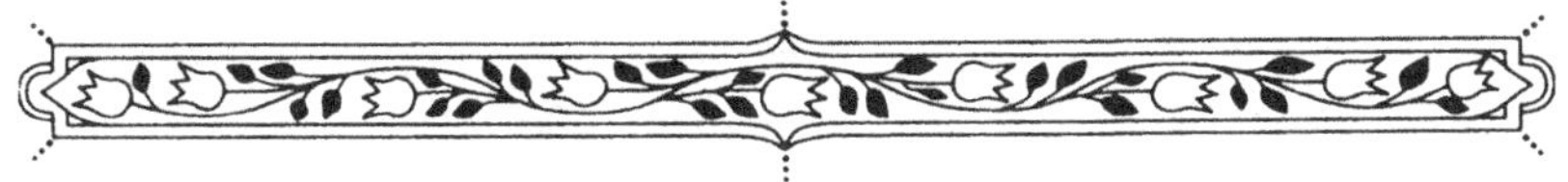

In the Āthi as the Friend,
Understanding that everything is in one state.
Realize the causal Āthi never falters in His justice,
Trust the Āthi with absolute faith
Then praise Him this way,
You will see Him with clarity.
When your mind receives the clarity of this state,
When you sing the truth of the eternal One,
Your heart must melt with His thoughts,
You must prostrate
To the resplendent, causal ocean of light,
You must prostrate before Him,
Live your life in that state, the state in which
Your mind has reached His beautiful qualities,
You must prostrate yourself
Before the great resplendent emperor,
You must prostrate, you must prostrate.
Understand the quickest way to correct yourself,
To realize yourself and worship Him,
You must do this before your time is up,
O my own born you must live your life this way!
The ocean which is man
Is greater than all the oceans with waves,
He is the noblest of creations,
He has the life of a human being,
He is a god in this world,
He is the eternal bliss
Which exists within justice,

He becomes precious
Because he has the gift of wisdom,
He makes the six-pointed house a temple,
Within it the Āthi exists as his Beloved
Who teaches, showing the ways of truth and justice,
Opening the path for all lives,
Making man acquire
The qualities of man-God, *manu-Īsan.*
Man is made great,
Ruling all living beings in the world,
This is the straight, true path
To the eternal treasure.
If you understand and truly worship within the *qalb*
You will see with clarity, you will realize
All lives are one O my own born, O my people,
Understand the explanation, find the way,
Love all lives as your own,
Know the right path and pray.
With a melting heart
Accept that all lives are equal,
With that understanding
Look at the laws of justice without wavering,
Keep reciting the Āthi is One, only One.
Recite well praising the grace of the Āthi,
Lord of the triple worlds,
Then He will grant you His grace and His truth
O my own born, then you will understand Him
With clarity O my brothers."

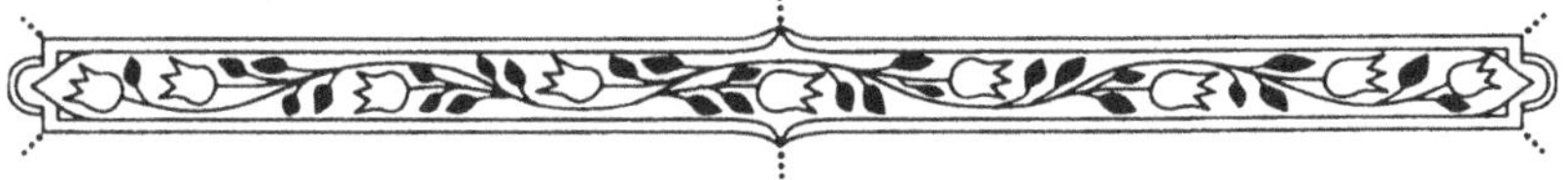

"O those who are born with me, those who love all lives equally are truly human gods, truly *manu-Īsan*. They look upon all lives as exalted, they have exalted wisdom, exalted qualities and flowing honeyed words, they resplend everywhere as *manu-Īsan*. Such beings offer divine love to all living things in the world and they in turn offer love to them. Such human beings are loved by all as gods, their hearts offer this kind of love and they trust all lives. The hearts of beings in this state should be like gods to them.

Appa, my friends, if you would like to know how man is supposed to live you should know that his work and his fatigue must become one. You always find fatigue setting in when you work — when you work fatigue follows. You have to work to satisfy the one-span stomach of everyone, including the lame or sick or tired who are all our own born, their fate written by God to conform with a drama acted out by their parents. Once He prints it, the Āthi gives a book their parents wrote to each person. This is the story, the drama we read today, a drama acted out to correspond with the book written by parents who might have been in a degraded or an elevated state.

What we have to understand in a loving way is that the different dramas written by each individual's parents are printed then handed over to this person who might also be in a degraded state, who might be lame or maimed, but just as we search for food to feed our own hunger we should understand that heart, that conscience, that face, that fatigue and feed it too. This is the truth within the truth. The primal Āthi created the world and *manu-Īsan* to rule the world, man was created to rule the world. *Manu-Īsan* rules the earth world and mighty God, the primal treasure rules man, He is the One who rules everything while man rules the earth. And so we must become *manu-Īsan* loving all lives as our own, we must not harbor vengeance or hurt others, we must not wound them, eat them or kill them. We must realize that man's life is the same as other lives.

My friends, we can attribute divisions within a tribe to the dramas of each individual, the history written by their parents. To illustrate, on earth you find mountains, plains, valleys, other realms buried deep in the earth and so on. The earth has gold and copper, it might also contain silver, iron, lead — many different things come from the earth. God created all living things from earth, but He sent down the light of the pure soul directly, this pure soul was planted in a pot of clay. That light will be united with light, earth will be united with earth. This is the way we must try to melt ourselves down and give back to earth what belongs to the earth. The first duty in man's birth is to trust and love all creations made of earth. Charity, justice, truth, patience, comfort and duty are all part of the laws of justice in our human conscience which is like a spear of power. This spear of power is conscience, conscience is God, God is the One who rules everything. Conscience rules the body and rules life, that primal luminosity exists within it and yet the all-pervading God of might is One, He has no equal, He has no partner. We are the female and He is the male, He is the One who watches over us, protecting us with love.

To one He gave a mouth, to another He gave eyes, to a third He gave strength of arms, to still others He gave strength of heart. You may ask yourself why some are poor and some are rich, and therefore wonder if God exists. Don't think that way, it is the consequence of a book written by the parents and presented to Him. The primal Āthi lives in the hearts of everyone as a servant, doing service to everyone, serving them according to the book already written by their parents. For this reason we see both good and evil acted out in the drama. He has also sent His slaves down to this earth one after another, those who have found clarity, to help others reach clarity. We should listen to them, we should achieve that clarity and since this is our condition, we must offer love, kindness, charity and affection to all living things.

If you have more food than you need for your one-span stomach give it to others. Understand that everything you seek, everything you keep for yourself belongs to the earth and will return to earth; understand what to save. Destroy arrogance, jealousy, vengeance, envy, hastiness and drive them away. Love and trust the primal, luminous treasure who exists within justice. This body is caught in the vilest of evils and the five sins, this body which is the house of maya will ultimately be a victim of earth, never trust it. What remains with us in the end as our capital are the good, the evil and what is born with us.

One day, in the same way we came together here, there will be a place where we meet again. Earth will remain with earth. One day we will meet again in another place and talk to each other. From wherever we came, from whatever people, when everything is over we have to go back one day, come together in that place. At this gathering there will be an inquiry concerning the good and evil we sought. When we come together in that place our profits will be weighed, there will be an inquiry concerning what is good, what is evil, what is true, all this will be shown to us by the God of might. So my own born, think carefully about each and every thing I have been saying, don't kill goats or cattle, don't harm other lives. The mayic evils mingled within you as a consequence of arrogance have been incorporated in the tricks of maya; this body made of the five letters can take so many different forms.

Our form is made of earth and like the earth has many colors, many qualities. To control all this, to reduce them to a single state we need God's grace and the spear of power, the certitude which is faith. Hold the spear of power and certitude in the hand which is faith, unite as one, all of you. Offer love to every living thing, offer love to every manifestation of earth. Show affection and kindness to every human life, love all lives as your own, understand the hunger of the one-span stomach, understand the

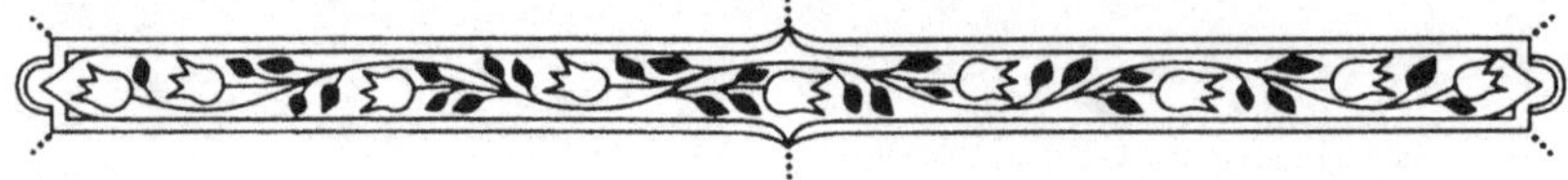

hunger of others and feed them. You must work, everyone must work. Go in search of all this before you leave the marketplace, and love those who cannot work because they are lame or blind or deaf, this is the consequence of a drama written by their parents, feed them with love and affection. Suppose you're walking along a path, and say someone has dug a hole in it because of the book written for him or her, what you should do is fill up the hole, level it and protect that person. You must love God who lives in cattle, goats, in everything.

Appa, there are countless things in the life of man, impossible for me to enumerate. This body entangled in the tricks of maya, wrapped in seventy thousand veils of maya has nine openings which are nine stars and nine astrological signs. All together there are twelve astrological signs, one of which is the navel which has been cut and closed, the others are the three eyes above. Two stars are the gnostic eyes. The twelve signs are also called the twelve astrological houses or twenty-seven stars. These twenty-seven stars have been brought down as twelve astrological signs, the twelve astrological signs are the twelve openings. Of the twelve openings, nine belong to maya *jālam,* the tricks of maya. These nine openings in the body cause it immense harm. Two openings are related to the way we finally merge with the Āthi. Try to find the right path with these two openings. The other ten are also equivalent to the ten signs of the zodiac which represent ten sins, a poisonous ten for this despicable body. The seventy thousand evil veils that cover them in a man make enticing sounds inside the man which are heard outwardly. Remove the veils, tear them off, discard them to see the primal Āthi. In the end there will be only one veil left, a veil made of earth. When you tear off that earthly veil you will see the Āthi. As long as you have that veil, love Him intensely. Loving the primal Āthi who has no equal means you shouldn't act against your conscience, for your own benefit. You shouldn't do things

for the sake of your stomach, you shouldn't deceive or harm others nor should you keep such evil qualities within you.

That iblīs who led our father Adam astray made idols of goats, cattle, horses, camels, donkeys, dogs and various other forms, placing devils in them to lead us astray. Some people have been caught by this, their form has changed, and as a result their good faith, their certitude have been ruined, destroyed. Even before these people die they behave like ghosts, demons and devils. There are thousands of such demonic ghosts, today in fact hundreds of thousands of such demons and ghosts possess human beings. Each human being makes room for seventy thousand demons, the seventy thousand evil veils have become seventy thousand demons. Just as iblīs lead Adam astray he keeps trying at every moment, at every second to lead us astray, he keeps asking God to be allowed to lead us all astray.

Iblīs said, 'O God, O vengeful One I was the leader of celestial beings in the heavens. You created this Adam from earth and decided to place me beneath him. I will never submit to his control, I know how to worship You. You created me from fire, Adam from earth and the five sins. He belongs to this earth which is hell while I belong to the heavens. I am a heavenly being, I was created from fire and under no circumstances will I take second place to him.' With an angry look God called out to him, 'O satan you demon, leave!' and cast him down from heaven to earth. Satan took his revenge and had Adam cast down to earth, his enemy's home. This enmity between satan and ourselves continues today. After tempting Adam to sin he asked God, 'Let me influence his wife and children, grant me that favor, let me lead them astray.' That vengeful *shaitān* argued for this from God.

To which God who has all the gracious names replied, 'You can go, your favor is granted.' And He proclaimed, 'Whoever follows Me will never follow you, whoever follows you will never follow Me.' After this iblīs was cast out. God said, 'Go *shaitān*!' and satan fell to the earth which he blends with today in a way that makes him seem invisible to the children of Adam.

That iblīs whose color is black appears as a black spot in the heart of every human being. If your heart is black it is symbolic of *shaitān's* presence in your heart, if your face is dark it means *shaitān* is there, if any dark spot appears on your face or hand it is symbolic of his presence. He enters you if you lack faith, certitude and determination. With His divine words of grace that mighty, all-pervasive God proclaimed those who become satan's slave will never be His slave, those who become His slave will never be satan's slave.

This is the reason satan long ago made idols of brass, stone and precious gems, then put ghosts inside to make them speak. He did this in the Arab countries too, creating mantras as well. To overcome *shaitān* six thousand, six hundred and sixty-six *āyats* or verses of the Qur'an were sent down to Muhammad, each *āyat* sent to control *shaitān*, each *āyat* also sent to tear off the seventy thousand evil veils. I believe it was said that a *nabī*, a prophet would come with the name Muhammad, and that all these *āyats* would be revealed to him in God's holy book." Muhammad ☪ said this and then his friends, the townspeople and others who had gathered there asked, "Is that Muhammad already born or not, where is he now?"

All for the One-Span Stomach

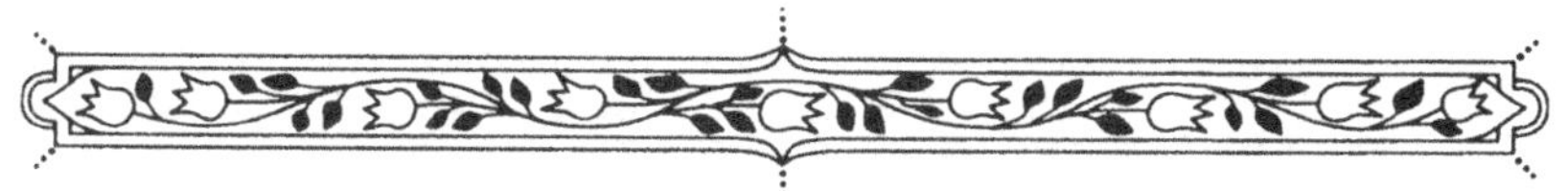

All for the One-Span Stomach

"Who will know, who will know the mystery
Of the Āthi O my fellow beings,
Who will ever know the mystery
Of the primal treasure permeating everything?
Who can understand it,
Who can understand the truth?
Can anyone understand
That mystery O my fellow beings?
Ages ago some elders proclaimed
A mighty prophet would be born,
This is merely a prediction,
This is merely a prediction.
I have uttered words from that God
Who exists completely in my heart,
Who reveals these honeyed words to me
In the form of advice, O my fellow beings.
A prophet with a melting heart will be born in Mecca,
His name will be Āthi Muhammad,
At the age of forty he will be crowned prophet
In the city of Mecca, six thousand,

Six hundred and sixty-six *āyats*, verses,
Will be revealed to him,
His bile will be removed,
He will be born as Muhammad, as a light,
That Āthi Muhammad will live in a form
On this earth, he will teach
So that *manu-Īsan* can tear off
The seventy thousand evil veils
Covering him on this earth.
His love will be drenched in happiness,
The sweetness of the Āthi's words
Will be like honey,
That causal Muhammad will come,
The Rasūl will come soon."

"The causal Muhammadur-Rasūl will come but the Āthi alone understands this mystery. How can I say who he is if I don't know? I only say what my heart tells me, *appa*, my brothers and sisters. Because he will be the last prophet all the evil veils can be ripped away through him. He, God who is mighty, who dwells in my heart has revealed this to me, He has revealed this in my heart. I don't know who that Muhammad is but my heart tells me he has already come, he has been born in Mecca. My heart tells me this but I do not know who he is. At some time in the future He will tell me, He will reveal that *nabī*, that prophet to me. Let us all follow him when the time comes O my fellow beings, and we will surely reach a high state."

Muhammadur-Rasūl replied to the question which had been asked with words of divine grace. His fellow beings gathered there

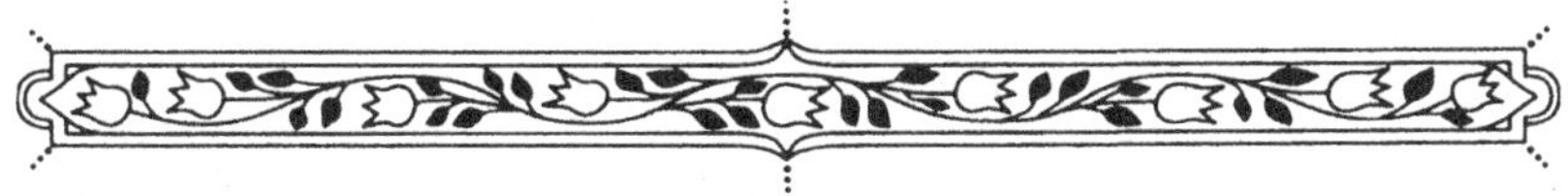

to listen became joyous, their hearts were blissful as they asked, "When will that *nabī* come?"

Then Muhammad ⊕ replied, "I believe he is already alive today yet I cannot say who he is, this question I can't answer. I know he will live in the city of Mecca, but we will only know who he is when the primal Āthi confers the mantle of prophethood on him, then let us follow him."

This is what he said to his friends and those who were born with him, "We must all live the secret of this life in a very exalted way, each of us trusting the one God who is without equal. Even while we are in this state iblīs may enter in so many forms, in idols to dogs, to demons, ghosts, cattle, bulls, goats, stones. By making idols speak like human beings he deceived each of the prophets. All these *śaktis* and mantras will be destroyed by the appearance of Nabī Muhammad, then the mouths of all the idols through whom iblīs speaks will be powerless. From that time on statues will no longer be able to speak, the mouths of all the ghosts will be powerless. When they lose their ability to speak this will be a sign the *nabī* has come: all the statues made by man, all the idols will be silent, will be like stone.

So instead of having certitude in their existence, have certitude in the primal Āthi, the Āthi who fills all lives, put all your trust in Him. Make every effort to fill the needs of others, to guide those who try to stay on the straight, true path, do not let them go astray. We must find the straight, true path and merge with the primal Āthi who exists within you, within me, in trees, bushes and stones. He is that complete treasure. I am instructing you now in a variety of ways, how human lives should be lived. If we offer love and affection to goats and cattle they will offer us love, they will speak to us. If we have absolute faith in the Āthi all lives will speak to us with love — it is therefore necessary to love and trust all lives. We must be in

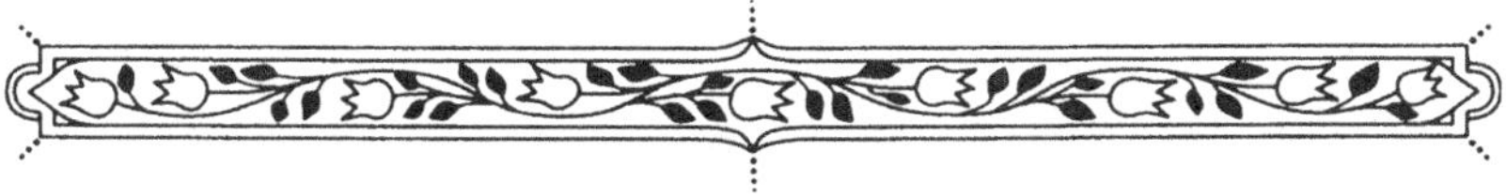

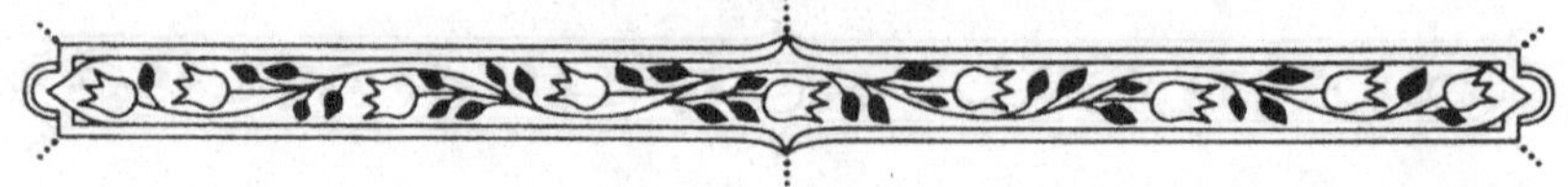

that state and love all lives, we must let our affection for all living
things be seen O my fellow beings."

"Even if it were a stone with certitude
In the words of the Āthi,
We should fall at its feet,
If even a piece of iron
Were to utter the words of the Āthi,
We should fall at its feet too
And walk along that path.
Have you not heard songs of praise
From all the Āthi's creations,
Including blades of grass, bushes on the earth,
Have you not heard them?
When blades of grass fall to the right
And then to the left, have you not understood
The words they say O my fellow beings?
Try to understand why these blades of grass
Bend to the right, bend to the left
And then bend forward."

"*Appa,* those long blades of grass near the pond are listening
to us, they turn to the right, to the left and bend forward. Try to
understand what this tells us. The blades of grass all move uni-
formly. What do they say when they move that way? They are
doing *ḍhikr,* reciting the remembrance of God, 'O my Āthi, my
Rahmān, *lā il,* nothing exists except You,' and then they say, *'Ill-*

Allāhu, You are Allah.' They recite this *dhikr, lā* is the negative, nothing, *ill-Allāhu,* You are Allah. This is what they say as they bend forward and repeat the *dhikr.* The large blades of grass near the pond worship that One. Can't you see? Look at them." As Muhammad ☪ looked in their direction every blade of grass and all the little plants near the pond bent forward to listen to him. They swayed to the north, they swayed to the south then bent forward facing west.

People who gathered around suggested, "They're moving because of the wind," but Muhammad ☪ said, "It's not that — well then, take a piece of cloth and see which way the wind blows." They found the wind blowing to the east. They asked, "Why are the blades of grass bending west if the wind is blowing to the east?" Muhammad ☪ replied, "If these blades of grass praise the Āthi, how much more should we with our six levels of wisdom praise Him? The grass is so filled with love, awe and worship of God, even after becoming mere blades of grass they still worship Him. Let us see just how many births this grass has taken, millions of births and still it worships. So try to understand the qualities of this grass."

> "*Appa,* the gracious Lord of three worlds
> Created a kind of grass called *sambai*
> In the digestive system of man,
> This particular grass grows in the large intestine,
> Crushing and dissolving all the food
> Taken in, digesting it
> While all the undigested food
> Is eliminated in the form of feces,
> Understand this digestive grass called *sambai.*

The Āthi, that most blissful Lord
Has placed this *sambai* which digests and filters
Food in the body of man, in his large intestine,
Realize this, understand it.
Look, understand this is that grass
You find in the intestine,
Fix yourself on the path of truth
As grass is fixed in the intestine,
Trust only that One, know Him,
Melt and become transcended man-God;
Try to understand it,
This grass connected to man
Has become part of his digestive tract,
It consumes, crushes and digests the food
In an exalted way and then eliminates the feces.
Manu-Īsan, man-God is the most exalted of forms,
Realize man is the most precious creation of the Āthi;
To take the exalted form of *manu-Īsan*
Know what the *sambai* grass does in the intestine
And know how to pray O my own born.

Know this as the prayer of completeness,
Those born with me, listen intently
And without fail to what I say,
Do not miss the least part of it,
Those who have the form of human beings,
Those who have analytic wisdom, that clarity,
Fix your intention on the eternal One

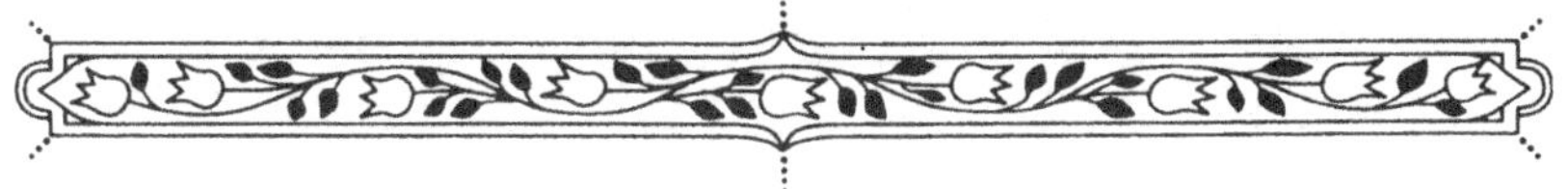

Who is always there,
Close your two eyes with this intention,
Discard the eyes of maya,
Cut away the demons of mind and desire,
Establish the plenitude of both worlds.
The treasure which is everywhere,
The treasure connected to all lives
Which looks upon all living things
As one within the heart,
With this understanding and this right, true thought
Understand the unique path, cut away multiple paths.
Discard evil, have clarity of intention,
Blind your two eyes and open the right, true eye,
Know with certitude that the lofty flame
Of true *gnānam* or wisdom
Is the only One who is Lord,
Have this joy, see this honey in the heart,
Know the taste of inner honey,
See that *katpaha virudcham*, the tree
Mingled in your intention as overwhelming joy.
Keep to your devotion,
There are fruits which do not ripen,
There are flowers which do not bloom,
This tree filled with merit is the *satchithananda*,
The being of eternal bliss
Who rules the eight with praise;
The One who is eternal grace
Is the *katpaha virudcham*,

That One, plenitude for everything,
The treasure of completeness for all things seen,
This divine tree which grants whatever you ask
Is the Āthi of exceeding grace.
Melt with the intention that this is a divine tree
Which grants whatever you ask, think and melt,
The Āthi will melt, He will mingle with you,
He will befriend you and fill you inwardly.
All those who were born with me,
Do not be caught
In the maya which makes your heart stone,
Do not be caught in the anger which destroys houses,
Do not linger in these evils
And do not lose your established place with that God,
May you not lose the place you have established,
May you establish the treasure
Which grants you this place in your intention,
Declare this in your intention.
As you go on polishing clarity will come,
Exalted beings who were born with me, listen,
Be that radiant, true heart
Which has the luminosity of true *gnānam*, wisdom,
May you mingle with the meaning within meaning.
Blind your two outer eyes,
Forget desire for things of the earth,
Reject desire for gold,
Do away with slander,
Say this is good, this is good

And it is always here.
Do not let go of Him, do not be separate from Him,
The Lord who is beyond anything sensual,
The luminous One, that form, that pure One,
The primal Rahmān, the Mercy, may you praise Him,
May you see His divine feet.
That Rahmān who is everywhere
Is a complete treasure
For those whose hearts are true,
He is the meaning
For those on the straight, true path.
He is the treasure, devotion is their remedy,
He is the treasure filled with endless merit,
He is the grace shining in the form of bliss,
Praise the primal One
Who is a treasure which fills the world,
This is plenitude, may you see that plenitude. *Amīn.*"

"Those who were born with me, how should you love the
primal One? As much as you love, to the extent of your devotion
you will see this beauty. You must have the clarity to see Him in
that state, you must grow, be truth within truth, become true man
within this lofty, true *gnānam* and He will be within true man, the
eternal One revealing a complete treasure. Acquire the quality
which praises Him without forgetting, be one-pointed and keep to
that one-pointedness. Do not invent different forms for the primal
One who rules beneath one umbrella, the eternal One who is in
the heart and never leaves. Don't be enchanted by the multiplicity

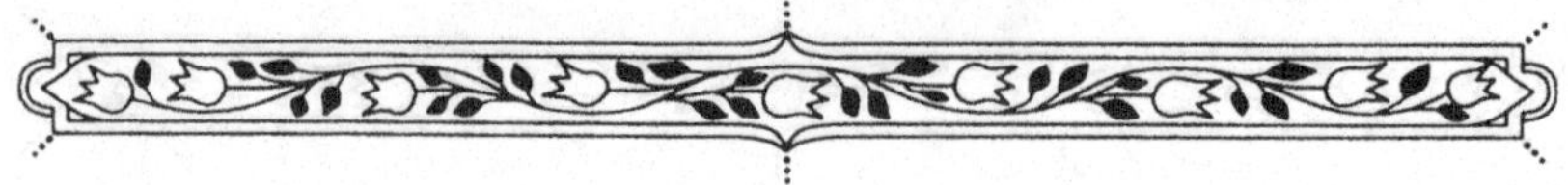

of things, the primal One who blossoms like a flower wherever you look has no parallel. If you look at all this seeing others as His equal, you will never see Him.

Can you keep the primal One who blossoms everywhere, who is fragrance everywhere in just one place? You can't do that. The unique treasure of repletion here, there and everywhere, the treasure who is here, there and everywhere, the treasure of grace and bliss has only one form. That treasure who exists fully in good qualities, in the integrity of understanding the point, the state, that God of grace, think of Him within your love with patience, peace and duty. Do this without fail.

Appa, God does His duty without fail — to have the grace of such a God, how exalted must we be? Man's life is filled with exaltedness, all lives are within him, all the heavenly beings and wise men are within man-God. The primal One is also within man-God, the primal One is everywhere as King. Love that One to whom all trust belongs, do not accept anyone as equal to the One who has no equal, do not think He can have partners, keep that unparalleled One as your help. The primal One is plenitude without picture or form, a treasure which can be caught by justice and honesty, a full treasure within patience, a rare treasure, the primal treasure of justice and honesty. This is an eternal treasure, this is the form of luminosity replete in all those resplendent beings. Unite with the One in your conscience. Think of it and melt. *Appa*, the Lord is there within it, may you see Him always, may you do your duty always. You need peace of mind to see Him always, this is plenitude. *Appa*, you must try."

The Rasūl ☪ sang this song to his brothers and all the people who were there. These people and his brothers then asked, "O noble Nabī Muhammad you went to Sham Nagar, to the city of Damascus on business. Describe your business, describe your travel. What was business like there?" To which he answered, "Ah,

are you asking about business? We went to Sham Nagar, my uncle, Abū Jahl and the others, we all went to do business there, many people, and each one sold his goods in a different way. I said what I had to say although they didn't listen, and I told them my share was to come to me. Now you want to know what business is like, I'll tell you."

"Freedom is business,
Comfort is the right of that treasure,
The treasure which is very rare,
That is business,
Something in which you are no one's slave.
What is the totality of this business,
Who is it we do business with?
We must know this well, all those born with me,
We must see that path O those born with me,
We must understand it, all those born with me,
We must digest it and understand,
We must have clarity
Whether business is with one person or many.
Those who are born with me,
It is for the sake of our stomach
And for clothes to cover this body,
A cover to protect our honor,
Clothing which covers this corpse
And food for our stomach,
That's what this business is for, to acquire these things.
We all came, we gathered in this market,

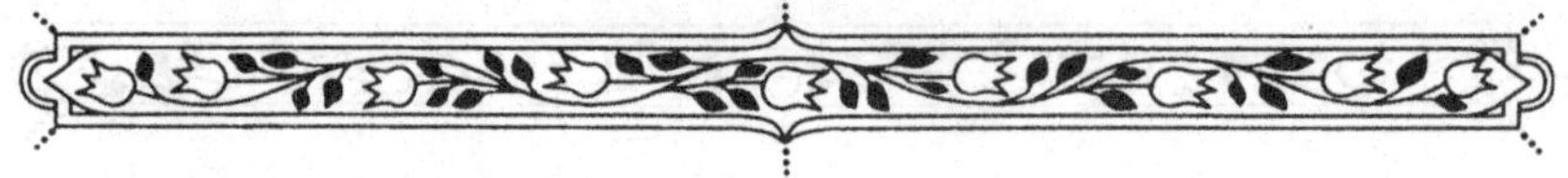

In this world we buy what we can then leave,
No matter what we buy,
No matter what we collect,
It's all for the one-span stomach
And clothing to cover our body.
This is what we do business for in the world
And this is what we took to sell."

"*Appa*, the things we took were food for the one-span stomach and clothing to cover the body. This is what they came to buy, they needed the same things too, clothing to cover the body, something to fill the one-span stomach. They came to buy the things they needed to cook their food with, and so you can say the business I went for was the one-span stomach and they came for that one-span stomach too.

Since this is the way things are we must not tell lies, we must not say this and that just to do business. There is no business beyond this. There is only one business we can do with the heart, the business of the Supreme Being. We must not bite when we buy for business, we must not collect money with lies and deceit. Now without telling lies, suppose we buy something for a half-cent and get three-quarters of a cent when we sell it. With this little profit we can feed our stomachs and they can feed theirs too. To buy for one cent and try to sell for ten is evil, that is deceiving others to take their money. Many did this and when I tried to stop them, Abū Jahl came along to thrash me saying, 'You have come to this world; now what are you doing to stop others from carrying on with their business?' He came to beat me because I told him the truth."

"'*Appa*, my brother, no matter what you collect,
The luminous One, the primal One
Who formed you gave you
So many states of joy, so many shining things,
He gave you so many resplendent things.
Everything you seek, everything you search for,
All these things are treasures of the primal One,
While you are just one thing on this earth;
To the hidden treasure,
Your *rūḥ*, your soul is one treasure,
May you realize the truth that
This is what is left at the end of everything.
All those lives who were born with me,
They came to that market to buy things,
All for the one-span stomach
And clothing to cover the body,
This is the reason they came.
Didn't you see how they came
Shouting as they walked?
For this one stomach we went from Mecca
To Sham, to Syria,
Only to fill this one-span stomach.
Just as we came, they did too,
To fill our one-span stomach, and they did too.
If you do not have clarity, others can be deceived,
If you double the price, claim two cents for one,
If you kill them, take them in and cheat them
The primal One will punish you one day;

On that day He will inquire then cut you down,
The primal One who is without equal or comparison,
Who created everything,
The primal One who is without compare,
The primal treasure within the resplendence
Of true *gnānam*, of grace awakened wisdom,
Who looks everywhere with that one eye,
The primal One who fills your body,
He will know you, He has this clarity,
He is within all lives.
Realize that the primal treasure
Who goes everywhere also has a share,
If you cut off that quality of yours
Filled with all the sins,
The primal One will come to help you.'
This is what I told Abū Jahl."

Noble Muhammad ⊕ said we have to explain
How to do business, how to encourage good qualities,
But when Abū Jahl heard these divine words
He rose up in anger, he leaped up with jealousy,
He spoke against
Noble Muhammad ⊕ without reason.
Muhammad ⊕ who was filled with patience,
Who had that exalted quality smiled,
His causal face bloomed like a lotus flower
As he raised his hands to ask the primal One,
"*Yā Rabbal-ʿālamīn*, O Lord of the universes

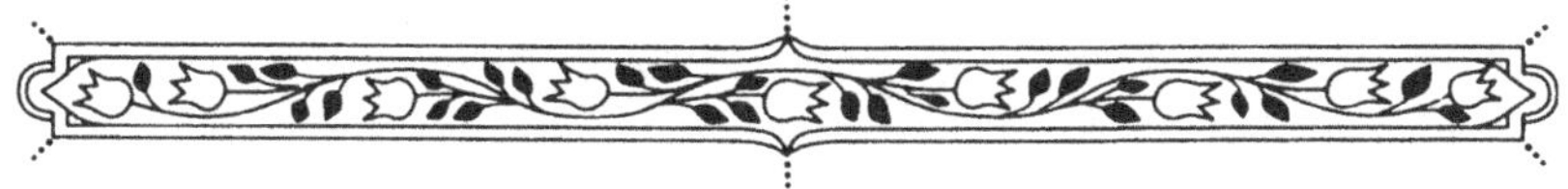

Who created me, may You protect
Those born with me in this world
From the influence of iblīs, of satan,
May You correct sinners
Who have lost their good qualities,
Make them hear what is said,
Make them understand good and evil,
May You show them the good, true path night and day,
May You dwell in their bodies
O primal One connected to all lives,
May You grant them good, true wisdom,
May You protect them night and day,
May You correct Abū Jahl's qualities and rule over him,
Yā Rabbal-'ālamīn."

He raised both hands in prayer
Supplicating the primal One.
Everyone saw this, everyone saw this
And smiled happily; some saw those golden feet
And prayed, their hearts melting,
And those businessmen
Who were reformed had clarity of heart,
They asked the right value for their goods,
For things which had cost one cent
They were given one-and-a-half,
They did business truthfully,
And so the people improved, correcting themselves
In the way they did business,

But Abū Jahl threw all this away,
Choosing the qualities of iblīs, of satan instead.
"When will the day come,
When will the primal One instill good qualities
In Abū Jahl, making him happy day and night?"
The noble Prophet ☙ repeated
The conversation he had with Abū Jahl,
Explaining what happened
When we went away on business,
Those were his divine words.

The companions of Muhammad ☙, those born with him asked, "If a thing cost them one cent, would they sell it to you for the same amount?" Muhammad ☙ replied, "Yes, and they had such trouble as they did business truthfully, collecting and traveling for the sake of this one-span stomach. If you are honest you can do that. They worked hard for their one-span stomachs and for clothing to cover their bodies too. All the creations of the primal One, cows, goats, they all search on behalf of the one-span stomach. Everything we collect remains on this earth, we have to understand that.

We went from Mecca to Sham Nagar, the city of Damascus, to earn something for this one-span stomach. What else is there? Everything belongs to Him. We have taken this human form which returns to earth in the end, and so all we really need is food for the one-span stomach and a piece of cloth to cover ourselves, to protect our honor, that's all we need profit for. What else do we need here? They came here to feed their one-span stomach, we went there to earn something for our one-span stomach. Why should

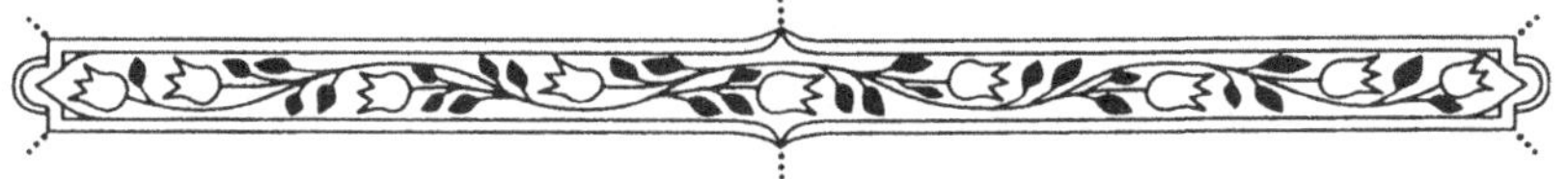

we tell lies just because we came to do business on its behalf? Why be jealous, why steal? We must understand if we are in business, no matter what kind of work we do, we can't do more than fill our one-span stomach, we can't take any of this back with us. Everyone tries to protect and feed a one-span stomach. If we do not deceive each other there will be no distinction between rich and poor, we will all be equal, all lives will have plenitude, God will dwell in all lives.

If one person deceives another, tells lies, utters falsehoods, then this evil happens. When we go on the path to God, when we are in this state we have to realize everything belongs to Him, everyone belongs to Him, we all belong to Him. The body belongs to the earth, it will return to earth, but the soul goes back to Him. And it is a one-week journey in this world, we have come to the market just to feed our one-span stomach. When the feast is over at the end of the week we have to return. We have only one week here for the feast. Then why do we have to tell lies, why do we have to deceive each other, and why murder, why all these sins just for one week's business to feed the stomach? We must understand this."

That is what Muhammad ☾ said to his companions as he explained it all. They asked, "O Muhammad, noble Muhammad in this state, who taught you such wisdom?" He answered, "The Lord who created me gave it to me." "Then how should a man lead his life, how should we live our lives?" they asked. "*Appa,* you ask how to live your lives? I'll tell you."

"You must have a clear heart,
Your heart and intention must be one,
The causal primal One, see that One as plenitude,

Your heart and eyes must be one,
See that causal primal One.
Your entire body must always
Carry out your duty to the world,
You will see the primal One in this joy,
You must see the primal One in this joy
Without deviating from good intentions,
Without forgetting His commands;
Do that service then you can receive the help
Of the primal One and receive what is yours by right,
You can see that One, this is the way,
This is the true treasure.
Consider other lives as your own,
The primal One who fills all lives,
The grace which is everywhere, that plenitude
Is the treasure, the eternal treasure,
And the place where the treasure lives
Is the temple where honesty and justice
Live in the human heart,
It is the temple which can change every evil
Although the temple itself cannot be changed,
This temple built of the nine kinds of gems,
This temple which makes us live in the truth,
This is the temple of creation and destruction.
To go on the straight, true path to the primal One,
To find peace, know the way and know the secret,
Know that justice, see it well,
See it with clarity, truly have compassion,

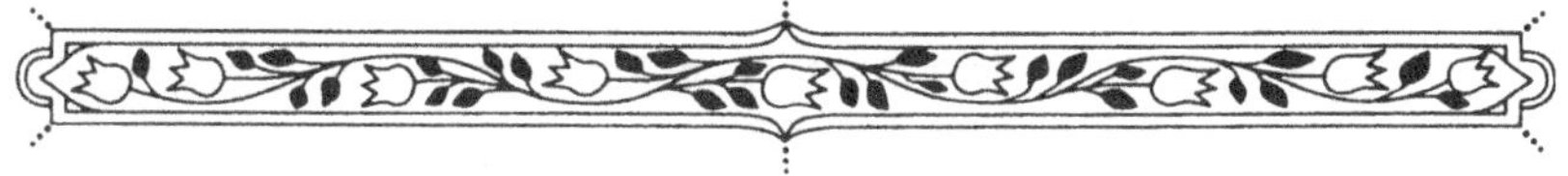

Have faith in that One
And know the state of justice with clarity.
Do this in the temple of three worlds,
The temple of Siva-Īsan,
The temple at Thiruppathi
Which is the heart of *manu-Īsan,* man-God.
If we open that heart, if we pray
To the primal One we will receive our due,
We will see, we will have clarity and see
The primal One within the heart, the temple of the heart,
That treasure of joy, this is that treasure of joy."

"*Appa,* He created so much within this temple, so many faces to help us on the straight, true path. Listen my brothers and sisters, you asked how man should live, I'll describe his state. How should a man conduct his life? He must take the form of the primal One, not the form of illusion, he must reach the state which is that divine form. The divine form of the triple flame appears within the illusion of the five letters. The place of illusion is the form of man, the features of the body belong to illusion, the divine form belongs to God, to man-God. There are two different areas we must identify with clarity and then behave in accordance with this knowledge. This is a treasure of truth, one area is the body, *suniyam* or illusion is the body and *sivamayam* or divine form is the state of the soul."

"This is the body made of illusory things
In a subtle way, understand this subtle state

259

And know the real state; this subtle state
Changes, reaching out to the real state.
We find every way, every deceit to nourish the body,
This body of illusion which does not resplend,
Which will perish.
The primal One, the luminous One
Made the soul, the soul
Which is a pure ray in the state of God,
Which is in the divine state of God,
The soul does have a state of divine resplendence
Which is that *śivam,* that purity, *manu-Īśan,* man-God.
The form mixed with the divine state of God
Is the one blissful lord who rules three worlds,
The treasure of three worlds, the complete treasure.
May you bring your soul to that divine state
With a melting heart, if you mingle
With that One you will be in a good, pure state,
A state which is rightfully yours,
On that straight, true path you will find clarity
And your body will have a divine form."

These were the divine words of Muhammad ⊕
Whose lips were like pearl;
Everyone listened to the words of grace,
The words of the guru, the jewel of *gnānam,* of wisdom,
They listened to the honeyed words with delight,
The words and teachings of the primal One.
Every day he told them how to keep their hearts

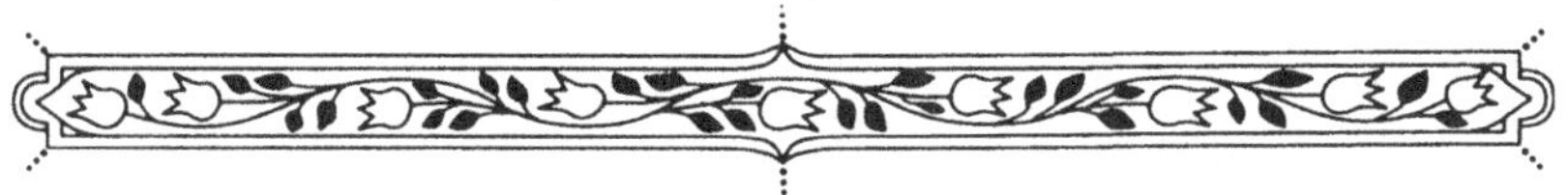

On the right path, he taught them that path openly,
The Prophet, the Rasūl, noble Muhammad.
Muhammadur-Rasūl was twenty years old
When he gave them all these teachings with joy,
The people understood the meaning
And washed their qualities clean.
You should never waste your time —
Those who had been wasting their lives
Wandering around the city of Mecca, losing their faith
Listened to the precious words of grace,
To the pearls of wisdom
The Prophet Muhammad gave them;
When these people saw this radiance of true wisdom
Their hearts melted, their intention never wavered
And their hearts melted,
They did service as they set out
On the straight, true path,
Accepting Muhammad as their help.
With melting hearts,
Without deviating from the straight, true path
They realized Muhammad was the gem of grace
Who would prescribe a remedy to clear their qualities
And send them on the straight, true path;
They praised this rare gem, this Āthi Muhammad,
The *guru mani* of the world, the treasure of bliss
Who is exalted among the exalted,
They came together in an exquisite way for that one
Whom they cherished and loved

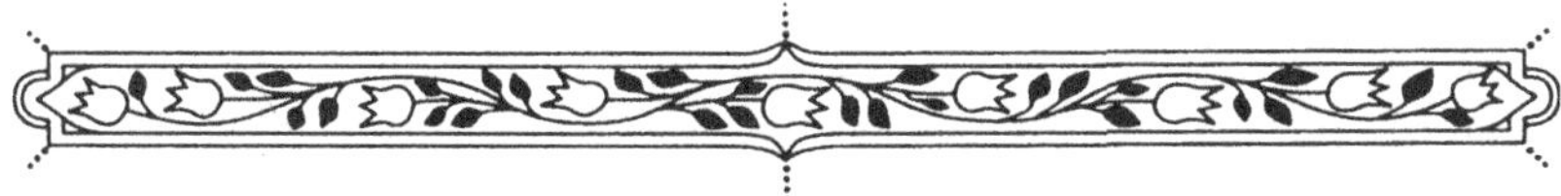

With a melting heart of joy;
With honey in their heart
They praised Muhammad ☪,
The noble one who shone everywhere.
At the age of twenty he showed them
Every state in which they could find
What was theirs by right,
How they could have permanent *īmān*, perfect faith,
He taught their hearts, revealing
The rich ways of *gnānam* or gnosis.
He approached them with detailed teachings
So they would know, would understand
The meaning of the five letters;
He explained how to find clarity,
He distilled his words, he gave explanations
About the form of man, a radiant ray of true *gnānam*.
Those who listened to the good, true words
Of that divine Prophet ☪
Established them in their hearts,
Making such sweetness flow.
Many listened with great care and tasted
Those divine words in this world.
He uttered precious words of wisdom about Īsan, God,
Words which were both subtle and rare,
The Rasūl Muhammad ☪
Uttered these words of grace.
O mind listen to these words of wisdom,
Have clarity in your heart.

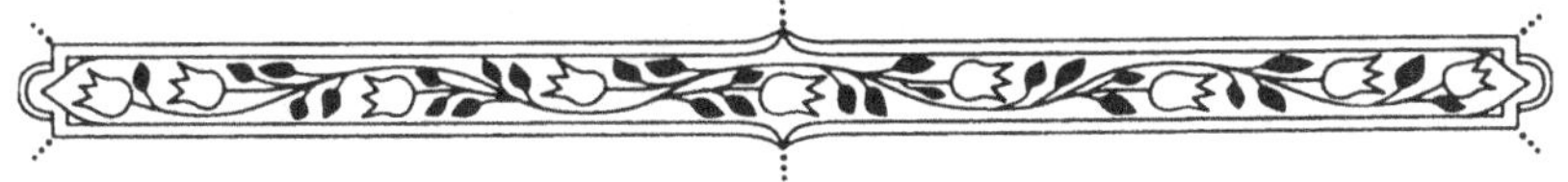

He spoke about these things to his close companions,
To those who were born with him,
To those with unequaled qualities of goodness,
Āthi Muhammad, the radiance uttered these pure words
Disclosing the treasure.
That silent guru within,
The Lord who shines at the center,
The silent Lord of wisdom,
The Lord who exists in fullness within the intellect,
That treasure, the primal One
Who is wealth, the plenitude of the eight praises,
Who is the effulgence granting grace,
The God who is caught within love,
The primal One, the treasure
Found in compassionate eyes
Showed them how to bring their hearts
To the straight, true path.
Exalted Muhammadur-Rasūl ﷺ
Had those who used to walk
With heads held high along the road
Walk instead with their heads lowered.
The One of six tastes, the divine gem of bliss,
The gem of wisdom,
The One of exalted qualities, the gem of grace,
The One who overflows as joy
Here, there and everywhere,
The One of the eight praises,
The word of wisdom which eliminates evil,

The One who has no prejudice of race,
The One who is the guru, the fragrance, the Friend,
The One who exists here, there, everywhere,
Millions and millions embraced Him without error.
To love that One, the great primal One
Was the advice the noble Prophet Rasūl ☽ gave.

"*Appa*, what is called *suṇīyam* or evil is our body, the body made of every deceptive thing, this body which is a test of the subtle states created by God. This body is filled with illusion, deceit, treachery, suffering, falsehood, jealousy, arrogance, anger; these are the qualities which fill the birth of this body. If you do not have clarity, if you do not clear your body of these inner evils your life is lost. Be sure of this, everything you search for, the joys of this body are only an illusion with bad qualities. If you go on searching for the body your life is lost.

The primal One created this body in a subtle way, this body was created with illusion, the four thousand, four hundred and forty-eight nerves are illusion. The human form is created with the subtle evils of the earth—we have to find clarity in this and take the true path. Until we do our body is filled with illusion, our body which is filled with illusion has such suffering while it lives and after death too. The five letters, the five deadly sins, the five elements are all caught in this illusion, caught in deceit and suffering; they will be burned to ashes.

We have to discard, we have to eliminate and be rid of these qualities of illusion to make the body divine. The power to make that change, to make it divine is within us; we must make the body of illusion a divine form. We can do this with the eternal One's words of wisdom. We must realize this divine state. Man has the

form of the divine. We have to know that, you and I, and if we have clarity we can find the good, true path. The life of man is very rare, a great treasure, greater than the ocean, beyond the oceans. There are so many inner secrets, the mind has more than seventy thousand horsepower. If it is caught by illusion it is subject to suffering, to hell, it is food for the earth. If this body of illusion is caught by maya it is food for maya. But if man can become *manu-Īṣan*, man-God, the divine form, he will see the divine treasure, he will reach that eternal God. Given this state we must improve, we must change, find a way to see the treasure of plenitude, the primal One permeating everything. This would be a good thing to do."

Mecca Opposes Muhammad ﷺ

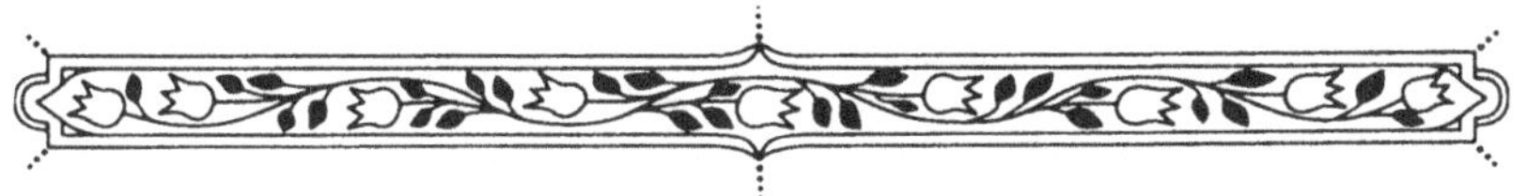

Mecca Opposes Muhammad ☾

"*Appa,* do not trust this illusory body
Which doesn't know the secret point,
This body filled with deceit,
With treachery and suffering
Is a corrosive medication which deceives you,
Then destroys you in the world.
All your relatives, your attachments and love
Are merely signs of a coming destruction.
Know the secret of this illusory body, the cause
Of every suffering, have clarity
Those who were born with me, know the secret
Of this illusory body and have clarity
Those who were born with me,
Understand the meaning,
Realize the state of *gnānam,* of wisdom,
And know that God who is invisible to the eyes,
Realize Him, clear all these illusions
And the force of illusion from your heart,
Chase it from your mind, realize Him,
The primal King; if you follow Him

You will see divine, eternal joy.
Without rain and without sunlight,
The primal One is a tree
Producing fruit in a hidden place,
If the heart is right, in a good state,
That tree will grant what it asks, what the heart asks,
It is the *katpaha virudcham*, the divine tree
Which grants whatever the heart asks,
If it asks from the right place.
No matter what you ask
It will give you shade and fruit,
It always grants you victory, that treasure
Which is the joy of six divine tastes
Conferring grace on every loving devotee,
That treasure conferring grace on those who love
Is the honey of joy, the ripened fruit,
It is everywhere, a treasure within the body,
That primal treasure is plenitude for everyone.
The primal One fills you this way —
If you love Him there are so many joys.
Those who were born with me,
Companions, beloved friends,
We are creations of the primal One,
We must step forward
To love the plenitude which has no blemish;
Given this state, to reach that treasure
We must behave without fault
On the straight, exalted path."

Primal Muhammad ㉛ sang this song at the age of twenty and all the people of the world heard his words, praising him, noble Muhammad ㉛. This is the song they sang to him then, the noble Prophet ㉛.

"Resplendent gem who came to be tested,
Causal ocean who is the cure for everyone,
That honey of taste,
The treasure of all three worlds,
A fruit which flourishes within the heart,
Light in the flame of steadfast, true *gnānam,*
Fruit, ripened fruit in the heart,
Light which gives light, light
Which is a flame at that secret point,
Which scrapes away the rust of our intentions,
The compassionate one, the treasure
Opening our eyes and revealing
A jeweled light, Muhammad,
Is the unique gem who tells us that everything,
All the blessings lie in reciting God's name.
The being who shines in two worlds,
Who knows before and after, who prays,
The being who shows us that primal point, Muhammad
Is the one who disperses darkness forever,
He is a lamp dispersing the darkness,
Honey of joy, lamp of both worlds,
Divine being within love, the comforter,

The gem who gives comfort, king of all the worlds
And a prophet for everyone.

He is the prophet of two worlds
Who can make a light burn without oil,
He is the one who fills every life,
Who is the light burning in all lives,
O our Prophet Muhammad, *Yā* Rasūl,
The earth hears your sounds and quakes with awe,
The trees bend down and listen
To you, in this world, in this *dunyā*
All lives hold out their hands,
They call out to you and clap,
They resonate, 'The Prophet
Who resplends in both worlds.'
They listen to your words, ants, fleas,
The eighty-four hundred thousand
Call out saying, 'O noble Prophet';
When they hear your voice they bow their heads
Listening to your words which proclaim equality,
Realizing the joy of the house to come.
O divine Prophet who is our only joy,
How can we praise your words of grace,
Your words of plenitude, O Prophet
Who was born to this world filled with exalted merit,
O Prophet who has come in this false body,
Every word you say is like fruit
Which is sweet as honey,

O how can we describe your magnitude
In these two worlds, how can we praise you?
You shine in *ākhirah*, the hereafter
And in the *dunyā*, this world,
You are the treasure of help O exalted guru,
You destroyed the ego, the *I*,
You destroyed all these illusions, the mantras,
You destroyed anger, all this hell,
You rejected everything which glitters.
You made us love the great primal One
As justice within justice, as treasure within treasure,
As merit, as the everywhere, the here and there,
As love within love, the joy which is everywhere,
O primal Muhammad how can we
Recite your praise in this world?
O light of the lamp, O shining treasure,
O golden one, the fullness everywhere
Who is ripened fruit for everyone,
O divine gem, the repletion of all eight directions!"

When they praised him this way Muhammad ⊕ heard it and said, "*Appa*, my sisters and brothers, the praise you sing so beautifully is like honey! May the primal One grant you that state so we will be able to sing the same words about you, so that we may all be praised in the same way.

How to live your householder's life, how to discard the eyes of illusion, the mantras, how to cut away all this deceit and understand the secret point, that treasure, this is what we have to sing about. If we believe in this illusory body we will not find the secret point, we will not see God; if we believe in this hell of the body we will suffer. We must find that point at which we look upon all lives as our own. Those who were born with me, exalted ones, precious jeweled lights of my eyes you must reach the primal One, travel the straight, true path. May He grant us His grace." This is what Muhammad ⊕ said to them.

All the words, the people of the world
Heard all the words spoken by the Prophet ⊕,
They received comfort
From this complete gem of the eye,
The Rasūl, Guru Muhammad ⊕
Overflowing with grace and bliss,
Their hearts were drenched in that strength
As they declared him
The resplendent Muhammadur-Rasūl ⊕
In this world and the next,
Upholding this state of *īmān*, of absolute faith.
The words of the Rasūl ⊕ flourished
As the words of the resplendent Āthi in the world,
The teachings of the noble Prophet ⊕
Were received by all living things,
The words of that divine Rasūl ⊕, the divine words
Filled all lives, settling deep in their hearts,
Making them realize, making them aware
Of that flame of true *gnānam*, of wisdom,
These words encouraged them showing them the path,

The words of the true Muhammadur-Rasūl ☺
Brought clarity to the four religions
And the four scriptures.
Understand this well, the words
Of the compassionate Prophet ☺
Are causal words.
The people believed the words
Of this extraordinary Prophet ☺ completely,
Their hearts melted in remembrance of them,
They heard words of love, joy flooded the world
And praise of the primal, compassionate One
Flourished in the fourteen worlds.
The primal Prophet ☺
Taught them these good words,
Words of truth for the true path,
All living things understood them with inner clarity,
Many lives pursued the meaning fully
And found clarity, realizing the primal One.

As they prayed Abū Jahl became jealous
Of all this; with evil qualities he rose up
In strength, gathering the people of the world,
Destruction his intention.
He collected an army by skillfully making them
Forget the words of truth,
He made them forget the feet of that lord
Who is beyond all sensual pleasure.
Abū Jahl was suffering in a burning hell, the hell

Of poking out your own eyes with a pointed stick.
He caused such evil in the city,
Trying to make them forget the words
Of the good Muhammadur-Rasūl ☙;
With deceit and treachery he rose up
To destroy the explanations
In the Prophet's words ☙,
To make them forget every good thing
Abū Jahl took the form of treachery.

Setting out to ruin them he fed the people of the world deceit and treachery, going from house to house saying, "O people of the world if you reach this state while you're still so young, our ancestral deities will be destroyed. Muhammad is a youth whose tricks you knew when he was a child. Don't follow him, he is the source of universal destruction, he has come to destroy the world. He lost his mother and father when he was young and now he's working to establish this vile hell, making trouble for our ancestral deities. Don't follow him, he curses our ancestral gods, insinuating things about them then claiming there is a God somewhere; he is trying to destroy our ancestral gods. This is what he teaches all day long, don't follow him or our ancestral deities will desert us. Our ancestors made these gods who speak to us, who are so good to us. Now he has begun our destruction. Let us come together to destroy him while he is still in his tender youth, may we all come together for this," and he collected his army.

Abū Tālib heard of this and said to Muhammad ☝,

"My son we don't need this country's hostility,

O Muhammad who has come as the primal Prophet,

Bringing good teachings and clear wisdom,

The Qasim family is against us,

The whole city is against us;

O my son they are all against you,

O my son the whole city is against you,

O Muhammad they have decided to kill you,

They have come together to kill you,

O my heart is melting, suffering,

O noble Muhammad, so many different interests

Have come together with Abū Jahl,

He has collected an army to kill you,

What can I do

O jeweled light of my eye, Muhammad?

My son Muhammad, do not engage

The enmity of the world, the Qasim family

Has joined Abū Jahl, they have decided to kill you,

Abū Jahl's family is coming together,

Joining forces to kill you.

They find fault with you

Because you are destroying all the gods, their gods;

It would be better not to interfere with them,

To proceed with the progress of your own soul.

When your mother died I took care of you

In an honest way and with great effort,

Now you are twenty years old and after so much time

I don't want to lose you to those wretched people.
My son, may you act with some clarity
And keep away from them,
Don't engage the enmity of this city."

Abū Tālib explained the situation to Muhammad ﷺ,
Then noble Muhammad ﷺ replied,
"O my Father who was born with my father,
Abū Jahl opposes the words of the primal One,
Whoever fails to understand the one path,
The true, complete path, is iblīs or satan,
Whoever does not melt, does not see with clarity
Of heart is the worst iblīs,
Whoever does not truthfully love the primal One,
The permanent One is a malicious person in this world,
Whoever does not learn justice and integrity,
Who does not have inner understanding and clarity
Is a satan gone astray,
This is what the elders of earlier times say.
The Āthi threw my father and mother out
Because they were tricked by iblīs,
Isn't this sort of creature malicious?
The Āthi rules everywhere from an unknown place,
When you pray He appears before you think,
He is the guru who always feeds you,
He is the grace, the completeness,
The treasure and clarity in everything,
He is the One who is close to you;

A sinner who does not realize the truth
Of this Āthi is iblīs, a satan.
If you pray on the straight, true path
In the right way, iblīs will show you another way;
To oppose or kill such an iblīs
Is a good thing to do O my Father.
The Āthi lives without illusion
Within love in the heart,
The One of justice without a body
Lives in all lives, permeating everywhere
As the form of peace, the form of good qualities.
Even if I have to fight a battle
With those sinners who do not love the Āthi
Who is repletion everywhere, I will have no fear,
O Father I will have no fear at all,
I will trust the Supreme Being
To put clarity and good qualities
In the words I say,
And I will praise the Āthi so that fragrance flows,
With faith I will come forward to do anything.
If they hit me or kill me,
If they strike me and keep striking me,
If they chop me into eight pieces
Or tie me up and kill me,
If they nail me down or cut me down,
If they pull out my roots,
Cut me down at the root,
O Father I will not deviate

From the words of the primal One.
My heart cannot bear opposition
To the words of the primal One,
Those who do not love the words of the Āthi,
Who do not know the meaning of divine words, *gnānam,*
Words of clarity, of divine grace, words
Of that primal treasure replete in all lives,
Those who do not love them,
No matter who they are
I will oppose them any way I can.
The One who created me, the One, the only treasure,
If that primal One is with me
I will fear nothing O Father,
I will have no fear, Father.

He is the Father of those who trust
The primal feet of the primal One,
And live their lives with that trust,
I will have no fear of those who forget His words
Even if they mean danger in my life.
I will embrace those O my Father,
Who walk straight and true on the path of justice,
Even though they make me fear,
If they are on the path of the primal One,
I will bow at their feet
If they are on the straight, true path,
But if they destroy human beings,
If they break their hearts,

If they ruin their good intentions by throwing stones
I will not fear such false people,
I will not fear such false people O my Father.
To those who walk the straight, true path,
To those who praise the eternal One,
Pointing out the true path,
To those true individuals I will bow down O my Father.
Those who recite mantras to feed their own stomachs,
Those who believe in idols which they claim are gods,
To those born with me who have such confusion
I will give clarity, I will make them bow down
To the exalted, primal One O my Father.
Should all these evils intertwine,
Should they destroy my body, trample me down,
Should the whole city unite to kill me
I have faith that the Lord, the primal One exists,
I have that faith O my Father.
I will embrace those who follow the cause of truth
No matter how many wars break out,
No matter how many battles are fought,
Even if I am alone I will have no fear,
That primal One will come as many O my Father,
He will fight, He will show them
The truth in everything O my Father.
To live for that straight, true path,
To pray to that eternal One,
To pray so that complete *gnānam* will grow,
So that divine grace will flourish

In the heavens, everywhere,
To stay on that straight, true path
And spread the grace of the eternal One everywhere
I will cause melting joy everywhere;
Even if they burn my body
I will have no fear O my Father.

So that they will consider all lives equal,
So that they will embrace the One who is everywhere
And be alone for the search,
I will have them acquire the grace
Of that deathless state O my Father, O my Father.
In this world where they chatter without point
And feed their stomachs with deceit,
I will always oppose the fools
Who are caught in this evil,
Even if it were the mother who gave birth to me
I would oppose her.
The One who exists fully in all lives,
The Father everywhere
Is the only Father, the primal One
Replete in the body — I will follow
Those who love that One,
Who are always victorious.
I will follow the words of the primal One
Even if they murder me, I will always oppose
Those who act against the words of the primal One
Even if they cut me to pieces and burn each part,

O my Father I will have no fear, O my Father."

Muhammad ☾ sang this song for Abū Talīb,

"O Father no matter what happens in this world

I will not be afraid, even if they crush me

I will not be afraid, my God exists

No matter what happens,

No matter how many armies appear,

My God, the One we have faith in, He exists.

I will not fight for my stomach or myself,

I will work for the primal One, I will follow

Those who work for the primal One,

I will always oppose

Those who forget God, who are selfish,

Who nurture their own stomachs, I will never hesitate

To wage war against them, I will not hold back

No matter what form they take,

I will not be afraid."

This is what Muhammad ☾

Said to Abū Talīb who replied,

"O my son you said all lives are like your own,

You said He exists completely in all lives,

He is everywhere, He is here, there, everywhere,

He exists fully in all lives, you said

They were all born with you, you said

They were all born with you, you say

Father and mother,

They were all born with you, you said

Those with melting hearts born in the *dunyā*, the world,

Are your own born, now whom are you going to fight,
Now whom will you fight?"

He answered, "O my Father I will tell you
The war I'll wage: there is no war
Against all those who are born with me, it is against
The demon who opposes the words of the primal One,
It is against the demon who opposes the words
Of our primal Father, against him I will wage war
Without fear, the demon
Who makes them change their minds,
Who leads them along the wrong path, that demon,
I will fight that demon
Without any confusion O my Father.
The God in whom I have faith,
The One who rules us every day,
The One who lives in the heart, He is that One,
The One who created every part of everything,
The One who gives us everything, the causal God,
I will fight those false people who do not remember
The causal One in their hearts,
They are the false people I will fight.

In the primal days Adam opened his eyes
Upon the heavens and made iblīs die,
I will fight this iblīs who deceives
Human beings and stains them, I will fight
This evil iblīs, the sinner who teases the truly just,

I will fight this evil demon O my Father,

Who utters vain words, who causes them suffering

At the point of a sword, this demon

Who steals and murders, who destroys everything it sees,

Who takes everything away, I will fight

This thieving demon, I will fight O my Father.

This thing which destroys a state of mind,

This creature who establishes

Different forms with disguises,

This creature who murders the primal One

Living in the heart, this satan who grows,

I will rush to fight him O my Father,

I will rush to fight him O my Father.

This creature who used every trick to feed his stomach

In the world, who used ego

To make mantras impressive,

This creature who crept into all those born with me,

Killing them without killing,

This creature, the source of these tricks,

I will fight this false demon O my Father.

This satan, the cause of suffering for those

With faith in the primal treasure, the shining treasure,

I will fight to destroy this demon and win.

The person who thinks himself important, who forgets

Justice and charity, the person who kills

The creations of the primal One, cutting them,

Eating them, I will fight this demon fearlessly,

I will fight him using the weapon of the primal One

And make him beg.
This creature who sins, who destroys
So that he, his wife and children
Can feed their stomachs and prosper,
I will fight this sinful satan
Even if it means my death.
When the primal One embraces me
I will fight without fear O my Father,
I will fearlessly fight
The creature who destroys truth,
The creature who tells lies,
The creature who slanders and deceives
Making these poor people suffer,
I will fight this hideous demon O my Father.

I will fight to correct those who kill without killing,
Those who murder and steal,
Those who sing without singing
And those sinners who tease, I will fight those sinners
O my Father; even if it means
My death I will be unafraid.
When the primal One is with me I will rush to fight
O my Father, without sleep or food,
Without fear I will take up the weapon
Of the One who is our right,
Without fear I will fight against the sinners
Who deceive those born with me,
I will fight to chase them from those born with me,

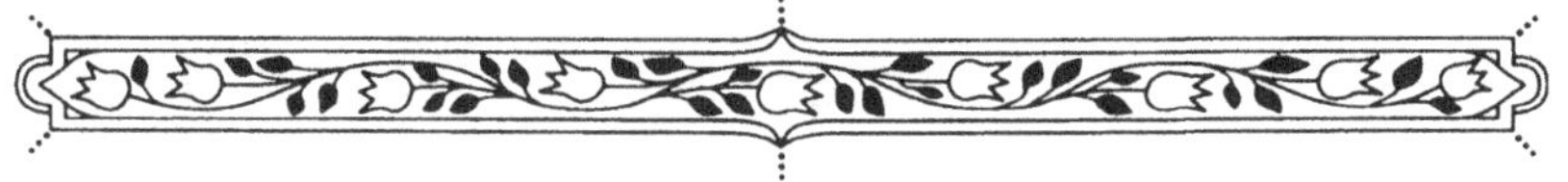

O my Father I will fight to rid them
Of the demon who has caught them.
The One who is without comparison, without help,
Sustainer of two worlds,
God who is love within love, who is beyond
The three states of charity, wealth and joy,
The One exalted in love, for Him I will fight
With pure intention and high purpose,
I will fight this filthy, deceiving satan
Who claims that wealth consists of gold and land
Or things, one kind or another,
Making the people live in a daze.
No matter how many forms this evil takes,
No matter how it comes,
I will rush out to fight; with the help
Of the primal One I will fight to destroy it
For the sake of the straight, true path,
Even if it costs me this body,
Even if I have no food or the whole city opposes me,
If they all turn against me, if they try to poison me,
I will not be afraid O my Father.
The primal One, the only One, the treasure
Within all treasures who protects us day and night,
The primal One who gives us everything, always,
I will fight to destroy those sinners
Who do not remember this treasure O my Father.
I will fight those who have believed all their life
That the world is the truth, I will fight

Those who spend their whole life
Searching for the world and gathering it all in.
Āmīn, āmīn, yā Rabbal-'ālamīn,
O Lord of all the universes."

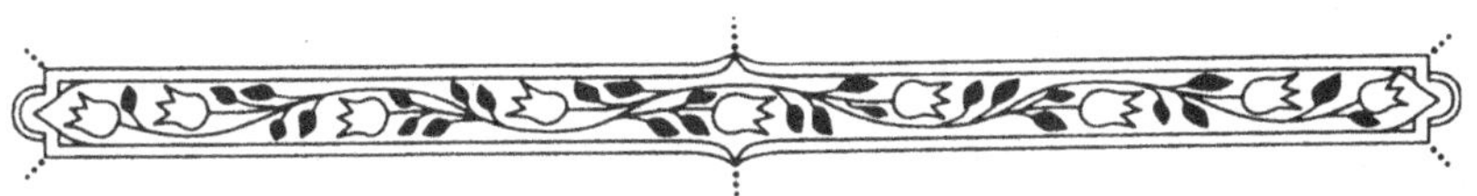

Glossary

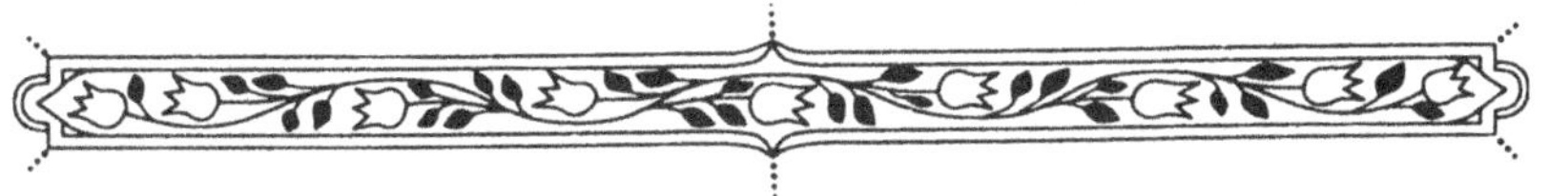

Glossary

The following traditional supplications in Arabic calligraphy are used throughout the text:

> ⌽ or (Sal.) following the Prophet Muhammad or Rasūlullāh stands for *ṣallallāhu 'alaihi wa ṣallam*, blessings and peace be upon him.

> ⌽ or (A.S.) following the name of a prophet or an angel stands for *'alaihis-ṣalām*, peace be upon him.

> ⌽ or (Ral.) following the name of a companion of the Prophet Muhammad, a saint or *khalīf* stands for *radiyallāhu 'anhu* or *'anhā*, may Allah be pleased with him or her.

(A) Indicates an Arabic word

(T) Indicates a Tamil word

aiyō (T) An exclamation of regret, sorrow.

Ahamed (A & T) Tamil variant of an Arabic name meaning the heart's beauty visible on the face.

ākhirah (A) The hereafter.

'ālam (A) The visible world, cosmos, universe.

Al-hamd (A) The praise, the heart of praise.

alif (A) The first letter of the Arabic alphabet. In the transformed man of wisdom, the *alif* represents Allah, the One.

Allāhu akbar (A) God is supreme.

Allāhu Nāyan (A & T) The Lord who is God.

Allāhu ta'ālā Nāyan (A & T) The exalted Lord who is God.

amma (T) Literally mother, also an address of endearment, respect.

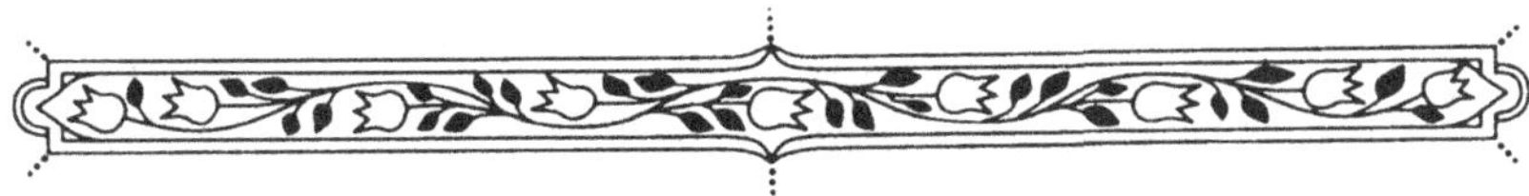

āmīn (A) So be it, amen.

anāthi (T) The beginningless beginning before creation.

annal (T) Noble, mighty.

appa (T) Literally father; also used in collective address meaning brothers and sisters.

'arsh (A) The throne of God.

aru muham (T) Six faces.

arwāh (A) The world of souls.

as-salāmu 'alaikum (A) May the peace of God be with you.

as-salāmu 'alaikum wa rahmatullāhi wa barakātuhu kulluhu (A) May the peace, the wealth and the blessings of God be with you.

Āthi (A) The primal One.

Āthi Nabī (A) The primal Prophet.

āthmām (T) The soul, life.

a'udhu billāhi minash-shaitānir-rajīm (A) I seek refuge in God from satan, the rejected.

awwal (A) The period when souls were created.

awwal kalimah (A) The first of the five *kalimahs, Lā ilāha ill-Allāhu Muhammadur-Rasūlullāh.* Nothing exists but God, You are God and Muhammad is Your messenger.

āyat (A) A verse in the Qur'an.

badushāh (Persian) Ruler, emperor.

Bawa (T) Father.

bhakti (T) Devotion.

Bismillāhir-rahmānir-rahīm (A) In the name of God, most merciful, most compassionate, the creator, sustainer and nourisher.

Bismin (A) A shortened form of *Bismillāhir-rahmānir-rahīm.*

Dastagīr (Persian) Lord, the helping hand.

dēva (T) A celestial being.

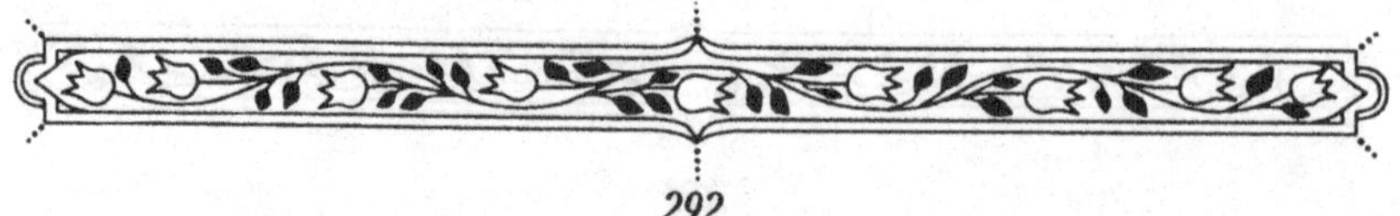

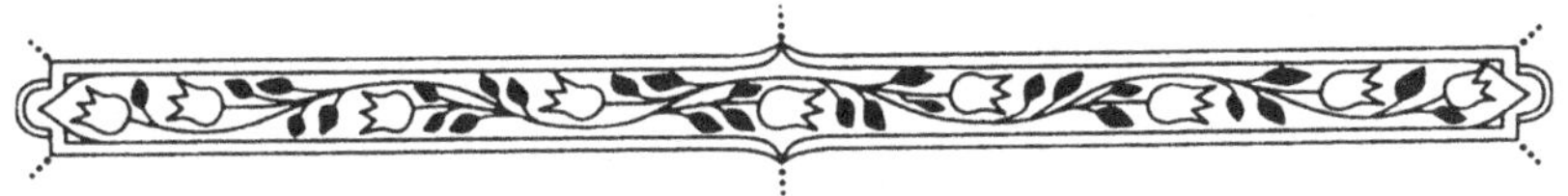

ðhikr (A) The recital of words in remembrance of God.

ðunyā (A) The world.

Furqān (A) Islam.

furūð (A) Obligatory duties known as the five pillars of Islam.

gnānam (T) Divine luminous wisdom.

gnāni (T) A gnostic of divine wisdom.

guru mani (T) A gem-like guru.

guru nāthan (T) A lord among gurus.

hāl (A) State.

Hānal (T) Fire worship.

Haqq (A) The Truth, God.

hayawān (A) A wild animal.

hikmat (A) Wisdom.

iblīs (A) Satan, a devil.

īmān (A) Absolute, complete and unshakable faith, certitude and determination.

Injīl (A) Christianity.

inʃān (A) Man, a human being.

Īswaran (T) The primal father of the Hindu tradition.

Īswari (T) The primal mother of the Hindu tradition.

Jabrāt (A) Fire worship.

jālam (T) Magic trick.

Jōthi (T) Radiant light.

Kab'ah (A) A cube-like building in the center of the mosque in Mecca. It was originally built by Prophet Abraham .

kalimah (A) A prayer, recitation of faith. Lit. a word.

kaʃtūri (T) The fragrance of musk.

katpaha viruðcham (T) The wish-fulfilling tree.

kursī (A) The gnostic eye.

lā (A) No, the negative.

Lā il (āha) (A) *Lā il (āha)* is the negation of all other than God. *Lā* is the world, *il* is for God.

Lā ilāha ill-Allāhu (A) Nothing exists but God, You are God.

lām (A) An Arabic letter. In the transformed man of wisdom, *lām* represents the *Nūr,* the resplendence of Allah.

mahabbah (A) Divine love.

Mahmūd (A) One who is praised by God.

mahshar (A) The gathering on Judgment Day.

malā'ikat (A) Angels; archangels.

mantra (T) An incantation.

manu-Īsan (T) Man-God.

maulid (A) A celebration in verse honoring a prophet, a *qutb* or saint.

maya (T) Illusion.

maya *jālam* (T) The tricks, the magic in the realm of illusion.

maya *saktis* (T) Energies of maya.

meignāna guru (T) A teacher of divine wisdom.

meignānam (T) True, divine wisdom.

mīm (A) An Arabic letter. In the transformed man of wisdom, the *mīm* represents Muhammad .

mubārakāt (A) Blessings.

Muhammadūay (A & T) A Tamil adaptation of the Arabic name, a term of endearment.

Muhammadūay Mustafar-Rasūl (A & T) The Chosen Messenger. *See also* Muhammadūay.

mukthar (T) A liberated being.

munivar (T) A being with occult powers.

mursalūn (A) Divine messengers.

nabī (A) A prophet.

nāthan (T) Lord.

Nāyan (T) The Ruler who protects and sustains.

Nūr (A) The resplendent light of God.

param (T) Universal.

qalam (A) The divine, recording pen.

qalb (A) The heart, the inner heart.

qiyāmah (A) The day of reckoning, of questioning.

qudrat (A) Allah's grace, His attributes in action. Lit. Allah's power.

Qutb (A) The divine luminous explanation, the axis or pole of the universe.

Rahīm (A) The most compassionate.

Rahmān (A) The most gracious.

rahmat (A) God's grace, His mercy.

rasūl (A) A messenger; the Rasūl—Allah's Messenger Muhammad .

rathina (T) Precious jewel.

rishi (A) Sage or poet, a wise being.

rūh (A) The soul.

sabūr (A) Absolute patience.

sakti (T) A force or energy.

salām (A) Peace, a greeting of peace.

salawāt (A) Prayers in praise and glorification.

satchithananda (T) A realized being of bliss.

satchithanandasivam (T) A realized being of bliss and purity.

shaitān (A) Satan, iblīs.

shakūr (A) Absolute contentment, intense gratitude.

sifāt (A) Form, creation, manifestation, descriptions.

sirātul-mustaqīm (A) The straight path, the straight path of righteousness.

sitthar (T) An illusionist.

Siva (T) In Hinduism, Siva represents the power, which is God.

sivam (T) Divine.

sivamayam (T) Divine form.

suniyam (T) The deception of evil.

tawakkul (A) Surrender to God, entrusting everything to God.

thambi (T) Younger brother.

thiru mani (T) Divine gem.

thiru nabi (T & A) Divine prophet.

waqt (A) A period of prayer.

Yā (A) The vocative, sometimes used as an actual part of a name.

Yā Rabbal-'ālamīn (A) O Lord of all the universes.

yaqīn (A) Certitude.

Zabūr (A) Used by Bawa Muhaiyaddeen to indicate Hinduism; also
means the Psalms of David (ﷺ).

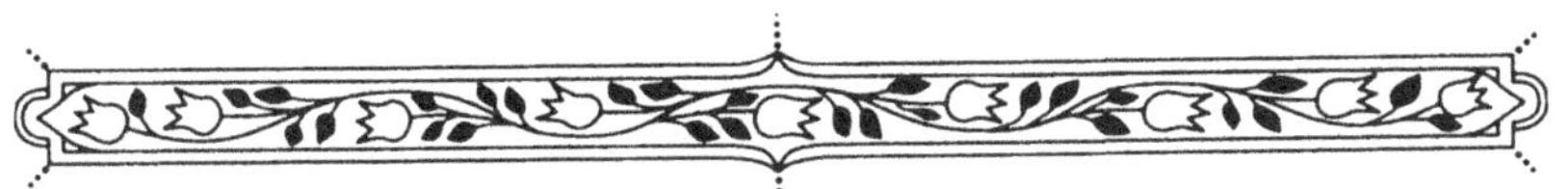

Books by
M. R. Bawa Muhaiyaddeen

Truth & Light: brief explanations

Songs of God's Grace

The Divine Luminous Wisdom That Dispels the Darkness

Wisdom of the Divine (Vols. 1, 2, 3, 4)

The Guidebook to the True Secret of the Heart (Vols. 1, 2)

God, His Prophets and His Children

Four Steps to Pure Iman

The Wisdom of Man

A Book of God's Love

My Love You My Children:
101 Stories for Children of All Ages

Come to the Secret Garden: Sufi Tales of Wisdom

The Golden Words of a Sufi Sheikh

The Tasty, Economical Cookbook (Vols. 1, 2)

Sheikh and Disciple

Maya Veeram or The Forces of Illusion

Asma'ul-Husna: The 99 Beautiful Names of Allah

Islam and World Peace: Explanations of a Sufi

A Mystical Journey

Questions of Life — Answers of Wisdom

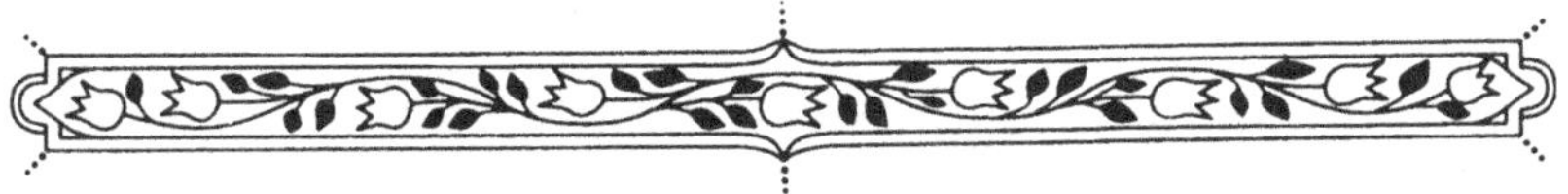

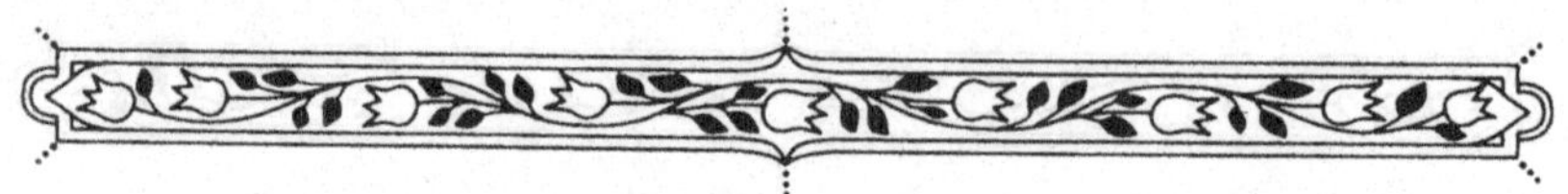

Treasures of the Heart: Sufi Stories for Young Children

To Die Before Death: The Sufi Way of Life

Gems of Wisdom series —
Vol. 1: The Value of Good Qualities
Vol. 2: Beyond Mind and Desire
Vol. 3: The Innermost Heart
Vol. 4: Come to Prayer

A Contemporary Sufi Speaks —
To Teenagers and Parents
On the Signs of Destruction
On Peace of Mind
On the True Meaning of Sufism
On Unity: The Legacy of the Prophets

Foreign Language Publications —

Ein Zeitgenössischer Sufi Spricht über Inneren Frieden
(A Contemporary Sufi Speaks On Peace of Mind)

Deux Discours tirés du Livre
L'Islam et la Paix Mondiale: Explications d'un Soufi
(Two Discourses from the Book
Islam & World Peace: Explanations of a Sufi)

For free catalog or book information call:
(215) 879-8604

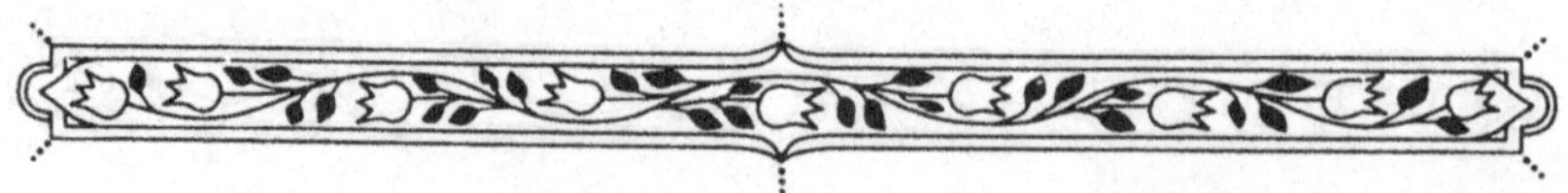

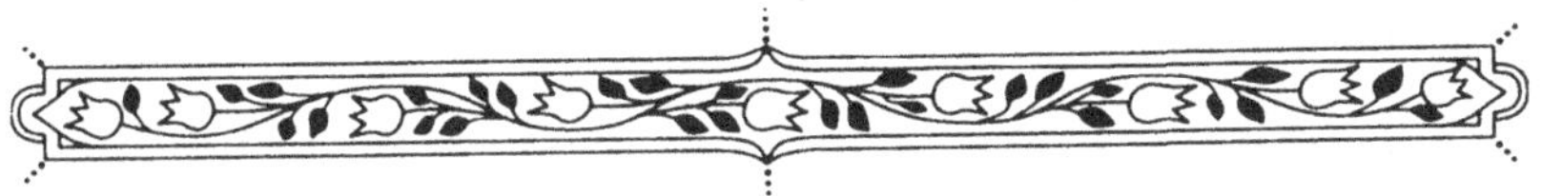

The central branch of the Bawa Muhaiyaddeen Fellowship is located in
Philadelphia, PA. The Fellowship serves as a meeting house
and as a reservoir of people and materials for all who are interested in the
teachings of M. R. Bawa Muhaiyaddeen.

For information, write or call:

The Bawa Muhaiyaddeen Fellowship
5820 Overbrook Avenue
Philadelphia, Pennsylvania 19131

Telephone: (215) 879-6300
or
(215) 879-8604
(24 hour answering machine)

E-Mail Address:
info@bmf.org

URL Web Address:
http://www.bmf.org

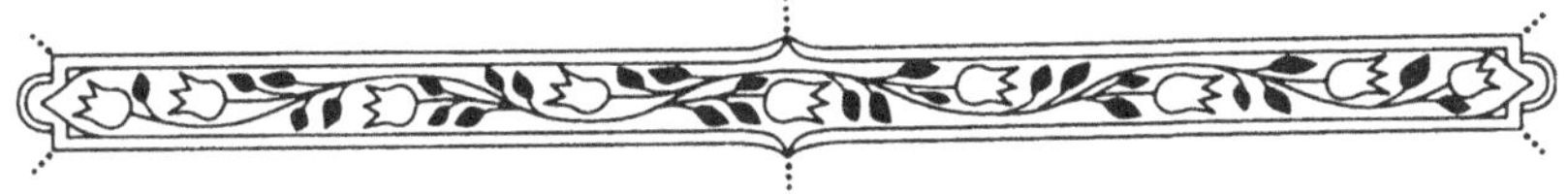

Made in the USA
Monee, IL
07 July 2026

56551544R00174